Searching For Immortality

Clayton B Carlson

Published by First Page Solutions (Canada)

ISBN: 1988226015
ISBN-13: 978-1988226019

Forward

I believe you and I have been given great potential. Our destiny is to become the children of God. Not only those who believe in him during this present life but all who have ever lived. The new born child, our parent, sibling, or friend, who died in unbelief, will at some point in their existence have the opportunity to accept the life giving sacrifice made by Jesus. Those who did not have the opportunity to hear the gospel of Jesus during this life, will at some point receive their one opportunity from God to come to Jesus. When we look into the scriptures they point out the plan God has in store for us and when this opportunity will arise. We all must make the choice between eternal life and death. God does not leave us adrift on the sea of false hope and fable. This bible study looks at the scriptures to show how they fit together to form the plan God has outlined.

As a biblist I regard the bible to be the highest authority on what I should believe about God. I believe that God has given his direction to us in this written form from a collection of books and letters passed down to us from those he used as instruments to write them. The bible is not a collection of fables written by men. It is the written word of God.

*Unless otherwise noted, all scriptures used in this book are quoted from the King James Version Bible.

Table of Contents

Chapter 1: INTRODUCTION

The ABC's of life. Airway, Breathing, Circulation. As taught in first aid, are the very basic essentials needed to sustain life. If you don't have these three, there is no need to work on the other things that may be wrong because the patient won't live long enough to worry about them. You need the essential things working. Then you can go on to the more peripheral problems. Christianity is like that. Without faith in Christ, how could anyone be a Christian? This would be essential. Faith is what will give spiritual life at its most basic level.

Consider the thief that was crucified beside Christ. He wasn't baptized. He didn't seem to have any great spiritual knowledge of God, no insight into his mysteries. By his own admission he was deserving of his punishment. He was a sinner worthy of a most gruesome death. Yet he has the promise of Jesus that he will be with him in Paradise.

Luke 23:40-43

40 But the other answering rebuked him, saying, Dost not thou fear God, seeing thou art in the same condemnation?

41 And we indeed justly; for we receive the due reward of our deeds: but this man hath done nothing amiss.

42 And he said unto Jesus, Lord, remember me when thou comest into thy kingdom.

43 And Jesus said unto him, Verily I say unto thee, Today shalt thou be

with me in paradise.

It is by faith we are saved.

Romans 5:1-2

5 Therefore being justified by faith, we have peace with God through our Lord Jesus Christ:

2 By whom also we have access by faith into this grace wherein we stand, and rejoice in hope of the glory of God.

Ephesians 2:8

8 For by grace are ye saved through faith; and that not of yourselves: it is the gift of God:

If there were any other requirement, how could there be any deathbed salvations? Or what if the new converts didn't have a complete and accurate Christian understanding? Would their salvation be compromised by their ignorance? Let's look at a short story about Paul and see.

Acts 19:1-7

19 And it came to pass, that, while Apollos was at Corinth, Paul having passed through the upper coasts came to Ephesus: and finding certain disciples,

2 He said unto them, Have ye received the Holy Ghost since ye believed? And they said unto him, We have not so much as heard whether there be any Holy Ghost.

3 And he said unto them, Unto what then were ye baptized? And they said, Unto John's baptism.

4 Then said Paul, John verily baptized with the baptism of repentance, saying unto the people, that they should believe on him which should come after him, that is, on Christ Jesus.

5 When they heard this, they were baptized in the name of the Lord Jesus.

6 And when Paul had laid his hands upon them, the Holy Ghost came on them; and they spake with tongues, and prophesied.

7 And all the men were about twelve.

It seems as though God wasn't concerned about their lack of knowledge on religious subjects. They worked with the understanding that they had in faith, and God accepted them. Here Jesus does not try to hinder others from working in his name, even if they weren't one of his disciples. He knew they couldn't do works in his name, and then talk badly of him.

Mark 9:38-41

38 And John answered him, saying, Master, we saw one casting out devils in thy name, and he followeth not us: and we forbad him, because he followeth not us.

39 But Jesus said, Forbid him not: for there is no man which shall do a miracle in my name, that can lightly speak evil of me.

40 For he that is not against us is on our part.

41 For whosoever shall give you a cup of water to drink in my name, because ye belong to Christ, verily I say unto you, he shall not lose his reward.

Luke 9:49-50

49 And John answered and said, Master, we saw one casting out devils in thy name; and we forbad him, because he followeth not with us.

50 And Jesus said unto him, Forbid him not: for he that is not against us is for us.

The essentials for Christianity appear to be very minimal. How is it then, that there are such deep divisions between churches that claim to be Christian? Between churches that use the same bible? Between churches that say they teach the bible truth? Between churches that claim the bible doesn't contradict itself?

I would like to humbly offer my opinion. The problem is Dogmas. Finding scripture in the bible that appear to be saying something on a subject, maybe several scriptures are found that seem to be all in support of one idea, then it is taken for gospel truth. It is then taught to parishioners who incorporate it into their personal beliefs. Once taught the doctrine, they won't give it up without a fight. Many churches will have their own non biblical traditions that they will not break. And they will all say that, “we're right, and the people in those other churches are wrong”. Dogmas divide. Being the special ones with the enlightened understanding of everything Godly, makes you exclusive, and arrogant. Not the best way to be if you want to love people.

Contrastingly, saying we need to agree on the essentials, but have freedom on the peripheral, is inclusive. Having freedom of thought is not only liberating to the thinker, but is stimulating and challenging to the listener. You will never learn more, or be as sure of your beliefs as when you need to prove them to yourself and to others. If you only associate with people that think, and believe the same as yourself you will never need to be able to prove what you believe, because no one will ever challenge you.

We need to not be afraid to say, this is what I find the bible to be saying about this topic. As opposed to, this is what the bible says. The first way invites discussion, the latter stifles it. Not being dogmatic doesn't make us wishy-washy, it makes us approachable. Saying, there are different ways to understand a scripture doesn't mean you don't know what you're talking about. Rather, it says that you've looked at the other thoughts, considered the options and made a choice that works for you. This leaves room for people to make their own choices, and not be afraid they will be going against God if they don't see it your way. Or worse yet, give up on being a Christian because they don't believe all of the peripheral things they've been told goes with being a Christian.

I've heard study results that say, 40% of Christian kids that go to university give up, or drop their Christian beliefs and faith. This is one reason why there is a push for creation science, and proving that the world is 7000 years old. The proponents of the creation science movement seem to think if they make strong arguments rebuffing the evolutionary time line of earth history being in the billions of years, then the time that evolution needs to work would vanish. I think that when we say the bible will only support one way of thinking to the exclusion of any other biblical possibility on a peripheral subject we alienate and loose those who don't agree with us. If they don't believe all they have been dogmatically taught on peripheral topics, then there is no other option given to them, but to leave. People need room to have their own opinions on the peripheral, and not be ostracized for them. It is the essential things that are truly important. We should be knowledgeable of some of the peripheral choices that are out there, even if we don't personally agree with them. That way we can tell others the reasons for the hope that is in us, which will foster growth in all that are involved in the conversation.

Christians used to teach that the world was the centre of the universe, and that all the other planets, stars, and our sun revolved around it. Of course the bible was used to prove this doctrine. All those who taught otherwise were not only considered heretics, but were libel to lose their life. Galileo finally got an official apology from the Vatican in the year 2000, a bit slow since his trial for this kind of heresy was in 1632. I haven't heard this bible truth taught lately. Was the bible wrong? Or was it our understanding of what the bible said, that was wrong?

Again I ask. What is essential to be a Christian? For the peripheral topics, why can't we say "This is how I see it."? If it doesn't make sense to you, that's ok it's a peripheral subject. Jesus never tied passing a test on creation facts, to salvation. There are plenty of verses on Love, Kindness, Forgiveness and Generosity. These subjects are more important to living a Christian life.

That doesn't mean you shouldn't hold strong opinions. Or be a passionate supporter of a particular doctrine. Just don't tell others they have to feel the same way to be a Christian. I went to a bible study put on by my church. It was billed as a college style course on end time events. I have an interest in that topic, and was looking forward to some discussion of biblical scriptures. I attend a church that agrees on the essentials and has freedom on the peripheral. Our church however isn't very good at giving a voice to the peripheral opinions of those in the minority. The moderator was great, but after my third critical scriptural point. An elderly lady gave me a scowling look, and said to the study leader. "Just tell us what we need to know."

I was there to discuss ideas. She was there to be indoctrinated. Now that really isn't such a bad thing. She had found a church she felt at home at. She wanted to know more about God, and how he was going to work it all out. How better to find out than to go to a class. The only problem from my perspective was the lack of options, or different points of view being covered. There are many differing scenarios of end time events held by Godly Christians, all using bible scripture to support their point of view. The one that is right, is the one that God opens your eyes to. I may not understand why you believe it, or agree with you. But will your belief in it keep you from Gods love. Would he lose you because of a misunderstanding? If he chooses to lead you to a new understanding then he will, in his time.

Here is another good reason to remain flexible on peripheral nonessential doctrine. If you hold tight to them it is harder for God to lead you to where he may want you. Maybe he will never have you move, but if you stay open to scriptural teaching it could happen. If you close yourself off to ideas the chances aren't very good you'll ever learn anything new.

I heard a friend's first sermon a long time ago. He talked about his cousin that had died young. He was disturbed by the thought that maybe she hadn't accepted Christ and was forever lost. The subject finally came up one day. I told him how I felt bad for him feeling like he should have done something more for her. I shared with him my understandings on what the bible teaches about death. He said, "ya, I have come to a deeper understanding of death and forgiveness. So I don't feel like that anymore." If he had stayed closed to any new thoughts, or closed to a different perspective for an old scripture, then a new insight wouldn't have been possible.

While visiting with our worship pastor one day after lunch, I asked him what he understood the bible taught about dieing and eternal life. He said he didn't give it much thought. He knew God had it covered, and that it would all work out in the end. This wasn't the answer that I was expecting. I wanted to know details. My mechanics mind wanted to know how things worked. Later while reading Heb.11 the faith chapter I wondered. Does he have more faith, because he doesn't feel compelled to know? Or am I more studious, because I want to look into the workings of Gods plan? I think the answer is neither. We are all unique, and God leads us, as we willingly follow him, to where ever he wants us to be. We all run the race on the course that he has laid out, especially for us.

Some people may think I'm saying what you believe isn't important. Not at all. If you have the essential faith in Christ, then you will have eternal life. Your beliefs and doctrines will determine how you live, and the kind of person you are. Just because a trauma patient, to use the first aid analogy, may have the essential ABC's of life, won't negate the fact they are paralysed. Will that affect the way they live their life, or interact with those around them? Of course it will. In the same way, the further our beliefs stray from God's word. The greater the negative affect will be on the way we live our lives, and interact with those around us. Having understanding and knowledge of biblical fundamentals is essential if we are trying to let Jesus live through us to positively influence the people we interact with.

Chapter 2: ESSENTIAL UNDERSTANDINGS

I believe there are two basic truths about God and how he interacts with mankind. These two truths will never change. They are fundamental. They are two of the core foundation blocks God has built his relationship with humanity on.

- FIRSTLY: God is love. That's his nature. He can't go against himself and do evil. God is bound by who he is, to have the best for others as his top priority. God will never force us to follow his ways.

Because God loves us, he will let us choose the wrong ways for life, if that is what we want to do. Just as the angels had a choice to make at Satan's rebellion, God will allow us to choose the path that leads to destruction. If he forced us to do his will, then God wouldn't be any better than a benevolent dictator. By allowing us to choose our own path, we can choose to be with God because we want to be there. As the old saying goes "You can't buy love", well you can't force anyone into it either.

1 John 4:8

8 He that loveth not knoweth not God; for God is love.

- SECONDLY: The only way to be reconciled to God and have our transgressions forgiven, is to accept the sacrifice Jesus made for us all.

Acts 4:10-12

10 Be it known unto you all, and to all the people of Israel, that by the name of Jesus Christ of Nazareth, whom ye crucified, whom God raised from the dead, even by him doth this man stand here before you whole.

11 This is the stone which was set at nought of you builders, which is become the head of the corner.

12 Neither is there salvation in any other: for there is none other name under heaven given among men, whereby we must be saved.

These two points are essential to understanding Gods plan for mankind. If our beliefs don't line up with either of them, then our beliefs are biblically inaccurate. I know that some people will find the second truth offensive, or painful. They may have known someone who never knew Jesus and are now dead. Maybe that person never had the opportunity to hear about Jesus. They could have lived in the wrong country. Or they could have lived in the wrong century. They could have been the nicest people possible, but the second truth is still there, and can be a stumbling block to many. The only biblically supported path to God is through Jesus. There is no other way.

Chapter 3: SATAN'S CONSPIRACY

Making a statement like, Jesus is the only way to be saved, very matter of factually can be what puts people off. They naturally assume, that if their dead loved one, or friend can't be with God. Presumably in heaven. Then the only other logical place for them, according to all they've heard from society, as well as Christianity is that they must be being tormented in hell. And we have all been taught that there is no escape from there, and it lasts forever. Little wonder, people can find the good news of Jesus, a bitter pill to swallow especially if you had loved ones, or friends that never knew him.

Take Oprah for Example. If you Google Oprah denies Jesus. You can hear her say that Jesus can't be the only way. Because if he was, how could someone who was in some unchristian country, living a loving life. Following Godly values, but never herd the name, or anything about Jesus. Ever get the chance to be reconciled to God. They would never be able to be in heaven. Now before we are too hard on Oprah.

Google, Billy Graham denies Jesus. In his conversation with Robert Schuller he says that people can be in the body of Christ and not know Jesus by name, but just know that they need something. And they turn to the only light that they can see. Is this very different than what Oprah said?

Why would people who say that they are Christians, say things like that? It goes against the basic core of Christianity. Rule number two, the need to accept Jesus. I think the reason people feel this way is because they think that it's not fair to send people to hell and be tormented for all eternity by Satan and the demons, if they never have the chance to accept Jesus. Christian religions predominately give no other possibility. So what are those people who see the injustice, to think about the great God of love?

Could there be some satanic conspiracy to trick people at work here? To make people misunderstand God. To lead them away from the plans that God has in store for them? To have them think that he is unfair and unjust?

Yes, I believe that it is a satanic conspiracy. The commonly held beliefs about life, death, and where we go when we die, are lies that Satin has tricked humanity into believing. You might think, that is quite a bold statement. Well maybe it is, but let's see what the bible has to say. After all, what I think is of little importance. It's what God say's that counts.

To start I would like to say that, in the end the evil people who reject God will be punished, and that those who accept Jesus will be with him in the paradise of his kingdom. But the path to get there is probably not the one you think. If you are one of the people who are put off by the exclusivity of Christianity then this may interest you in a good way. If you have those in your life who don't know Jesus, or died before they could hear about him, then take heart, and see what Gods word has to say from a different, yet biblical point of view.

I find bible studies can be a bit of a letdown. Not that I don't like what the bible has to say, but a lot of the time the people who write them only use scripture that appear to prove their point. Much like the class I attended at church. So I want to look at all the relevant scriptures I can find. I am not interested in indoctrination, but rather finding out what God has to say throughout the bible. Carefully looking at each verse to see how it blends in with the others, for I firmly believe that the bible will not contradict itself. If it appears to then the problem lies with our interpretation, or understanding of the verse.

Most anthropologists say that every culture has a belief of an afterlife. I suppose the only ones who don't would be the evolutionists. Though I have heard them say their energy will not quit but will go on into other things. But not to be too picky, it is a commonly held belief worldwide that there is some form of life after death. It crosses religious and economic divides. But where does this belief come from. If only from the bible, then why do the Buddhists, and Hindus have it? They had little to no historical contact with the bible.

Chapter 4: DID GOD CREATE MANKIND IMORTAL

Let's look at the beginning of mankind, and study through the bible till we find where mankind becomes immortal. After all, it would take immortality to live for ever, either in heaven or hell. The question should not be, is there a heaven or hell, but how, and when do we get there. The bible account of creation in Genesis is where God first makes man. Did God create mankind immortal? Or was it gifted to us by God later? Or do we even have it yet?

Genesis 2:7

King James Version

7 And the LORD God formed man of the dust of the ground, and breathed into his nostrils the breath of life; and man became a living soul.

Genesis 2:7

Common English Bible (CEB)

7 the LORD God formed the human[a] from the topsoil of the fertile land[b] and blew life's breath into his nostrils. The human came to life.

Genesis 2:7

Expanded Bible (EXB)

7 Then the LORD God took dust from the ground and formed a man from

it [C⍰there is wordplay between “ground” (adama) and “man” (adam)]. He breathed the breath of life into the man’s nose, and the man became a living person.

Genesis 2:7

Lexham English Bible (LEB)

7 when[a] Yahweh God formed the man[b] of dust from the ground, and he blew into his nostrils the breath of life, and the man became a living creature.

I used these different translations to highlight a point. We can debate the merits of each translation or we can go directly to the source, the Hebrew that it was written in. Pay close attention to the last part of the verse. We go from, a living soul, came to life, living person, to living creature. These don't say that man was created immortal. Soul as in the KJV gets interpreted by people and denominations as meaning immortal, but is that what the KJV scholars meant? I'm a mechanic. Not a scholar of ancient Hebrew. If I have a problem fixing a vehicle, I check the manua to see how the designers and engineers want it fixed. Let’s see what the experts that wrote the KJV have to say. Luckily we can use the Strong’s concordance to see what the Hebrew word was, where it was used, and all the different ways it got interpreted.

Genesis 2:7

IHOT(i) (In English order)

7 H3335 וייצר formed H3068 יהוה And the LORD H430 אלהים God H853 את H120 האדם man H6083 עפר the dust H4480 מן of H127 האדמה the ground, H5301 ויפח and breathed H639 באפיו into his nostrils H5397 נשמת the breath H2416 חיים of life; H1961 ויהי became H120 האדם and man H5315 לנפש soul. H2416 חיה: a living

H5315 נפש - Strong's Hebrew Lexicon Number

Previous Strong's #H5314 Next Strong's #H5316

נפש

nephesh

neh'-fesh

From H5314; properly a breathing creature, that is, animal or (abstractly) vitality; used very widely in a literal, accommodated or figurative sense (bodily or mental)

KJV Usage: any, appetite, beast, body, breath, creature, X dead (-ly), desire, X [dis-] contented, X fish, ghost, + greedy, he, heart (-y), (hath, X jeopardy of) life (X in jeopardy), lust, man, me, mind, mortality, one, own, person, pleasure, (her-, him-, my-, thy-) self, them (your) -selves, + slay, soul, + tablet, they, thing, (X she) will, X would have it.

Brown-Driver-Briggs' Hebrew Definitions

נפש

1. soul, self, life, creature, person, appetite, mind, living being, desire, emotion, passion

a. that which breathes, the breathing substance or being, soul, the inner being of man

b. living being

c. living being (with life in the blood)

d. the man himself, self, person or individual

e. seat of the appetites

f. seat of emotions and passions

g. activity of mind

1. dubious

h. activity of the will

1. dubious

i. activity of the character

1. dubious

Origin: from H5314

TWOT: 1395a

Parts of Speech: Noun Feminine

We see that the word used as soul is nephesh. It means a breathing creature, an animal, describing the physical body or mental functions. The KJV scholars translated it many times in reference to physical life as well as to intellect or emotions. They also used it to mean mortality. Not immortality. Wouldn't it be a bit silly to let one word mean the exact opposite of itself?

I can see how they may have wanted to differentiate man from a cow or some other animal. We are different in the way we think and reason. But this verse does not say that we are immortal, but rather that we are mortal, the same as any other animal is mortal. This is not me, making up something. Check your own concordance, maybe I have missed something. I'm not the expert, I'm just reading the manual.

If there is some mistake about immortality, the next verses should help make it clearer.

Genesis 3:22-24

KJV Strongs(i)

22 H3068 And the LORD H430 God H559 said [H8799] H2005 , Behold H120 , the man H259 is become as one H3045 of us, to know [H8800] H2896 good H7451 and evil H7971 : and now, lest he put forth [H8799] H3027 his hand H3947 , and take [H8804] H6086 also of the tree H2416 of life H398 , and eat [H8804] H2425 , and live [H8804] H5769 for ever:

23 H3068 Therefore the LORD H430 God H7971 sent him forth [H8762] H1588 from the garden H5731 of Eden H5647 , to till [H8800] H127 the ground H3947 from whence he was taken [H8795].

24 H1644 So he drove out [H8762] H120 the man H7931 ; and he placed [H8686] H6924 at the east H1588 of the garden H5731 of Eden H3742 Cherubims H3858 , and a flaming H2719 sword H2015 which turned every way [H8693] H8104 , to keep [H8800] H1870 the way H6086 of the tree H2416 of life.

Notice God is saying that man, now after eating of the tree of knowledge, has become as one of us, to know good and evil. Mankind gained knowledge from their sin. Mankind didn't gain immortality. He was still mortal, just as he had been created in chapter 2:7. He hadn't eaten from the tree of life, and live for ever.3: 22/B. To make sure that mankind couldn't eat from the tree of life, God guarded it with Cherubim and a flaming sword.3:24.

Here after being sent out of the Garden of Eden by God, man is still mortal. The tree of life isn't available to mankind again until Jesus comes and establishes his kingdom. There is no other time mentioned in the bible where the tree of life is made available to mankind.

Revelation 22:1-5

KJV Strongs(i)

1 G2532 And G1166 he shewed [G5656] G3427 me G2513 a pure G4215
river G5204 of water G2222 of life G2986 , clear G5613 as G2930 crystal
G1607 , proceeding [G5740] G1537 out of G2362 the throne G2316 of
God G2532 and G721 of the Lamb.

2 G1722 In G3319 the midst G4113 of the street G846 of it G2532 , and
G2532 on either G1782 side G1782 G4215 of the river G3586 , was there
the tree G2222 of life G4160 , which bare [G5723] G1427 twelve G2590
manner of fruits G591 , and yielded [G5723] G846 her G2590 fruit G2596
every G1538 G1520 G3376 month G2532 : and G5444 the leaves G3586 of
the tree G1519 were for G2322 the healing G1484 of the nations.

3 G2532 And G2071 there shall be [G5704] G3756 no G2089 more G3956
G2652 curse G2532 : but G2362 the throne G2316 of God G2532 and
G721 of the Lamb G2071 shall be [G5704] G1722 in G846 it G2532 ; and
G846 his G1401 servants G3000 shall serve [G5692] G846 him:

4 G2532 And G3700 they shall see [G5695] G846 his G4383 face G2532 ;
and G846 his G3686 name G1909 shall be in G846 their G3359 foreheads.

5 G2532 And G2071 there shall be [G5704] G3756 no G3571 night G1563
there G2532 ; and G5532 they need G3756 no G3088 candle G2192
[G5719] G2532 , neither G5457 light G2246 of the sun G3754 ; for G2962
the Lord G2316 God G5461 giveth G846 them G5461 light [G5719] G2532
: and G936 they shall reign [G5692] G1519 for G165 ever G165 and ever.

Chapter 5: WHERE DOES THE IDEA OF IMMORTALITY COME FROM?

So where did the idea that we are immortal come from? Why is it so pervasive throughout humanity? The first reference to not dieing is in Genesis 3:4 but the source of the quote is untrustworthy. I think that you'll see what I mean when you read it.

Genesis 3:1-7

KJV Strongs(i)

1 H5175 Now the serpent H1961 was [H8804] H6175 more subtil H2416 than any beast H7704 of the field H3068 which the LORD H430 God H6213 had made [H8804] H559 . And he said [H8799] H802 unto the woman H637 , Yea H430 , hath God H559 said [H8804] H398 , Ye shall not eat [H8799] H6086 of every tree H1588 of the garden?

2 H802 And the woman H559 said [H8799] H5175 unto the serpent H398 , We may eat [H8799] H6529 of the fruit H6086 of the trees H1588 of the garden:

3 H6529 But of the fruit H6086 of the tree H8432 which is in the midst H1588 of the garden H430 , God H559 hath said [H8804] H398 , Ye shall not eat [H8799] H5060 of it, neither shall ye touch [H8799] H6435 it, lest H4191 ye die [H8799].

4 H5175 And the serpent H559 said [H8799] H802 unto the woman H4191 , Ye shall not surely [H8800] H4191 die [H8799]:

5 H430 For God H3045 doth know [H8802] H3117 that in the day H398 ye eat [H8800] H5869 thereof, then your eyes H6491 shall be opened [H8738] H430 , and ye shall be as gods H3045 , knowing [H8802] H2896 good H7451 and evil.

6 H802 And when the woman H7200 saw [H8799] H6086 that the tree H2896 was good H3978 for food H1931 , and that it H8378 was pleasant H5869 to the eyes H6086 , and a tree H2530 to be desired [H8737] H7919 to make one wise [H8687] H3947 , she took [H8799] H6529 of the fruit thereof H398 , and did eat [H8799] H5414 , and gave [H8799] H1571 also H376 unto her husband H398 with her; and he did eat [H8799].

7 H5869 And the eyes H8147 of them both H6491 were opened [H8735] H1992 , and they H3045 knew [H8799] H5903 that they were naked H8609 ; and they sewed H8384 fig H5929 leaves H8609 together [H8799] H6213 , and made themselves [H8799] H2290 aprons.

It is said that the best lies have truth embedded in them, add a little distraction, and misdirection for good measure to create the whole lie package. I included the whole story for context. Here we find Satan cleverly wrapping the lie that they wouldn't die, 3:4-5 in the truth that the tree of knowledge would give them the ability to know good and evil. Note they would be as {small g} gods knowing good from evil. Rejecting divine direction by God, and taking the responsibility of moral decisions into their own hands. This is the same power that Satan craved when he rebelled against God. He to, rejected the authority of God over his life.

We are familiar with the idea of original sin. But have we given any thought to the original lie. Where it came from, what it was. As I stated earlier, I do believe that there is a satanic conspiracy to keep us from the truth about Gods love and his plan for humanity. It is the oldest lie, and the most pervasive. Since most people on earth have it engrained into their culture in one form or another. After they die they aren't finished, “But wait there’s more!” is the most difficult lie to eradicate. And the brilliance of Satan’s lie is that it has a touch of truth to it. Because it isn't the end of us. We do have an afterlife, but it is dependent upon God to bring us back in his time frame. It's not something that we have built into us, that will occur naturally by itself. Rather something that God has promised he will do for us.

Once we understand that when we die; we do just that, we die. Then the thoughts of loved ones in the proverbial torture chamber of Hell at the moment of death aren't disturbing. Because we understand that they couldn't be there, they are dead in the grave. No medians talking to dead people. They may be talking to spirits pretending to be dead people. But the dead are just that, dead. Not mentally conscious somewhere looking down on us, or in great distress down below.

Chapter 6: TERMS USED FOR LIVED, DIED, IMMORTAL

So far we've only looked at three small sections of scripture. Let's continue through the OT and see what else we can find, then we can recap. I know that there are lots of references in the NT and we will get to them and see how they affect the mix. But it is important to know what happened to the people pre Jesus. It gives us the big picture. Maybe we'll find the key to immortality yet. And please feel free to disagree with the thoughts so far. This is a peripheral topic after all. I do ask that you'll be gentle in your criticism of the KJV and Strong's scholars as they are not able to defend themselves over any errors they may have made.

Genesis 5:26-27 Strongs

26 H4968 And Methuselah H2421 lived [H8799] H310 after H3205 he begat [H8687] H3929 Lamech H7651 seven H3967 hundred H8141 H8084 eighty H8147 and two H8141 years H3205 , and begat [H8686] H1121 sons H1323 and daughters:

27 H3117 And all the days H4968 of Methuselah H8672 were nine H3967 hundred H8141 H8346 sixty H8672 and nine H8141 years H4191 : and he died [H8799].

H2421 Chayah - Lived s used 235 times

H4191 Muth - Died is used 694 times

Previous Strong's #H2420 Next Strong's #H2422

חיה

châyâh

khaw-yaw'

A prim root (compare H2331, H2424); to live, whether literally or figuratively; causatively to revive

KJV Usage: keep (leave, make) alive, X certainly, give (promise) life, (let, suffer to) live, nourish up, preserve (alive), quicken, recover, repair, restore (to life), revive, (X God) save (alive, life, lives), X surely, be whole.

Previous Strong's #H4190 Next Strong's #H4192

מוּת

mûth

mooth

A primitive root; to die (literally or figuratively); causatively to kill

KJV Usage: X at all, X crying, (be) dead (body, man, one), (put to, worthy of) death, destroy (-er), (cause to, be like to, must) die, kill, necro [-mancer], X must needs, slay, X surely, X very suddenly, X in [no] wise.

These words live, and die seem to be in reference to mortal life. I won't be referencing them again do to time and space. They don't seem to pertain to immortality, or obtaining it.

Next we find God saying man is flesh. Some insist that God doesn't say that man isn't immortal, Only that he's made of flesh, man still could have immortality built in. That logic would also require God to say that reincarnation is false, along with any other belief not found in the bible.

God doesn't tell us what isn't true. He tells us what is true. We have to follow his truth as it is revealed to us. People trained in spotting counterfeit money don't study counterfeits, they study the real thing. Then they spot the fake bills by what's not there.

Genesis 6:3 Strongs

3 H3068 And the LORD H559 said [H8799] H7307 , My spirit H5769 shall not always H1777 strive [H8799] H120 with man H1571 , for that he also [H8677] H7683 [H8800] H1320 is flesh H3117 : yet his days H3967 shall be an hundred H6242 and twenty H8141 years.

H1320 בּשׂר - Strong's Hebrew Lexicon Number

Previous Strong's #H1319 Next Strong's #H1321

בּשׂר

bâśâr

baw-sawr'

From H1319; flesh (from its freshness); by extension body, person; also (by euphemism) the pudenda of a man

KJV Usage: body, [fat, lean] flesh [-ed], kin, [man-] kind, + nakedness, self, skin.

Jacob gives up the ghost. KJV uses the word ghost to mean die, or perish. It doesn't say it is eternal. He gives it up. It goes away from him. He didn't have it anymore. Which made him dead.

Genesis 49:33 Strongs

33 H3290 And when Jacob H3615 had made an end [H8762] H6680 of commanding [H8763] H1121 his sons H622 , he gathered up [H8799] H7272 his feet H4296 into the bed H1478 , and yielded up the ghost

[H8799] H622 , and was gathered [H8735] H5971 unto his people.

Previous Strong's #H1477 Next Strong's #H1478

גוע

gâvaʻ

gaw-vah'

A primitive root; to breathe out, that is, (by implication) expire

KJV Usage: die, be dead, give up the ghost, perish.

Brown-Driver-Briggs' Hebrew Definitions

גוע

1. to expire, die, perish, give up the ghost, yield up the ghost, be dead, be ready to die

a. (Qal) to expire, die, be about to die

Origin: a primitive root

TWOT: 328

Parts of Speech: Verb

Here is an example for the words life and death. Both referring to mortality.

Deuteronomy 30:19 Strongs

19 H5749 I call H8064 heaven H776 and earth H5749 to record [H8689] H3117 this day H5414 against you, that I have set [H8804] H6440 before H2416 you life H4194 and death H1293 , blessing H7045 and cursing H977

: therefore choose [H8804] H2416 life H2233 , that both thou and thy seed H2421 may live [H8799]:

H2416 Chay - Reference to mortal life. Used 452 times.

Previous Strong's #H2415 Next Strong's #H2417

חי

chay

khah'ee

From H2421; alive; hence raw (flesh); fresh (plant, water, year), strong; also (as noun, especially in the feminine singular and masculine plural) life (or living thing), whether literally or figuratively

KJV Usage: + age, alive, appetite, (wild) beast, company, congregation, life (-time), live (-ly), living (creature, thing), maintenance, + merry, multitude, + (be) old, quick, raw, running, springing, troop.

H4194 Maveth - Death, or the opposite to life. Used 155 Times.

Previous Strong's #H4193 Next Strong's #H4195

מות

mâveth

maw'-veth

From H4191; death (natural or violent); concretely the dead, their place or state (hades); figuratively pestilence, ruin

KJV Usage: (be) dead ([-ly]), death, die (-d).

Brown-Driver-Briggs' Hebrew Definitions

מות

1. death, dying, Death (personified), realm of the dead

a. death

b. death by violence (as a penalty)

c. state of death, place of death

Origin: from H4191

TWOT: 1169a

Parts of Speech: Noun Masculine

Choose life, so you can live. These words talk of physical mortal life. It isn't referring to eternal life. The Israelites never had eternal life. When Jesus talked about eternal life, the people wanted to know how to get it. {We'll see those references when we get to the NT.} They knew they had no access to immortality. Only physical blessings with a hope, or faith of more to come in the future.

Joshua is talking of dieing and turning back to dirt. No mention of an eternal afterlife, to be experienced immediately after death.

Joshua 23:14 Strongs

14 H3117 And, behold, this day H1980 I am going [H8802] H1870 the way H776 of all the earth H3045 : and ye know [H8804] H3824 in all your hearts H5315 and in all your souls H259 , that not one H1697 thing H5307 hath failed [H8804] H2896 of all the good H1697 things H3068 which the LORD H430 your God H1696 spake [H8765] H935 concerning you; all are

come to pass [H8804] H259 unto you, and not one H1697 thing H5307 hath failed [H8804] thereof.

Chapter 7: CAN SATAN RAISE THE DEAD?

This is a very interesting storey about Saul. It's the night before he dies. He goes to see a median so that he could talk to the prophet Samuel who was dead. Let's read it, and then ask some questions about it.

1 Samuel 28:9-20 Strongs

9 H802 And the woman H559 said [H8799] H3045 unto him, Behold, thou knowest [H8804] H7586 what Saul H6213 hath done [H8804] H3772 , how he hath cut off [H8689] H178 those that have familiar spirits H3049 , and the wizards H776 , out of the land H5367 : wherefore then layest thou a snare [H8693] H5315 for my life H4191 , to cause me to die [H8687]?

10 H7586 And Saul H7650 sware [H8735] H3068 to her by the LORD H559 , saying [H8800] H3068 , As the LORD H2416 liveth H518 , there shall H5771 no punishment H7136 happen [H8799] H1697 to thee for this thing.

11 H559 Then said [H8799] H802 the woman H5927 , Whom shall I bring up [H8686] H559 unto thee? And he said [H8799] H5927 , Bring me up [H8685] H8050 Samuel.

12 H802 And when the woman H7200 saw [H8799] H8050 Samuel H2199 , she cried [H8799] H1419 with a loud H6963 voice H802 : and the woman H559 spake [H8799] H7586 to Saul H559 , saying [H8800] H7411 , Why hast thou deceived [H8765] H7586 me? for thou art Saul.

13 H4428 And the king H559 said [H8799] H3372 unto her, Be not afraid

[H8799] H7200 : for what sawest [H8804] H802 thou? And the woman H559 said [H8799] H7586 unto Saul H7200 , I saw [H8804] H430 gods H5927 ascending [H8802] H776 out of the earth.

14 H559 And he said [H8799] H8389 unto her, What form H559 is he of? And she said [H8799] H2205 , An old H376 man H5927 cometh up [H8802] H5844 ; and he is covered [H8802] H4598 with a mantle H7586 . And Saul H3045 perceived [H8799] H8050 that it was Samuel H6915 , and he stooped [H8799] H639 with his face H776 to the ground H7812 , and bowed [H8691] himself.

15 H8050 And Samuel H559 said [H8799] H7586 to Saul H7264 , Why hast thou disquieted [H8689] H5927 me, to bring me up [H8687] H7586 ? And Saul H559 answered [H8799] H3966 , I am sore H6887 distressed [H8804] H6430 ; for the Philistines H3898 make war [H8737] H430 against me, and God H5493 is departed [H8804] H6030 from me, and answereth [H8804] H3027 me no more, neither by H5030 prophets H2472 , nor by dreams H7121 : therefore I have called [H8799] H3045 thee, that thou mayest make known [H8687] H6213 unto me what I shall do [H8799].

16 H559 Then said [H8799] H8050 Samuel H7592 , Wherefore then dost thou ask [H8799] H3068 of me, seeing the LORD H5493 is departed [H8804] H6145 from thee, and is become thine enemy?

17 H3068 And the LORD H6213 hath done [H8799] H1696 to him, as he spake [H8765] H3027 by me H3068 : for the LORD H7167 hath rent [H8799] H4467 the kingdom H3027 out of thine hand H5414 , and given [H8799] H7453 it to thy neighbour H1732 , even to David:

18 H834 Because H8085 thou obeyedst [H8804] H6963 not the voice H3068 of the LORD H6213 , nor executedst [H8804] H2740 his fierce H639 wrath H6002 upon Amalek H3068 , therefore hath the LORD H6213 done [H8804] H1697 this thing H3117 unto thee this day.

19 H3068 Moreover the LORD H5414 will also deliver [H8799] H3478 Israel H3027 with thee into the hand H6430 of the Philistines H4279 : and

to morrow H1121 shalt thou and thy sons H3068 be with me: the LORD H5414 also shall deliver [H8799] H4264 the host H3478 of Israel H3027 into the hand H6430 of the Philistines. 20 H7586 Then Saul H5307 fell [H8799] H4116 straightway [H8762] H4393 all H6967 along H776 on the earth H3966 , and was sore H3372 afraid [H8799] H1697 , because of the words H8050 of Samuel H3581 : and there was no strength H398 in him; for he had eaten [H8804] H3899 no bread H3117 all the day H3915 , nor all the night.

Some people may try to use this passage to show that Samuel was conscious somewhere. But note that Saul didn't see him, but asked the median what she saw. He took it to be Samuel. The woman had a familiar spirit. She talked to satanic forces. That is why God wanted all medians killed. The message that was given was foretold already by Samuel. It was also very demoralizing to Saul and it made him very afraid. Note she said that she saw him rising out of the ground rather than descending out of heaven. As well there is the question can Satan bring people back from the dead? Or more troubling, drag them back to earth from heaven? The implications can get deep if you believe that it was really Samuel. I believe that it was a spirit, pretending to be Samuel, to an ungodly king.

Chapter 8: SLEEP WITH THY FATHERS

The next few verses are very similar, so I have lumped them together. 2 Samuel 12 is often used to show that babies go directly to heaven when they die because the passage says David would go to his dead infant son. However we can see by other verses that David is sleeping in his grave along with his relatives. This fact would put the child in his own grave asleep. David would be rightly expecting to go and be with his son, they both are asleep in their graves.

2 Samuel 7:12 Strongs

12 H3117 And when thy days H4390 be fulfilled [H8799] H7901 , and thou shalt sleep [H8804] H1 with thy fathers H6965 , I will set up [H8689] H2233 thy seed H310 after H3318 thee, which shall proceed [H8799] H4578 out of thy bowels H3559 , and I will establish [H8689] H4467 his kingdom.

2 Samuel 12:19-23

19 But when David saw that his servants whispered, David perceived that the child was dead: therefore David said unto his servants, Is the child dead? And they said, He is dead.

20 Then David arose from the earth, and washed, and anointed himself, and changed his apparel, and came into the house of the LORD, and worshipped: then he came to his own house; and when he required, they set bread before him, and he did eat.

21 Then said his servants unto him, What thing is this that thou hast done? thou didst fast and weep for the child, while it was alive; but when the child was dead, thou didst rise and eat bread.

22 And he said, While the child was yet alive, I fasted and wept: for I said, Who can tell whether GOD will be gracious to me, that the child may live?

23 But now he is dead, wherefore should I fast? can I bring him back again? I shall go to him, but he shall not return to me.

1 Kings 2:10 Strongs

10 H1732 So David H7901 slept [H8799] H1 with his fathers H6912 , and was buried [H8735] H5892 in the city H1732 of David.

1 Kings 11:43 Strongs

43 H8010 And Solomon H7901 slept [H8799] H1 with his fathers H6912 , and was buried [H8735] H5892 in the city H1732 of David H1 his father H7346 : and Rehoboam H1121 his son H4427 reigned [H8799] in his stead.

SLEPT. H7901

--Decease, to lie down, to stay.-Used 194 times in reference to people who died. Notably David, and Solomon, two peoplewho you would think would be in heaven. But they are described as sleeping with their fathers. For space and time I probably won't use this word again. You can see that if nothing else, they aren't pictured as conscious and aware of their surroundings.

Previous Strong's #H7900 Next Strong's #H7902

שׁכב

shâkab

shaw-kab'

A primitive root; to lie down (for rest, sexual connection, decease or any other purpose)

KJV Usage: X at all, cast down, ([over-]) lay (self) (down), (make to) lie (down, down to sleep, still, with), lodge, ravish, take rest, sleep, stay.

Brown-Driver-Briggs' Hebrew Definitions

שׁכב

1. to lie down

a. (Qal)

1. to lie, lie down, lie on

2. to lodge

3. to lie (of sexual relations)

4. to lie down (in death)

5. to rest, relax (fig)

b. (Niphal) to be lain with (sexually)

c. (Pual) to be lain with (sexually)

d. (Hiphil) to make to lie down

e. (Hophal) to be laid

Origin: a primitive root

TWOT: 2381

Parts of Speech: Verb

Chapter 9: IN THE MOMENT LIFE RESTORATION

The soul is the same one that we saw in Gen. Nephesh. God brought the boy back to life, as a mortal. The boy wasn't from Israel so hadn't taken part in sacrifices to God. Nor would he have kept the laws of God. He was just the son of the widow that Elijah was staying with in a foreign land. So he wouldn't have been doing anything Godly or faithful to deserve resurrection.

1 Kings 17:22 Strongs

22 H3068 And the LORD H8085 heard [H8799] H6963 the voice H452 of Elijah H5315 ; and the soul H3206 of the child H7725 came H7130 into him H7725 again [H8799] H2421 , and he revived [H8799].

Here is a story of Elisha bringing another child back to life. Again no immortality is mentioned or referred to.

2 Kings 4:32-35 Strongs

32 H477 And when Elisha H935 was come [H8799] H1004 into the house H5288 , behold, the child H4191 was dead [H8801] H7901 , and laid [H8716] H4296 upon his bed.

33 H935 He went in [H8799] H5462 therefore, and shut [H8799] H1817

the door H8147 upon them twain H6419 , and prayed [H8691] H3068 unto the LORD.

34 H5927 And he went up [H8799] H7901 , and lay [H8799] H3206 upon the child H7760 , and put [H8799] H6310 his mouth H6310 upon his mouth H5869 , and his eyes H5869 upon his eyes H3709 , and his hands H3709 upon his hands H1457 : and he stretched [H8799] H1320 himself upon the child; and the flesh H3206 of the child H2552 waxed warm [H8799].

35 H7725 Then he returned [H8799] H3212 , and walked [H8799] H1004 in the house H259 to H2008 H259 and fro H2008 H5927 ; and went up [H8799] H1457 , and stretched [H8799] H5288 himself upon him: and the child H2237 sneezed [H8779] H7651 seven H6471 times H5288 , and the child H6491 opened [H8799] H5869 his eyes.

Sometimes to be restored to life you didn't need any faith or anything at all. Just the happenstance of touching the bones of a dead prophet of God.

2 Kings 13:21 Strongs

21 H6912 And it came to pass, as they were burying [H8802] H376 a man H7200 , that, behold, they spied [H8804] H1416 a band H7993 of men; and they cast [H8686] H376 the man H6913 into the sepulchre H477 of Elisha H376 : and when the man H3212 was let down [H8799] H5060 , and touched [H8799] H6106 the bones H477 of Elisha H2421 , he revived [H8799] H6965 , and stood up [H8799] H7272 on his feet.

Previous Strong's #H2420 Next Strong's #H2422

חיה

châyâh

khaw-yaw'

A prim root (compare H2331, H2424); to live, whether literally or figuratively; causatively to revive

KJV Usage: keep (leave, make) alive, X certainly, give (promise) life, (let, suffer to) live, nourish up, preserve (alive), quicken, recover, repair, restore (to life), revive, (X God) save (alive, life, lives), X surely, be whole.

Brown-Driver-Briggs' Hebrew Definitions

חיה

1. to live, have life, remain alive, sustain life, live prosperously, live for ever, be quickened, be alive, be restored to life or health

a. (Qal)

1. to live 1a

b. to have life 1a

c. to continue in life, remain alive 1a

d. to sustain life, to live on or upon 1a

e. to live (prosperously)

1. to revive, be quickened 1a

f. from sickness 1a

g. from discouragement 1a

h. from faintness 1a

i. from death

j. (Piel)

1. to preserve alive, let live

2. to give life

3. to quicken, revive, refresh 1b

k. to restore to life 1b

l. to cause to grow 1b

m. to restore 1b

n. to revive

o. (Hiphil)

1. to preserve alive, let live

2. to quicken, revive 1c

p. to restore (to health) 1c

q. to revive 1c

r. to restore to life

Origin: a primitive root [compare H2331, H2421]

TWOT: 644

Parts of Speech: Verb

Chapter 10: WHAT DOES JOB TELL US?

Here man is described as mortal. How can it be that we would be mortal, and immortal at the same time?

Job 4:17 Strongs

17 H582 Shall mortal man H6663 be more just [H8799] H433 than God H1397 ? shall a man H2891 be more pure [H8799] H6213 than his maker [H8802] ?

In this verse Job talks of where he expects to go when he dies. To be fair he was very melancholy at the time. It was a very dark time in his life, and he is talking metaphorically.

Job 10:20-22 Strongs

20 H3117 Are not my days H4592 few H2308 ? cease [H8798] [H8675] H2308 [H8799] H7896 then, and let me alone [H8798] [H8675] H7896 [H8799] H1082 , that I may take comfort [H8686] H4592 a little,

21 H3212 Before I go [H8799] H7725 whence I shall not return [H8799] H776 , even to the land H2822 of darkness H6757 and the shadow of death;

22 H776 A land H5890 of darkness H652 , as darkness H6757 itself; and of the shadow of death H5468 , without any order H3313 , and where the light [H8686] H652 is as darkness.

Here Job talks about waiting for his change, all the days of his appointed time. Definition C relief from death. He doesn't get that relief instantaneously, he has to wait for it.

Job 14:14 Strongs

14 H1397 If a man H4191 die [H8799] H2421 , shall he live [H8799] H3117 again ? all the days H6635 of my appointed time H3176 will I wait [H8762] H2487 , till my change H935 come [H8800].

Previous Strong's #H2486 Next Strong's #H2488

חליפה

chălîyphâh

khal-ee-faw'

From H2498; alternation

KJV Usage: change, course.

Brown-Driver-Briggs' Hebrew Definitions

חליפה

1. a change, change (of garments), replacement

a. change (of raiment)

b. relays

c. relief (from death)

d. changing, varying (course of life)

Origin: from H2498

TWOT: 666c

Parts of Speech: Noun Feminine

Job expecting death to come.

Job 16:22 Strongs

22 H4557 When a few H8141 years H857 are come [H8799] H1980 , then I shall go [H8799] H734 the way H7725 whence I shall not return [H8799].

Previous Strong's #H1979 Next Strong's #H1981

I think that he's saying in a few years he will die and go down a path leading to God and he won't turn off of it. Look through the definitions and see which one you would use to describe the words.

הלך

hâlak

haw-lak'

Akin to H3212; a primitive root; to walk (in a great variety of applications, literally and figuratively)

KJV Usage: (all) along, apace, behave (self), come, (on) continually, be conversant, depart, + be eased, enter, exercise (self), + follow, forth, forward, get, go (about, abroad, along, away, forward, on, out, up and down), + greater, grow, be wont to haunt, lead, march, X more and more, move (self), needs, on, pass (away), be at the point, quite, run (along), + send, speedily, spread, still, surely, + tale-bearer, + travel (-ler), walk (abroad, on, to and fro, up and down, to places), wander, wax, [way-] faring man, X be weak, whirl.

Brown-Driver-Briggs' Hebrew Definitions

הלך

1. to go, walk, come

a. (Qal)

1. to go, walk, come, depart, proceed, move, go away

2. to die, live, manner of life (fig.)

b. (Piel)

1. to walk

2. to walk (fig.)

c. (Hithpael)

1. to traverse

2. to walk about

d. (Niphal) to lead, bring, lead away, carry, cause to walk

Origin: akin to H3212, a primitive root

TWOT: 498

Previous Strong's #H7724 Next Strong's #H7726

שׁוּב

shûb

shoob

A primitive root; to turn back (hence, away) transitively or intransitively, literally or figuratively (not necessarily with the idea of return to the starting point); generally to retreat; often adverbially again

KJV Usage: ([break, build, circumcise, dig, do anything, do evil, feed, lay down, lie down, lodge, make, rejoice, send, take, weep]) X again, (cause to) answer (+ again), X in any case (wise), X at all, averse, bring (again, back, home again), call [to mind], carry again (back), cease, X certainly, come again (back) X consider, + continually, convert, deliver (again), + deny, draw back, fetch home again, X fro, get [oneself] (back) again, X give (again), go again (back, home), [go] out, hinder, let, [see] more, X needs, be past, X pay, pervert, pull in again, put (again, up again), recall, recompense, recover, refresh, relieve, render (again), X repent, requite, rescue, restore, retrieve, (cause to, make to) return, reverse, reward, + say nay, send back, set again, slide back, still, X surely, take back (off), (cause to, make to) turn (again, self again, away, back, back again, backward, from, off), withdraw.

Brown-Driver-Briggs' Hebrew Definitions

שׁוּב

1. to return, turn back

a. (Qal)

1. to turn back, return 1a

b. to turn back 1a

c. to return, come or go back 1a

d. to return unto, go back, come back 1a

e. of dying 1a

f. of human relations (fig) 1a

g. of spiritual relations (fig) 1a

1. to turn back (from God), apostatise 1a

2. to turn away (of God) 1a

3. to turn back (to God), repent 1a

4. turn back (from evil) 1a

h. of inanimate things 1a

i. in repetition

j. (Polel)

1. to bring back

2. to restore, refresh, repair (fig)

3. to lead away (enticingly)

4. to show turning, apostatise

k. (Pual) restored (participle)

l. (Hiphil) to cause to return, bring back

1. to bring back, allow to return, put back, draw back, give back, restore, relinquish, give in payment

2. to bring back, refresh, restore

3. to bring back, report to, answer

4. to bring back, make requital, pay (as recompense)

5. to turn back or backward, repel, defeat, repulse, hinder, reject, refuse

6. to turn away (face), turn toward

7. to turn against

8. to bring back to mind

9. to show a turning away 1d

2. to reverse, revoke

a. (Hophal) to be returned, be restored, be brought back

b. (Pulal) brought back

Origin: a primitive root

TWOT: 2340

Parts of Speech: Verb

Here is a great verse supporting a resurrection. His faith is that even though his body will be eaten by worms, he will see God on earth, in his flesh, in the end times. {Day of the Lord} How could this scripture work in the traditional understanding of heaven, and hell?

Job 19:25-26 Strongs

25 H3045 For I know [H8804] H1350 that my redeemer [H8802] H2416 liveth H6965 , and that he shall stand [H8799] H314 at the latter H6083 day upon the earth:

26 H310 And though after H5785 my skin H5362 worms destroy [H8765] H1320 this body, yet in my flesh H2372 shall I see [H8799] H433 God:

This tells us where we go when we die. A physical grave awaits our physical bodies. Nothing about immortality here. The wicked are reserved to the day of destruction, laying in the dust, remaining in the tomb.

Job 21:22-33 Strongs

22 H3925 Shall any teach [H8762] H410 God H1847 knowledge H8199 ? seeing he judgeth [H8799] H7311 those that are high [H8802].

23 H4191 One dieth [H8799] H8537 in his full H6106 strength H7946 , being wholly at ease H7961 and quiet.

24 H5845 His breasts H4390 are full [H8804] H2461 of milk H6106 , and his bones H8248 are moistened [H8792] H4221 with marrow.

25 H4191 And another dieth [H8799] H4751 in the bitterness H5315 of his soul H398 , and never eateth [H8804] H2896 with pleasure.

26 H7901 They shall lie down [H8799] H3162 alike H6083 in the dust H7415 , and the worms H3680 shall cover [H8762] them.

27 H3045 Behold, I know [H8804] H4284 your thoughts H4209 , and the devices H2554 which ye wrongfully imagine [H8799] against me.

28 H559 For ye say [H8799] H1004 , Where is the house H5081 of the prince H4908 ? and where are the dwelling H168 places H7563 of the wicked?

29 H7592 Have ye not asked [H8804] H5674 them that go [H8802] H1870 by the way H5234 ? and do ye not know [H8762] H226 their tokens,

30 H7451 That the wicked H2820 is reserved [H8735] H3117 to the day H343 of destruction H2986 ? they shall be brought forth [H8714] H3117 to the day H5678 of wrath.

31 H5046 Who shall declare [H8686] H1870 his way H6440 to his face H7999 ? and who shall repay [H8762] H6213 him what he hath done [H8804]?

32 H2986 Yet shall he be brought [H8714] H6913 to the grave H8245 , and shall remain [H8799] H1430 in the tomb.

33 H7263 The clods H5158 of the valley H4985 shall be sweet [H8804]

H120 unto him, and every man H4900 shall draw [H8799] H310 after H4557 him, as there are innumerable H6440 before him.

What spirit is being referred to? It is the breath of life that comes from God.

Job 27:3 Strongs

3 H5750 All the while H5397 my breath H7307 is in me, and the spirit H433 of God H639 is in my nostrils;

Previous Strong's #H7306 Next Strong's #H7308

רוּח

rûach

roo'-akh

From H7306; wind; by resemblance breath, that is, a sensible (or even violent) exhalation; figuratively life, anger, unsubstantiality; by extension a region of the sky; by resemblance spirit, but only of a rational being (including its expression and functions)

KJV Usage: air, anger, blast, breath, X cool, courage, mind, X quarter, X side, spirit ([-ual]), tempest, X vain, ([whirl-]) wind (-y).

Brown-Driver-Briggs' Hebrew Definitions

רוּח

1. wind, breath, mind, spirit

a. breath

b. wind

1. of heaven

2. quarter (of wind), side

3. breath of air

4. air, gas

5. vain, empty thing

c. spirit (as that which breathes quickly in animation or agitation)

1. spirit, animation, vivacity, vigour

2. courage

3. temper, anger

4. impatience, patience

5. spirit, disposition (as troubled, bitter, discontented)

6. disposition (of various kinds), unaccountable or uncontrollable impulse

7. prophetic spirit

d. spirit (of the living, breathing being in man and animals)

1. as gift, preserved by God, God's spirit, departing at death, disembodied being

e. spirit (as seat of emotion)

1. desire

2. sorrow, trouble

f. spirit

1. as seat or organ of mental acts

2. rarely of the will

3. as seat especially of moral character

g. Spirit of God, the third person of the triune God, the Holy Spirit, coequal, coeternal with the Father and the Son

1. as inspiring ecstatic state of prophecy

2. as impelling prophet to utter instruction or warning

3. imparting warlike energy and executive and administrative power

4. as endowing men with various gifts

5. as energy of life

6. as manifest in the Shekinah glory

7. never referred to as a depersonalised force

Origin: from H7306

TWOT: 2131a

Parts of Speech: Noun Feminine

Chapter 11: PSALMS AND PROVERBS TALK ABOUT ETERNAL LIFE?

We have no memory of, nor do we thank God. Sounds like it's describing a dead mortal. Void of any conscious thought.

Psalms 6:5 Strongs

5 H4194 For in death H2143 there is no remembrance H7585 of thee: in the grave H3034 who shall give thee thanks [H8686] ?

Who is our redeemer? When will we have victory over the grave? As these questions need the NT for a proper answer, we will get to them. But for now, his soul would not be redeemed at death, as his redeemer had not yet redeemed it. Rule two would apply. Mankind is only saved by the atoning sacrifice of Jesus. The whole of humanity is saved by Jesus blotting out our sins on the cross. To say that anyone from before Christ could have been reconciled to God makes a mockery of what Christ did for us all, and cheapens his sacrifice. Wasn't Jesus pleading for another way in the garden of Gethsemane? No other way was found, as there is no other way. But here in Psalms the author has faith that he will be redeemed at some point in the future.

Psalms 49:15 Strongs

15 H430 But God H6299 will redeem [H8799] H5315 my soul H3027 from the power H7585 of the grave H3947 : for he shall receive [H8799] H5542

me. Selah.

I'm including this verse as a representation for the use of the word hell. It was used 63 times. The definitions range from place of the dead, to punishment for the sinful. Both are accurate. It is a place for the dead, the grave. Where the body is consumed by worms and we go back to the earth that we were made from. Later when God brings us back to life, and we see him in our flesh. Then the wicked who reject God, will go to hell. That is their punishment. Till the day of wrath comes we wait in our graves. Some wait for rejoicing, some wait for punishment.

Psalms 55:15 Strongs

15 H4194 Let death H5377 seize [H8686] [H8675] H3451 H3381 upon them, and let them go down [H8799] H2416 quick H7585 into hell H7451 : for wickedness H4033 is in their dwellings H7130 , and among them.

Previous Strong's #H7584 Next Strong's #H7586

שְׁאוֹל שְׁאֹל

she 'ôl she 'ôl

sheh-ole', sheh-ole'

From H7592; hades or the world of the dead (as if a subterranian retreat), including its accessories and inmates

KJV Usage: grave, hell, pit.

Brown-Driver-Briggs' Hebrew Definitions

שְׁאוֹל שְׁאֹל

1. sheol, underworld, grave, hell, pit

a. the underworld

b. Sheol - the OT designation for the abode of the dead

1. place of no return

2. without praise of God

3. wicked sent there for punishment

4. righteous not abandoned to it

5. of the place of exile (fig)

6. of extreme degradation in sin

Origin: from H7592

TWOT: 2303c

Parts of Speech: Noun Feminine

I think this verse ties in quite nicely with my thoughts on the above scripture. Judgement is yet to come. The dead have to wait in their graves till then.

Psalms 98:8-9 Strongs

8 H5104 Let the floods H4222 clap [H8799] H3709 their hands H2022 : let the hills H7442 be joyful [H8762] H3162 together

9 H6440 Before H3068 the LORD H935 ; for he cometh [H8804] H8199 to judge [H8800] H776 the earth H6664 : with righteousness H8199 shall he judge [H8799] H8398 the world H5971 , and the people H4339 with equity.

No eternal life mentioned here.

Psalms 115:17 Strongs

17 H4191 The dead [H8301] H1984 praise [H8762] H3050 not the LORD H3381 , neither any that go down [H8802] H1745 into silence.

This next verse talks about the path to immortality. And how to find it. It doesn't say that we have it. I have included three modern translations to help clarify the meaning. Google some other translations and see what you come up with.

New International Version (©2011)

In the way of righteousness there is life; along that path is immortality.

New Living Translation (©2007)

The way of the godly leads to life; that path does not lead to death.

Holman Christian Standard Bible (©2009)

There is life in the path of righteousness, but another path leads to death.

Proverbs 12:28 Strongs

28 H734 In the way H6666 of righteousness H2416 is life H5410 ; and in the pathway H1870 H4194 thereof there is no death.

Chapter 12: SOLOMON IN ALL HIS WISDOM DIDN'T HAVE IMMORTALITY

Again I will include some other translations in an attempt to clarify what is being said. Look up alternate translations for yourself and see if you agree. Remember that all of the scriptures should be able to blend together to give the overall picture of our subject.

Ecclesiastes.3:21

New Living Translation (©2007)

For who can prove that the human spirit goes up and the spirit of animals goes down into the earth?

New American Standard Bible (©1995)

Who knows that the breath of man ascends upward and the breath of the beast descends downward to the earth?

King James Version (Cambridge Ed.)

Who knoweth the spirit of man that goeth upward, and the spirit of the beast that goeth downward to the earth?

International Standard Version (©2012)

Who knows whether the spirit of human beings ascends, and whether the spirit of animals descends to the earth?

GOD'S WORD® Translation (©1995)

Who knows whether a human spirit goes upward or whether an animal spirit goes downward to the earth?

All return to dust. Beast and man. All go to the same place.

Ecclesiastes 3:19-22 Strongs

19 H4745 For that which befalleth H1121 the sons H120 of men H4745 befalleth H929 beasts H259 ; even one thing H4745 befalleth H4194 them: as the one dieth H4194 , so dieth H2088 the other H259 ; yea, they have all one H7307 breath H120 ; so that a man H4195 hath no preeminence H929 above a beast H1892 : for all is vanity.

20 H1980 All go [H8802] H259 unto one H4725 place H6083 ; all are of the dust H7725 , and all turn H6083 to dust H7725 again [H8804].

21 H3045 Who knoweth [H8802] H7307 the spirit H1121 of man H120 H5927 that goeth [H8802] H4605 upward H7307 , and the spirit H929 of the beast H3381 that goeth [H8802] H4295 downward H776 to the earth?

22 H7200 Wherefore I perceive [H8804] H2896 that there is nothing better H120 , than that a man H8055 should rejoice [H8799] H4639 in his own works H2506 ; for that is his portion H935 : for who shall bring [H8686] H7200 him to see [H8800] H310 what shall be after him?

Again the dead are unaware of what is going on in the land of the living. They are described as not knowing anything, and will be forgotten in time, by those left alive.

Ecclesiastes 9:5-6 Strongs

5 H2416 For the living H3045 know [H8802] H4191 that they shall die [H8799] H4191 : but the dead [H8801] H3045 know [H8802] H3972 not

any thing H7939 , neither have they any more a reward H2143 ; for the memory H7911 of them is forgotten [H8738].

6 H160 Also their love H8135 , and their hatred H7068 , and their envy H3528 , is now H6 perished [H8804] H2506 ; neither have they any more a portion H5769 for ever H6213 in any thing that is done [H8738] H8121 under the sun.

Spirit is used 348 times. This scripture is talking about death and turning back into dirt. We can probably agree on the first part. To see what is being said about the spirit, we should consult our concordance. What is the spirit, according to the experts who study Hebrew?

Below are the definitions. The first ones say that it is our breath. Next our vivacity or physical attributes. It's the power that makes us go. Then it could also be our emotions. We have the spirit to win, or we lost our spirit to live when things looked to be too overwhelming for us.

Definition *d. spirit (of the living, breathing being in man and animals)

This is probably not the definition most people would choose as it puts people on par with animals.

Definition *1. as gift, preserved by God, God's spirit, departing at death, disembodied being.

This is probably the definition that most people would use.

So, what is the spirit? Firstly it's a gift. God gives it to us. It belongs to him, God's spirit. Not man's spirit, God's. It leaves us at death, where does it go? "Shall return unto God who gave it." God is getting his spirit back from us when we die. It is not man's spirit. It is not some part of us that is immortal. It is the spirit that God gave us at birth, going back to him. If we were asked to give a short description of God's spirit. We might say it was a disembodied being.

There are other definitions for spirit in the Strong's concordance. None of them say that man possesses one that is immortal and belongs to him. Also when coming to your understanding of this verse, don't forget about fitting it in with the other scriptures on the same subject. Will your understanding blend with what the other scriptures have to say?

Ecclesiastes 12:7 Strongs

7 H6083 Then shall the dust H7725 return [H8799] H776 to the earth H7307 as it was: and the spirit H7725 shall return [H8799] H430 unto God H5414 who gave [H8804] it.

Previous Strong's #H7306 Next Strong's #H7308

רוּח

rûach

roo'-akh

From H7306; wind; by resemblance breath, that is, a sensible (or even violent) exhalation; figuratively life, anger, unsubstantiality; by extension a region of the sky; by resemblance spirit, but only of a rational being (including its expression and functions)

KJV Usage: air, anger, blast, breath, X cool, courage, mind, X quarter, X side, spirit ([-ual]), tempest, X vain, ([whirl-]) wind (-y).

Brown-Driver-Briggs' Hebrew Definitions

רוּח

1. wind, breath, mind, spirit

a. breath

b. wind

1. of heaven

2. quarter (of wind), side

3. breath of air

4. air, gas

5. vain, empty thing

c. spirit (as that which breathes quickly in animation or agitation)

1. spirit, animation, vivacity, vigour

2. courage

3. temper, anger

4. impatience, patience

5. spirit, disposition (as troubled, bitter, discontented)

6. disposition (of various kinds), unaccountable or uncontrollable impulse

7. prophetic spirit

*d. spirit (of the living, breathing being in man and animals)

*1. as gift, preserved by God, God's spirit, departing at death, disembodied being

e. spirit (as seat of emotion)

1. desire

2. sorrow, trouble

f. spirit

1. as seat or organ of mental acts

2. rarely of the will

3. as seat especially of moral character

g. Spirit of God, the third person of the triune God, the Holy Spirit, coequal, coeternal with the Father and the Son

1. as inspiring ecstatic state of prophecy

2. as impelling prophet to utter instruction or warning

3. imparting warlike energy and executive and administrative power

4. as endowing men with various gifts

5. as energy of life

6. as manifest in the Shekinah glory

7. never referred to as a depersonalised force

Origin: from H7306

TWOT: 2131a

Parts of Speech: Noun Feminine

Chapter 13: RESSURECTIONS OF THE DEAD AND WHERE THEY WILL BE LIVING

The Hebrew words here all refer to a physical, mortal rebirth. It describes them awakening from sleeping in the earth. The dead arising out of the earth to life. Verse 21 of the passage seams to place this event in the end times, during Gods punishment of mankind for their iniquity.

As we are looking for the source of eternal life, this doesn't seem to be it. It is however a step along the path. If you'd like to, try some other translations on your own for further clarification.

Isaiah 26:19-21 Strongs

19 H4191 Thy dead [H8801] H2421 men shall live [H8799] H5038 , together with my dead body H6965 shall they arise [H8799] H6974 . Awake [H8685] H7442 and sing [H8761] H7931 , ye that dwell [H8802] H6083 in dust H2919 : for thy dew H2919 is as the dew H219 of herbs H776 , and the earth H5307 shall cast out [H8686] H7496 the dead.

20 H3212 Come [H8798] H5971 , my people H935 , enter [H8798] H2315 thou into thy chambers H5462 , and shut [H8798] H1817 thy doors H2247 about thee: hide [H8798] H4592 thyself as it were for a little H7281 moment H2195 , until the indignation H5674 be overpast [H8799].

21 H3068 For, behold, the LORD H3318 cometh out [H8802] H4725 of his place H6485 to punish [H8800] H3427 the inhabitants [H8802] H776 of

the earth H5771 for their iniquity H776 : the earth H1540 also shall disclose [H8765] H1818 her blood H3680 , and shall no more cover [H8762] H2026 her slain [H8803].

These next verses tell us a bit about what it will be like after Christ returns and establishes the kingdom of God here on earth. Verse 20 shows how those in the second resurrection will live out a full life of up to one hundred years in order to decide if they will choose Gods way of life, or not. We will be revisiting these verses as we get into the New Testament scriptures.

Isaiah 65:17-25

17 For, behold, I create new heavens and a new earth: and the former shall not be remembered, nor come into mind.

18 But be ye glad and rejoice for ever in that which I create: for, behold, I create Jerusalem a rejoicing, and her people a joy.

19 And I will rejoice in Jerusalem, and joy in my people: and the voice of weeping shall be no more heard in her, nor the voice of crying.

20 There shall be no more thence an infant of days, nor an old man that hath not filled his days: for the child shall die an hundred years old; but the sinner being an hundred years old shall be accursed.

21 And they shall build houses, and inhabit them; and they shall plant vineyards, and eat the fruit of them.

22 They shall not build, and another inhabit; they shall not plant, and another eat: for as the days of a tree are the days of my people, and mine elect shall long enjoy the work of their hands.

23 They shall not labour in vain, nor bring forth for trouble; for they are the seed of the blessed of the LORD, and their offspring with them.

24 And it shall come to pass, that before they call, I will answer; and while they are yet speaking, I will hear.

25 The wolf and the lamb shall feed together, and the lion shall eat straw like the bullock: and dust shall be the serpent's meat. They shall not hurt nor destroy in all my holy mountain, saith the LORD.

Isaiah 66:22-24

22 For as the new heavens and the new earth, which I will make, shall remain before me, saith the LORD, so shall your seed and your name remain.

23 And it shall come to pass, that from one new moon to another, and from one sabbath to another, shall all flesh come to worship before me, saith the LORD.

24 And they shall go forth, and look upon the carcases of the men that have transgressed against me: for their worm shall not die, neither shall their fire be quenched; and they shall be an abhorring unto all flesh.

Here during the Kingdom of God. The transgressors of God will be dead. The usage of the word carcases makes it plain that they are dead.

Isaiah 66:24 Strongs

24 H3318 And they shall go forth [H8804] H7200 , and look [H8804] H6297 upon the carcases H582 of the men H6586 that have transgressed [H8802] H8438 against me: for their worm H4191 shall not die [H8799] H784 , neither shall their fire H3518 be quenched [H8799] H1860 ; and they shall be an abhorring H1320 unto all flesh.

פגר

peger

peh'-gher

From H6296; a carcase (as limp), whether of man or beast; figuratively an idolatrous image

KJV Usage: carcase, corpse, dead body.

Brown-Driver-Briggs' Hebrew Definitions

פגר

1. corpse, carcass, monument, stela

a. corpse (of man)

b. carcass (of animals)

These next verses describe how Ezekiel was shown by God how the resurrection of the dead would occur. Verse 9 is reminiscent of how Adam was formed, and then came to life, after the breath of life came into him. Ezekiel 37:1-14

1 The hand of the LORD was upon me, and carried me out in the spirit of the LORD, and set me down in the midst of the valley which was full of bones,

2 And caused me to pass by them round about: and, behold, there were very many in the open valley; and, lo, they were very dry.

3 And he said unto me, Son of man, can these bones live? And I answered, O Lord GOD, thou knowest.

4 Again he said unto me, Prophesy upon these bones, and say unto them, O ye dry bones, hear the word of the LORD.

5 Thus saith the Lord GOD unto these bones; Behold, I will cause breath to

enter into you, and ye shall live:

6 And I will lay sinews upon you, and will bring up flesh upon you, and cover you with skin, and put breath in you, and ye shall live; and ye shall know that I am the LORD.

7 So I prophesied as I was commanded: and as I prophesied, there was a noise, and behold a shaking, and the bones came together, bone to his bone.

8 And when I beheld, lo, the sinews and the flesh came up upon them, and the skin covered them above: but there was no breath in them.

9 Then said he unto me, Prophesy unto the wind, prophesy, son of man, and say to the wind, Thus saith the Lord GOD; Come from the four winds, O breath, and breathe upon these slain, that they may live.

10 So I prophesied as he commanded me, and the breath came into them, and they lived, and stood up upon their feet, an exceeding great army.

11 Then he said unto me, Son of man, these bones are the whole house of Israel: behold, they say, Our bones are dried, and our hope is lost: we are cut off for our parts.

12 Therefore prophesy and say unto them, Thus saith the Lord GOD; Behold, O my people, I will open your graves, and cause you to come up out of your graves, and bring you into the land of Israel.

13 And ye shall know that I am the LORD, when I have opened your graves, O my people, and brought you up out of your graves,

14 And shall put my spirit in you, and ye shall live, and I shall place you in your own land: then shall ye know that I the LORD have spoken it, and performed it, saith the LORD.

Chapter 14: A WARNING FOR THE UNGODLY OF THE FUTURE WORLD

God sends a waring to Gog.

Ezekiel 38:1-23

1 And the word of the LORD came unto me, saying,

2 Son of man, set thy face against Gog, the land of Magog, the chief prince of Meshech and Tubal, and prophesy against him,

3 And say, Thus saith the Lord GOD; Behold, I am against thee, O Gog, the chief prince of Meshech and Tubal:

4 And I will turn thee back, and put hooks into thy jaws, and I will bring thee forth, and all thine army, horses and horsemen, all of them clothed with all sorts of armour, even a great company with bucklers and shields, all of them handling swords:

5 Persia, Ethiopia, and Libya with them; all of them with shield and helmet:

6 Gomer, and all his bands; the house of Togarmah of the north quarters, and all his bands: and many people with thee.

7 Be thou prepared, and prepare for thyself, thou, and all thy company that are assembled unto thee, and be thou a guard unto them.

8 After many days thou shalt be visited: in the latter years thou shalt

come into the land that is brought back from the sword, and is gathered out of many people, against the mountains of Israel, which have been always waste: but it is brought forth out of the nations, and they shall dwell safely all of them.

9 Thou shalt ascend and come like a storm, thou shalt be like a cloud to cover the land, thou, and all thy bands, and many people with thee.

10 Thus saith the Lord GOD; It shall also come to pass, that at the same time shall things come into thy mind, and thou shalt think an evil thought:

11 And thou shalt say, I will go up to the land of unwalled villages; I will go to them that are at rest, that dwell safely, all of them dwelling without walls, and having neither bars nor gates,

12 To take a spoil, and to take a prey; to turn thine hand upon the desolate places that are now inhabited, and upon the people that are gathered out of the nations, which have gotten cattle and goods, that dwell in the midst of the land.

13 Sheba, and Dedan, and the merchants of Tarshish, with all the young lions thereof, shall say unto thee, Art thou come to take a spoil? hast thou gathered thy company to take a prey? to carry away silver and gold, to take away cattle and goods, to take a great spoil?

14 Therefore, son of man, prophesy and say unto Gog, Thus saith the Lord GOD; In that day when my people of Israel dwelleth safely, shalt thou not know it?

15 And thou shalt come from thy place out of the north parts, thou, and many people with thee, all of them riding upon horses, a great company, and a mighty army:

16 And thou shalt come up against my people of Israel, as a cloud to cover the land; it shall be in the latter days, and I will bring thee against my land, that the heathen may know me, when I shall be sanctified in thee, O Gog, before their eyes.

17 Thus saith the Lord GOD; Art thou he of whom I have spoken in old time by my servants the prophets of Israel, which prophesied in those days many years that I would bring thee against them?

18 And it shall come to pass at the same time when Gog shall come against the land of Israel, saith the Lord GOD, that my fury shall come up in my face.

19 For in my jealousy and in the fire of my wrath have I spoken, Surely in that day there shall be a great shaking in the land of Israel;

20 So that the fishes of the sea, and the fowls of the heaven, and the beasts of the field, and all creeping things that creep upon the earth, and all the men that are upon the face of the earth, shall shake at my presence, and the mountains shall be thrown down, and the steep places shall fall, and every wall shall fall to the ground.

21 And I will call for a sword against him throughout all my mountains, saith the Lord GOD: every man's sword shall be against his brother.

22 And I will plead against him with pestilence and with blood; and I will rain upon him, and upon his bands, and upon the many people that are with him, an overflowing rain, and great hailstones, fire, and brimstone.

23 Thus will I magnify myself, and sanctify myself; and I will be known in the eyes of many nations, and they shall know that I am the LORD.

These warnings are forerunners of similar events found in the NT.

Ezekiel 39:1-29

1 Therefore, thou son of man, prophesy against Gog, and say, Thus saith the Lord GOD; Behold, I am against thee, O Gog, the chief prince of Meshech and Tubal:

2 And I will turn thee back, and leave but the sixth part of thee, and will

cause thee to come up from the north parts, and will bring thee upon the mountains of Israel:

3 And I will smite thy bow out of thy left hand, and will cause thine arrows to fall out of thy right hand.

4 Thou shalt fall upon the mountains of Israel, thou, and all thy bands, and the people that is with thee: I will give thee unto the ravenous birds of every sort, and to the beasts of the field to be devoured.

5 Thou shalt fall upon the open field: for I have spoken it, saith the Lord GOD.

6 And I will send a fire on Magog, and among them that dwell carelessly in the isles: and they shall know that I am the LORD.

7 So will I make my holy name known in the midst of my people Israel; and I will not let them pollute my holy name any more: and the heathen shall know that I am the LORD, the Holy One in Israel.

8 Behold, it is come, and it is done, saith the Lord GOD; this is the day whereof I have spoken.

9 And they that dwell in the cities of Israel shall go forth, and shall set on fire and burn the weapons, both the shields and the bucklers, the bows and the arrows, and the handstaves, and the spears, and they shall burn them with fire seven years:

10 So that they shall take no wood out of the field, neither cut down any out of the forests; for they shall burn the weapons with fire: and they shall spoil those that spoiled them, and rob those that robbed them, saith the Lord GOD.

11 And it shall come to pass in that day, that I will give unto Gog a place there of graves in Israel, the valley of the passengers on the east of the sea: and it shall stop the noses of the passengers: and there shall they bury Gog and all his multitude: and they shall call it The valley of Hamongog.

12 And seven months shall the house of Israel be burying of them, that they may cleanse the land.

13 Yea, all the people of the land shall bury them; and it shall be to them a renown the day that I shall be glorified, saith the Lord GOD.

14 And they shall sever out men of continual employment, passing through the land to bury with the passengers those that remain upon the face of the earth, to cleanse it: after the end of seven months shall they search.

15 And the passengers that pass through the land, when any seeth a man's bone, then shall he set up a sign by it, till the buriers have buried it in the valley of Hamongog.

16 And also the name of the city shall be Hamonah. Thus shall they cleanse the land.

17 And, thou son of man, thus saith the Lord GOD; Speak unto every feathered fowl, and to every beast of the field, Assemble yourselves, and come; gather yourselves on every side to my sacrifice that I do sacrifice for you, even a great sacrifice upon the mountains of Israel, that ye may eat flesh, and drink blood.

18 Ye shall eat the flesh of the mighty, and drink the blood of the princes of the earth, of rams, of lambs, and of goats, of bullocks, all of them fatlings of Bashan.

19 And ye shall eat fat till ye be full, and drink blood till ye be drunken, of my sacrifice which I have sacrificed for you.

20 Thus ye shall be filled at my table with horses and chariots, with mighty men, and with all men of war, saith the Lord GOD.

21 And I will set my glory among the heathen, and all the heathen shall see my judgment that I have executed, and my hand that I have laid upon them.

22 So the house of Israel shall know that I am the LORD their God from that day and forward.

23 And the heathen shall know that the house of Israel went into captivity for their iniquity: because they trespassed against me, therefore hid I my face from them, and gave them into the hand of their enemies: so fell they all by the sword.

24 According to their uncleanness and according to their transgressions have I done unto them, and hid my face from them.

25 Therefore thus saith the Lord GOD; Now will I bring again the captivity of Jacob, and have mercy upon the whole house of Israel, and will be jealous for my holy name;

26 After that they have borne their shame, and all their trespasses whereby they have trespassed against me, when they dwelt safely in their land, and none made them afraid.

27 When I have brought them again from the people, and gathered them out of their enemies' lands, and am sanctified in them in the sight of many nations;

28 Then shall they know that I am the LORD their God, which caused them to be led into captivity among the heathen: but I have gathered them unto their own land, and have left none of them any more there.

29 Neither will I hide my face any more from them: for I have poured out my spirit upon the house of Israel, saith the Lord GOD.

Chapter 15: FINAL THOUGHTS FROM THE OLD TESTEMANT

This is an interesting description of dead people. It talks of them being asleep in the dust of the earth. Then at the time of trouble like never before, they are to be awakened. Some to everlasting life. If they are being woken up to everlasting life at this point, then it stands to reason that they didn't have everlasting life previously. And if they did. Why would they be sleeping {dead} in the dust of the earth? And then awakened to everlasting life?

Notice also, that those awaken to shame, aren't said to have eternal life. Only everlasting contempt. Contempt isn't something that you have. But rather, something that others have towards you. Those with eternal life, can have everlasting contempt for the ones that are dead. They are to awaken and be ashamed that they will be held in everlasting contempt. It doesn't say that they will have eternal life. Only the wise and righteous will receive eternal life.

Verse 3 gives us a glimpse of what our glorified bodies might look like. Or is it purely metaphorical? Give it some thought. There will be other verses later on the subject.

Daniel 12:2-3 Strongs

2 H7227 And many H3463 of them that sleep H6083 in the dust H127 of the earth H6974 shall awake [H8686] H5769 , some to everlasting H2416 life H2781 , and some to shame H5769 and everlasting H1860 contempt.

3 H7919 And they that be wise [H8688] H2094 shall shine [H8686] H2096 as the brightness H7549 of the firmament H7227; and they that turn many H6663 to righteousness [H8688] H3556 as the stars H5769 for ever H5703 and ever.

Who paid our ransom for sin? Who is our redeemer from death? Christ is the answer. If we are to be redeemed from death, then we have to be dead. Which would preclude eternal life being innate within us.

Hosea 13:14 Strongs

14 H6299 I will ransom [H8799] H3027 them from the power H7585 of the grave H1350 ; I will redeem [H8799] H4194 them from death H4194 : O death H165 , I will H1698 be thy plagues H7585 ; O grave H165 , I will H6987 be thy destruction H5164 : repentance H5641 shall be hid [H8735] H5869 from mine eyes.

Zechariah here describes the vision that he had of Christs return. It is interesting that the one fighting against the nations is the LORD. When the NT writings give that role to Christ. Would this make Jesus Christ the LORD of the OT?

Zechariah 14:1-21 Strongs

1 H3117 Behold, the day H3068 of the LORD H935 cometh [H8804] H7998 , and thy spoil H2505 shall be divided [H8795] H7130 in the midst of thee.

2 H622 For I will gather [H8804] H1471 all nations H3389 against Jerusalem H4421 to battle H5892 ; and the city H3920 shall be taken [H8738] H1004 , and the houses H8155 rifled [H8738] H802 , and the women H7901 ravished [H8735] [H8675] H7693 [H8735] H2677 ; and half H5892 of the city H3318 shall go forth [H8804] H1473 into captivity H3499

, and the residue H5971 of the people H3772 shall not be cut off [H8735] H5892 from the city.

3 H3068 Then shall the LORD H3318 go forth [H8804] H3898 , and fight [H8738] H1471 against those nations H3117 , as when H3898 he fought [H8736] H3117 in the day H7128 of battle.

4 H7272 And his feet H5975 shall stand [H8804] H3117 in that day H2022 upon the mount H2132 of Olives H6440 , which is before H3389 Jerusalem H6924 on the east H2022 , and the mount H2132 of Olives H1234 shall cleave [H8738] H2677 in the midst H4217 thereof toward the east H3220 and toward the west H3966 , and there shall be a very H1419 great H1516 valley H2677 ; and half H2022 of the mountain H4185 shall remove [H8804] H6828 toward the north H2677 , and half H5045 of it toward the south.

5 H5127 And ye shall flee [H8804] H1516 to the valley H2022 of the mountains H1516 ; for the valley H2022 of the mountains H5060 shall reach [H8686] H682 unto Azal H5127 : yea, ye shall flee [H8804] H5127 , like as ye fled [H8804] H6440 from before H7494 the earthquake H3117 in the days H5818 of Uzziah H4428 king H3063 of Judah H3068 : and the LORD H430 my God H935 shall come [H8804] H6918 , and all the saints with thee.

6 H3117 And it shall come to pass in that day H216 , that the light H3368 shall not be clear H7087 , nor dark [H8675] H7087 [H8799] :

7 H259 But it shall be one H3117 day H3045 which shall be known [H8735] H3068 to the LORD H3117 , not day H3915 , nor night H6153 : but it shall come to pass, that at evening H6256 time H216 it shall be light.

8 H3117 And it shall be in that day H2416 , that living H4325 waters H3318 shall go out [H8799] H3389 from Jerusalem H2677 ; half H6931 of them toward the former H3220 sea H2677 , and half H314 of them toward the hinder H3220 sea H7019 : in summer H2779 and in winter shall it be.

9 H3068 And the LORD H4428 shall be king H776 over all the earth H3117 : in that day H259 shall there be one H3068 LORD H8034 , and his name H259 one.

10 H776 All the land H5437 shall be turned [H8735] H6160 as a plain H1387 from Geba H7417 to Rimmon H5045 south H3389 of Jerusalem H7213 : and it shall be lifted up [H8804] H3427 , and inhabited [H8804] H1144 in her place, from Benjamin's H8179 gate H4725 unto the place H7223 of the first H8179 gate H6434 , unto the corner H8179 gate H4026 , and from the tower H2606 of Hananeel H4428 unto the king's H3342 winepresses.

11 H3427 And men shall dwell [H8804] H2764 in it, and there shall be no more utter destruction H3389 ; but Jerusalem H983 shall be safely H3427 inhabited [H8804] .

12 H4046 And this shall be the plague H3068 wherewith the LORD H5062 will smite [H8799] H5971 all the people H6633 that have fought [H8804]H3389 against Jerusalem H1320 ; Their flesh H4743 shall consume away [H8687] H5975 while they stand [H8802] H7272 upon their feet H5869 , and their eyes H4743 shall consume away [H8735] H2356 in their holes H3956 , and their tongue H4743 shall consume away [H8735] H6310 in their mouth.

13 H3117 And it shall come to pass in that day H7227 , that a great H4103 tumult H3068 from the LORD H2388 shall be among them; and they shall lay hold [H8689] H376 every one H3027 on the hand H7453 of his neighbour H3027 , and his hand H5927 shall rise up [H8804] H3027 against the hand H7453 of his neighbour.

14 H3063 And Judah H3898 also shall fight [H8735] H3389 at Jerusalem H2428 ; and the wealth H1471 of all the heathen H5439 round about H622 shall be gathered together [H8795] H2091 , gold H3701 , and silver H899 , and apparel H3966 , in great H7230 abundance.

15 H4046 And so shall be the plague H5483 of the horse H6505 , of the

mule H1581 , of the camel H2543 , and of the ass H929 , and of all the beasts H1992 that shall be in these H4264 tents H4046 , as this plague.

16 H3498 And it shall come to pass, that every one that is left [H8737] H1471 of all the nations H935 which came [H8802] H3389 against Jerusalem H5927 shall even go up [H8804] H1767 from H8141 year H8141 to year H7812 to worship [H8692] H4428 the King H3068 , the LORD H6635 of hosts H2287 , and to keep [H8800] H2282 the feast H5521 of tabernacles.

17 H5927 And it shall be, that whoso will not come up [H8799] H4940 of all the families H776 of the earth H3389 unto Jerusalem H7812 to worship [H8692] H4428 the King H3068 , the LORD H6635 of hosts H1653 , even upon them shall be no rain.

18 H4940 And if the family H4714 of Egypt H5927 go not up [H8799] H935 , and come [H8804] H4046 not, that have no rain; there shall be the plague H3068 , wherewith the LORD H5062 will smite [H8799] H1471 the heathen H5927 that come not up [H8799] H2287 to keep [H8800] H2282 the feast H5521 of tabernacles.

19 H2403 This shall be the punishment H4714 of Egypt H2403 , and the punishment H1471 of all nations H5927 that come not up [H8799] H2287 to keep [H8800] H2282 the feast H5521 of tabernacles.

20 H3117 In that day H4698 shall there be upon the bells H5483 of the horses H6944 , HOLINESS H3068 UNTO THE LORD H5518 ; and the pots H3068 in the LORD'S H1004 house H4219 shall be like the bowls H6440 before H4196 the altar.

21 H5518 Yea, every pot H3389 in Jerusalem H3063 and in Judah H6944 shall be holiness H3068 unto the LORD H6635 of hosts H2076 : and all they that sacrifice [H8802] H935 shall come [H8804] H3947 and take [H8804] H1310 of them, and seethe [H8765] H3117 therein: and in that day H3669 there shall be no more the Canaanite H1004 in the house H3068 of the LORD H6635 of hosts.

The wicked will be burned up and become ashes under the feet of the righteous.

Malachi 4:1-3 Strongs

1 H3117 For, behold, the day H935 cometh [H8802] H1197 , that shall burn [H8802] H8574 as an oven H2086 ; and all the proud H6213 , yea, and all that do [H8802] H7564 wickedly H7179 , shall be stubble H3117 : and the day H935 that cometh [H8802] H3857 shall burn them up [H8765] H559 , saith [H8804] H3068 the LORD H6635 of hosts H5800 , that it shall leave [H8799] H8328 them neither root H6057 nor branch.

2 H3373 But unto you that fear H8034 my name H8121 shall the Sun H6666 of righteousness H2224 arise [H8804] H4832 with healing H3671 in his wings H3318 ; and ye shall go forth [H8804] H6335 , and grow up [H8804] H5695 as calves H4770 of the stall.

3 H6072 And ye shall tread down [H8804] H7563 the wicked H665 ; for they shall be ashes H3709 under the soles H7272 of your feet H3117 in the day H6213 that I shall do [H8802] H559 this, saith [H8804] H3068 the LORD H6635 of hosts.

Chapter 16: ALTERNATE THOUGHTS PERIFERAL TOPICS ON IMORTALITY

This concludes the scriptures that I could find dealing with eternal life or how and when the dead are resurrected, in the Old Testament. When I analyze them individually, and then collectively as a whole. I can't find a verse where mankind has immortality, or eternal life innately built into them. Using the concordance and the definitions used by the KJV translators, clearly demonstrates to me that mankind is mortal.

I can find verses where the people look forward to having life again at a future time. I can find hope of a resurrection, and the faith that God will work it out. But none that puts eternal life into mankind's possession within the time frame of the Old Testament.

So do we have access to eternal life? We most certainly do. But it isn't made available till the New Testament. So where are those who died in the O/T times? Well as we have read in the previous scriptures, they are dead and in their graves, awaiting their change. Let's now look through the N/T and find the scriptures that describe this life everlasting, and see who can obtain it, how and when they get it.

My goal here isn't to convince people into agreeing with me. My main objective is to show that the bible gives clear scriptural direction of another way, other than the traditional thoughts on this subject. My hope is that my arguments will persuade people to at least be less dogmatic in their thinking, and give other scripturally supported ideas a second thought.

When speaking we should use inclusive language. Allowing room for others to have their opinions on peripheral issues. Statements like "the bible says" tend to stop conversation. Or start arguments. "The bible tells me" or "I understand the bible to say" encourages conversation, and makes room for the other party to have a different point of view.

As Christians we should be as inviting and open to the widest range of people as possible, especially other Christians. If we are to learn from each other and let our iron sharpen each other, then we need to be as inclusive as possible. That doesn't mean we shouldn't have a point of view, but rather that we should be cordial in our conversations. Letting the Holy Spirit convict, rather than us. When we talk to people like Oprah who aren't satisfied with our answers. Let them know there are other scriptural possibilities they might agree with. After all, these are peripheral topics, and there are many different purposes, functions, and parts in the Christian body. We are bound to have different ideas. We are to be recognized most of all by our love. Not by our ideology, or theology. But by our love for one another.

Chapter 17: BOOK OF MATHEW

JESUS SAVES

This first verse from Mathew doesn't talk specifically about eternal life. It does foretell of what is to come. God has already displayed his thoughts on how he feels towards sinners. So if Jesus is to be the one to save his people from their sins, it would be prudent to be one of Jesus' people.

Matthew 1:21 Strongs

21 G1161 And G5088 she shall bring forth [G5695] G5207 a son G2532 , and G2564 thou shalt call [G5692]G846 his G3686 name G2424 JESUS G1063 : for G846 he G4982 shall save [G5692]G846 his G2992 people G575 from G846 their G266 sins.

BETTER TO LOSE A LITTLE BIT THAN EVERYTHING

In his teaching here Jesus uses the word γέεννα or ge-henna. It is a deep, narrow glen to the south of Jerusalem, where the idolatrous Jews offered their children in sacrifice to Molech 2 Chronicles 28:3; 33:6; Jeremiah 7:31; 19:2-6. This valley afterwards became a common receptacle for the bodies of dead animals, criminals, and all kinds of filth, that were cast into it.

It gets translated into hell, by the KJV translators. It is unfortunate the word hell has lots of misleading imagery tied to it. Beliefs from various religions and philosophy's can be found attached to the word hell. Many of the attributes of hell aren't biblically based, and are out of context when used in reference to the human experience.

In the OT hell was a place your dead body was put into. It also could be used as a reference to eternal punishment. It could be one or the other, or both. Interesting to note that here our body is to be cast into it. The KJV translators talk of everlasting punishment should we be put there. It doesn't say it will be everlasting punishing. As described in Mal. 4:1-3 they will become ashes under foot. No other opportunity will be given for redemption. They will cease to exist. Not exist in eternal torment, which would require eternal life which is reserved for the righteous.

12 occurrences of G1067 γέεννα Hell

Matthew 5:29-30 Strongs

29 G1161 And G1487 if G4675 thy G1188 right G3788 eye G4624 offend [G5719]G4571 thee G1807 , pluck G846 it G1807 out [G5628]G2532 , and G906 cast [G5628]G575 it from G4675 thee G1063 : for G4851 it is profitable [G5719]G4671 for thee G2443 that G1520 one G4675 of thy G3196 members G622 should perish [G5643]G2532 , and G3361 not G4675 that thy G3650 whole G4983 body G906 should be cast [G5686]G1519 into G1067 hell.

30 G2532 And G1487 if G4675 thy G1188 right G5495 hand G4624 offend [G5719] G4571 thee G1581 , cut G846 it G1581 off [G5657] G2532 , and G906 cast [G5628] G575 it from G4675 thee G1063 : for G4851 it is profitable [G5719] G4671 for thee G2443 that G1520 one G4675 of thy G3196 members G622 should perish [G5643] G2532 , and G3361 not G4675 that thy G3650 whole G4983 body G906 should be cast [G5686] G1519 into G1067 hell.

Previous Strong's #G1066 Next Strong's #G1068

γέεννα

ge-hinnom

γέεννα valley of (the son of) Hinnom; ge-henna (or Ge-Hinnom), a valley of Jerusalem, used (figuratively) as a name for the place (or state) of everlasting punishment

γέεννα

geenna

gheh'-en-nah

Of Hebrew origin ([H1516] and [H2011]); valley of (the son of) Hinnom; gehenna (or Ge-Hinnom), a valley of Jerusalem, used (figuratively) as a name for the place (or state) of everlasting punishment

Was Jesus here teaching about the human fate of eternal punishment? Or was he saying it was better to cut off your arm and throw it away, if it causes you to sin, rather than have your whole body destroyed. Better to suffer a small painful loss, than suffer total annihilation.

Regardless of the way you look at it, it still doesn't talk of eternal life. We still haven't found the passage giving us immortality.

DON'T FEAR MAN, FEAR GOD

Some people will use this verse to show we have a soul that is eternal, lives on after our bodies die. I think it is making a distinction between our physical bodies, and our emotions and intellect. If we had an immortal soul how could it be destroyed?

Matthew 10:28 Strongs

28 G2532 And G5399 fear [G5676] G575 G3361 not G3588 them which G615 kill [G5723] G4983 the body G1161, but G1410 are G3361 not G1410 able [G5740] G615 to kill [G5658] G5590 the soul G1161: but G3123 rather G5399 fear [G5676] G3588 him which G1410 is able [G5740] G622 to destroy [G5658] G2532 both G5590 soul G2532 and G4983 body G1722 in G1067 hell.

G5590

Previous Strong's #G5589 Next Strong's #G5591

ψυχή

breath

ψυχή breath, i.e. (by implication) spirit, abstractly or concretely (the animal sentient principle only; thus distinguished on the one hand from G4151, which is the rational and immortal soul; and on the other from G2222, which is mere vitality, even of plants: these terms thus exactly correspond respectively to the Hebrew H5315, H7307 and H2416)

Derivation: from G5594;

KJV Usage: heart (+ -ily), life, mind, soul, + us, + you.

G5594 G4151 G2222 H5315 H7307 H2416

1) breath

1a) the breath of life

1a1) the vital force which animates the body and shows itself in breathing

1a1a) of animals

1a12) of men

1b) life

1c) that in which there is life

1c1) a living being, a living soul

2) the soul

2a) the seat of the feelings, desires, affections, aversions (our heart, soul etc.)

2b) the (human) soul in so far as it is constituted that by the right use of the aids offered it by God it can attain its highest end and secure eternal blessedness, the soul regarded as a moral being designed for everlasting life

2c) the soul as an essence which differs from the body and is not dissolved by death (distinguished from other parts of the body)

Notice 2b. We are designed for everlasting life. That is our purpose. That is the destiny God has for us if we choose to live his way. That is what he wants for us. Let's keep looking, to see how he makes it available to us.

WHERE THE WICKED GO

Here Jesus is telling us plainly what will happen to wicked people when the kingdom of God is established. They are to be cast into a furnace of fire, and be burned up, as the tares are in his analogy.

Matthew 13:40-42 Strongs

40 G5618 As G3767 therefore G2215 the tares G4816 are gathered [G5743] G2532 and G2618 burned [G5743] G4442 in the fire G3779; so G2071 shall it be [G5704] G1722 in G4930 the end G5127 of this G165 world.

41 G5207 The Son G444 of man G649 shall send forth [G5692] G846 his G32 angels G2532, and G4816 they shall gather [G5692] G1537 out of G846 his G932 kingdom G3956 all things G4625 that offend G2532 , and G4160 them which do [G5723] G458 iniquity;

42 G2532 And G906 shall cast [G5692] G846 them G1519 into G2575 a furnace G4442 of fire G1563 : there G2071 shall be [G5704] G2805 wailing G2532 and G1030 gnashing G3599 of teeth

This verse parallels Malachi nicely. Mortal physical people will be cremated in these flames and just end up as ashes.

Malachi 4:1-3 Strongs

1 H3117 For, behold, the day H935 cometh [H8802] H1197 , that shall burn [H8802] H8574 as an oven H2086 ; and all the proud H6213 , yea, and all that do [H8802] H7564 wickedly H7179 , shall be stubble H3117 : and the day H935 that cometh [H8802] H3857 shall burn them up [H8765] H559 , saith [H8804] H3068 the LORD H6635 of hosts H5800 , that it shall leave [H8799] H8328 them neither root H6057 nor branch.

2 H3373 But unto you that fear H8034 my name H8121 shall the Sun H6666 of righteousness H2224 arise [H8804] H4832 with healing H3671 in his wings H3318 ; and ye shall go forth [H8804] H6335 , and grow up [H8804] H5695 as calves H4770 of the stall.

3 H6072 And ye shall tread down [H8804] H7563 the wicked H665 ; for they shall be ashes H3709 under the soles H7272 of your feet H3117 in the day H6213 that I shall do [H8802] H559 this, saith [H8804] H3068 the LORD H6635 of hosts.

This verse is similar to the ones above.

Matthew 13:49-50 Strongs

49 G3779 So G2071 shall it be [G5704] G1722 at G4930 the end G165 of the world G32 : the angels G1831 shall come forth [G5695] G2532 , and G873 sever [G5692] G4190 the wicked G1537 from G3319 among G1342 the just,

50 G2532 And G906 shall cast [G5692] G846 them G1519 into G2575 the furnace G4442 of fire G1563 : there G2071 shall be [G5704] G2805 wailing G2532 and G1030 gnashing G3599 of teeth.

TRANSFIGURATION PART ONE

Did the disciples see the resurrected Moses and Elias? How would they know if it was them? Had they seen them before? Or was this a vision imparting on them that this was who they were?

Matthew 17:3 Strongs

3 G2532 And G2400 , behold [G5628] G3700 , there appeared [G5681] G846 unto them G3475 Moses G2532 and G2243 Elias G4814 talking [G5723] G3326 with G846 him.

Jesus tells them not to talk about their experience with others until his resection.

Matthew 17:9 Strongs

9 G2532 And G846 as they G2597 came down [G5723] G575 from G3735 the mountain G2424 , Jesus G1781 charged [G5662] G846 them G3004 , saying [G5723] G2036 , Tell [G5632] G3705 the vision G3367 to no man G2193 , until G3739 G5207 the Son G444 of man G450 be risen again [G5632] G1537 from G3498 the dead.

This discussion between Jesus and his disciples makes it even more convoluted. Did they see Elias alive? Did they see something they perceived to be Elias? Was it a vision they had? Was it the Elias of the OT or was it someone who represented Elias, like John the Baptist? This scriptural passage doesn't talk about eternal life, but it is used by some to say that the dead Moses and Elias must be alive in heaven to be able to appear with Jesus in this transfiguration. Is this conclusion supported by the rest of the scriptures we have read? Remember the bible will not contradict itself.

Matthew 17:10-13 Strongs

10 G2532 And G846 his G3101 disciples G1905 asked [G5656] G846 him G3004 , saying [G5723] G5101 , Why G3767 then G3004 say [G5719] G1122 the scribes G3754 that G2243 Elias G1163 must [G5748] G4412 first G2064 come [G5629]?

11 G1161 And G2424 Jesus G611 answered [G5679] G2036 and said [G5627] G846 unto them G2243 , Elias G3303 truly G4412 shall first G2064 come [G5736] G2532 , and G600 restore [G5692] G3956 all things.

12 G1161 But G3004 I say [G5719] G5213 unto you G3754 , That G2243 Elias G2064 is come [G5627] G2235 already G2532 , and G1921 they knew [G5627] G846 him G3756 not G235 , but G4160 have done [G5656] G1722 unto G846 him G3745 whatsoever G2309 they listed [G5656] G3779 . Likewise G3195 shall [G5719] G2532 also G5207 the Son G444 of man G3958 suffer [G5721] G5259 of G846 them.

13 G5119 Then G3101 the disciples G4920 understood [G5656] G3754 that G2036 he spake [G5627] G846 unto them G4012 of G2491 John G910 the Baptist.

The transfiguration was not a teaching moment for where the dead go, or instruction on eternal life. The reason for it, was to build the faith and spiritual insight of those who were present. The divinity of Jesus was established firmly to them when God spoke.

Matthew 17:5-7 Strongs

5 G846 While he G2089 yet G2980 spake [G5723] G2400 , behold [G5628] G5460 , a bright G3507 cloud G1982 overshadowed [G5656] G846 them G2532 : and G2400 behold [G5628] G5456 a voice G1537 out of G3507 the cloud G3004 , which said [G5723] G3778 , This G2076 is [G5748] G3450 my G27 beloved G5207 Son G1722 , in G3739 whom G2106 I am well pleased [G5656] G191 ; hear ye [G5720] G846 him.

6 G2532 And G3101 when the disciples G191 heard [G5660] G4098 it, they fell [G5627] G1909 on G846 their G4383 face G2532 , and G4970 were sore G5399 afraid [G5675].

7 G2532 And G2424 Jesus G4334 came [G5631] G680 and touched [G5662] G846 them G2532 , and G2036 said [G5627] G1453 , Arise [G5682] G2532 , and G5399 be G3361 not G5399 afraid [G5737].

ALIVE AND CRIPPLED BETTER THAN DEAD AND WHOLE

Here the fire is everlasting, not those thrown into it.

Matthew 18:7-9 Strongs

7 G3759 Woe G2889 unto the world G575 because of G4625 offences G1063 ! for G318 it must needs G2076 be [G5748] G4625 that offences G2064 come [G5629] G4133 ; but G3759 woe G444 to that man G1565 by G1223 whom G3739 G4625 the offence G2064 cometh [G5736]!

8 G1161 Wherefore G1487 if G4675 thy G5495 hand G2228 or G4675 thy G4228 foot G4624 offend thee [G5719] G1581 , cut G846 them G1581 off [G5657] G2532 , and G906 cast [G5628] G575 them from G4571 thee G4675 G2076 : it is [G5748] G2570 better G4671 for thee G1525 to enter into [G5629] G1519 G2222 life G5560 halt G2228 or G2948 maimed G2228 , rather than G2192 having [G5723] G1417 two G5495 hands G2228 or G1417 two G4228 feet G906 to be cast [G5683] G1519 into G166 everlasting G4442 fire.

9 G2532 And G1487 if G4675 thine G3788 eye G4624 offend [G5719] G4571 thee G1807 , pluck G846 it G1807 out [G5628] G2532 , and G906 cast [G5628] G575 it from G4675 thee G2076 : it is [G5748] G2570 better G4671 for thee G1525 to enter [G5629] G1519 into G2222 life G3442 with one eye G2228 , rather than G2192 having [G5723] G1417 two G3788 eyes G906 to be cast [G5683] G1519 into G1067 hell G4442 fire.

HOW TO OBTAIN ELUSIVE ETERNAL LIFE

This rich young leader didn't know how to obtain eternal life. It was a mystery to him. He didn't already possess it. He knew he wasn't immortal.

Matthew 19:16 Strongs

16 G2532 And G2400 , behold [G5628] G1520 , one G4334 came [G5631] G2036 and said [G5627] G846 unto him G18 , Good G1320 Master G5101 , what G18 good thing G4160 shall I do [G5661] G2443 , that G2192 I may have [G5725] G166 eternal G2222 life?

Eternal life is something we can inherit if we give up earthly things for Jesus' sake. Not something we already possess innately within ourselves. Also note the believers follow Jesus in the regeneration, they don't precede him.

The OT people aren't to be changed until after Jesus has been resurrected, and when he is sitting on his throne in glory, in the Kingdom of God. For clear directions on how to have eternal life see verse 29.

Matthew 19:27-30 Strongs

27 G5119 Then G611 answered [G5679] G4074 Peter G2036 and said [G5627] G846 unto him G2400 , Behold [G5628] G2249 , we G863 have forsaken [G5656] G3956 all G2532 , and G190 followed [G5656] G4671 thee G5101 ; what G2254 shall we G2071 have [G5704] G686 therefore?

28 G1161 And G2424 Jesus G2036 said [G5627] G846 unto them G281 , Verily G3004 I say [G5719] G5213 unto you G3754 , That G5210 ye G3588 which G190 have followed [G5660] G3427 me G1722 , in G3824 the regeneration G3752 when G5207 the Son G444 of man G2523 shall sit [G5661] G1909 in G2362 the throne G846 of his G1391 glory G5210 , ye G2532 also G2523 shall sit [G5695] G1909 upon G1427 twelve G2362 thrones G2919 , judging [G5723] G1427 the twelve G5443 tribes G2474 of Israel.

29 G2532 And G3956 every G3739 one G863 that hath forsaken [G5656]
G3614 houses G2228 , or G80 brethren G2228 , or G79 sisters G2228 , or
G3962 father G2228 , or G3384 mother G2228 , or G1135 wife G2228 , or
G5043 children G2228 , or G68 lands G3450 , for my G3686 name's G1752
sake G2983 , shall receive [G5695] G1542 an hundredfold G2532 , and
G2816 shall inherit [G5692] G166 everlasting G2222 life.

30 G1161 But G4183 many G4413 that are first G2071 shall be [G5704]
G2078 last G2532 ; and G2078 the last G4413 shall be first.

THE POWER OF GOD. IF HE SAYS HE'LL DO IT, IT'S AS GOOD AS DONE.

This next passage of scripture, as well as the parallel passages in the corresponding gospels are some or the most contentious I've come across yet. On reading it I get the impression, as do most people that Abraham, Isaac, and Jacob, are in heaven somewhere. Verses 29-32. I looked into some essays on the passage and there are interesting yet contradictory points of view. It's a good thing these are peripheral issues, but as we have covered before all of the scriptures need to blend together and not contradict each other.

My conflict is, even though it seems to say the patriarchs are alive, we need to be sure what is being taught. I can't find any verse making them that way until after Jesus ransomed us from sin at his crucifixion. As he prayed in the garden before his arrest and crucifixion "father if there be some other way, take this cup from me." But no other way was available to save humanity. Jesus had to be crucified to gain our redemption. So how could anyone be in heaven with God before he died? Some will say time to God isn't the same as it is to us, and it isn't linear. I find that to be a poor argument. The fact Jesus is said to be the first fruits, the first to be resurrected to new life makes time lineal. We are to follow after Jesus into new life, he is our example of how it will work. This puts him first. It only stands to reason, if he was to be the first, then there would have to be a time line that would follow after him. He can't be the first, if the OT believers are already in heaven with God.

The question still remains about what is being said in the passage. What was Jesus telling them? In some of the articles I have read, the point is made the Sadducees didn't believe in the resurrection. Jesus tells them firstly, they not only didn't know the scriptures, but they didn't know the power of God either. He is in support of a biblical resurrection of the dead. This resurrection is said to happen on the Day Of The Lord, at his return. Not at death.

Some will say we have an immortal soul that doesn't die. Only our bodies die separate from our soul. As covered earlier, I don't find this idea to be supported by the bible.

Next Jesus gives a glimpse of what it will be like after being resurrected. We won't be getting married but we will be like the angels. Does this mean we will be sexless? Or just not in small nuclear families, rather thinking of ourselves as children of God in a large family context?

Verse 31. A. Jesus contextualizes the second half of the verse by saying. "But as touching the resurrection of the dead". So when he says "God is the God of the living not the dead", he is referring to the time in the resurrection. He is reinforcing to the Sadducees, there will be a resurrection from the dead, just as the OT describes, and God is a God of the living not the dead. The dead will be resurrected, and he will be their God, and they will be his people, after the resurrection occurs at the coming of the Lord. If the passage is understood in this way then it still blends with other scriptures that pertain to the subject. If it is viewed as teaching the dead are alive with God, I can't see how it doesn't contradict numerous other scriptures.

Matthew 22:23-32 Strongs

23 G1722 The same G1565 G2250 day G4334 came [G5656] G846 to him G4523 the Sadducees G3588 , which G3004 say [G5723] G1511 that there is [G5750] G3361 no G386 resurrection G2532 , and G1905 asked [G5656]

G846 him,

24 G3004 Saying [G5723] G1320 , Master G3475 , Moses G2036 said [G5627] G1437 , If G5100 a man G599 die [G5632] G2192 , having [G5723] G3361 no G5043 children G846 , his G80 brother G1918 shall marry [G5692] G846 his G1135 wife G2532 , and G450 raise up [G5692] G4690 seed G846 unto his G80 brother.

25 G1161 Now G2258 there were [G5713] G3844 with G2254 us G2033 seven G80 brethren G2532 : and G4413 the first G1060 , when he had married a wife [G5660] G5053 , deceased [G5656] G2532 , and G2192 , having [G5723] G3361 no G4690 issue G863 , left [G5656] G846 his G1135 wife G846 unto his G80 brother:

26 G3668 Likewise G1208 the second G2532 also G2532 , and G5154 the third G2193 , unto G2033 the seventh.

27 G1161 And G5305 last G3956 of all G1135 the woman G599 died [G5627] G2532 also.

28 G3767 Therefore G1722 in G386 the resurrection G5101 whose G1135 wife G2071 shall she be [G5704] G2033 of the seven G1063 ? for G3956 they all G2192 had [G5627] G846 her.

29 G2424 Jesus G611 answered [G5679] G1161 and G2036 said [G5627] G846 unto them G4105 , Ye do err [G5744] G3361 , not G1492 knowing [G5761] G1124 the scriptures G3366 , nor G1411 the power G2316 of God.

30 G1063 For G1722 in G386 the resurrection G3777 they neither G1060 marry [G5719] G3777 , nor G1547 are given in marriage [G5743] G235 , but G1526 are [G5748] G5613 as G32 the angels G2316 of God G1722 in G3 772 heaven.

31 G1161 But G4012 as touching G386 the resurrection G3498 of the dead G314 , have ye G3756 not G314 read [G5627] G3588 that which G4483 was spoken [G5685] G5213 unto you G5259 by G2316 God G3004 ,

saying [G5723],

32 G1473 I G1510 am [G5748] G2316 the God G11 of Abraham G2532 , and G2316 the God G2464 of Isaac G2532 , and G2316 the God G2384 of Jacob G2316 ? God G2076 is [G5748] G3756 not G2316 the God G3498 of the dead G235 , but G2198 of the living [G5723].

THE RAPTURE? I WANT TO BE LEFT BEHIND.

These next verses are talking about Christs return to the earth, not specifically about eternal life. Some people say this text supports the doctrine of the rapture. I'm not inclined to agree with them. I do believe in the technical meaning of the word rapture, as taken from the Latin translation of the verb [caught-up] found in 1 Thessalonians 4:17. We will be caught-up at the return of Christ. I don't agree with all of the trappings people have associated with the word rapture.

When you say rapture in reference to the end times, it is generally understood you are talking about the belief Jesus will secretively return and take his believers to heaven, so they can escape the brutal reign of the Antichrist. This rapture is to take place before his final public return to the earth. V. 40-42 are used to support this doctrine. The proponents of the rapture doctrine will tell us we want to be with those who are taken. Those left behind will suffer under the antichrist. Is this what the scripture is telling us?

Looking at it in the context of the conversation, Jesus is explaining no one knows when his return will take place. Then he uses the analogy of the flood to describe how it will take everyone by surprise. V.39 the flood came and took them all away. Took the evil of mankind away, all the wicked were taken away by the flood. Noah and his family were left behind. So as the analogy goes, also the coming of the son of man shall be. V. 40-41 those who are taken would be the wicked. Why would you want to be one of the taken in the story that he told about Noah? You wouldn't want to be with them and lose your life. You would want to be with Noah, and be left behind. To say that those taken is the better group to be in, is to understand the analogy opposite to the way it is told by Jesus.

V.42 urges us to be vigilant and to watch for we don't know the hour that our Lord will come. For if we knew the hour then we would be sure to be ready. By not knowing, we need to always be ready. Always at our best, living a life worthy of Jesus.

Matthew 24:36-44 Strongs

36 G1161 But G4012 of G1565 that G2250 day G2532 and G5610 hour G1492 knoweth [G5758] G3762 no G3761 man, no, not G32 the angels G3772 of heaven G1508 , but G3450 my G3962 Father G3441 only.

37 G1161 But G5618 as G2250 the days G3575 of Noe G3779 were, so G2071 shall G2532 also G3952 the coming G5207 of the Son G444 of man G2071 be [G5704].

38 G1063 For G5618 as G1722 in G2250 the days G2258 that were [G5713] G4253 before G2627 the flood G5176 they were eating [G5723] G2532 and G4095 drinking [G5723] G1060 , marrying [G5723] G2532 and G1547 giving in marriage [G5723] G891 , until G2250 the day G3739 that G3575 Noe G1525 entered [G5627] G1519 into G2787 the ark,

39 G2532 And G1097 knew [G5627] G3756 not G2193 until G2627 the flood G2064 came [G5627] G2532 , and G142 took G537 them all G142 away [G5656] G3779 ; so G2071 shall G2532 also G3952 the coming G5207 of the Son G444 of man G2071 be [G5704].

40 G5119 Then G2071 shall G1417 two G2071 be [G5704] G1722 in G68 the field G1520 ; the one G3880 shall be taken [G5743] G2532 , and G1520 the other G863 left [G5743].

41 G1417 Two G229 women shall be grinding [G5723] G1722 at G3459 the mill G3391 ; the one G3880 shall be taken [G5743] G2532 , and G3391 the other G863 left [G5743].

42 G1127 Watch [G5720] G3767 therefore G3754 : for G1492 ye know [G5758] G3756 not G4169 what G5610 hour G5216 your G2962 Lord G2064 doth come [G5736].

43 G1161 But G1097 know [G5719] G1565 this G3754 , that G1487 if G3617 the goodman of the house G1492 had known [G5715] G4169 in what G5438 watch G2812 the thief G2064 would come [G5736] G302 , he would G1127 have watched [G5656] G2532 , and G302 would G3756 not G1439 have suffered [G5656] G846 his G3614 house G1358 to be broken up [G5650].

44 G1223 Therefore G5124 G1096 be [G5737] G5210 ye G2532 also G2092 ready G3754 : for G3739 in such G5610 an hour G1380 as ye think [G5719] G3756 not G5207 the Son G444 of man G2064 cometh [G5736].

RIGHTIOUS LIVE, SINNERS DIE, SATAN ETERNALLY TORMENTED

These verses are talking about the fate of those who are righteous, and those who are cursed. The cursed are thrown into the everlasting fire prepared for the devil. The devil is a spirit being, he will be tormented forever in his punishment. He will have no escape from it.

The cursed humans are mortal physical people. Their punishment will be eternal. When they die they will have no other opportunity to be brought back to life. They will cease to exist forever. They will go into everlasting punishment. Not everlasting punishing.

The righteous will go into life eternal. This is when they get eternal life. If they were already immortal wouldn't they be just receiving their new glorious bodies? If you read the Strongs meanings for word G2222 it talks about real life, active, genuine, full of vitality, the absolute fullness of life. If this is the kind of life they receive at the resurrection from the dead at the last day, what kind of life were they experiencing before the resurrection? If they were alive with God in heaven since the time of their physical bodies death, there would be no need to give them this fullness of life and vitality. They would only need a form to put it into at the return of Jesus.

Matthew 25:41-46 Strongs

41 G5119 Then G2046 shall he say [G5692] G2532 also G1537 unto them on G2176 the left hand G4198 , Depart [G5737] G575 from G1700 me G2672 , ye cursed [G5772] G1519 , into G166 everlasting G4442 fire G2090 , prepared [G5772] G1228 for the devil G2532 and G846 his G32 angels:

42 G1063 For G3983 I was an hungred [G5656] G2532 , and G1325 ye gave [G5656] G3427 me G3756 no G5315 meat [G5629] G1372 : I was thirsty [G5656] G2532 , and G4222 ye gave G3165 me G3756 no G4222 drink [G5656]:

43 G2252 I was [G5713] G3581 a stranger G2532 , and G4863 ye took G3165 me G3756 not G4863 in [G5627] G1131 : naked G2532 , and G4016 ye clothed [G5627] G3165 me G3756 not G772 : sick G2532 , and G1722 in G5438 prison G2532 , and G1980 ye visited [G5662] G3165 me G3756 not.

44 G5119 Then G846 shall they G2532 also G611 answer [G5700] G846 him G3004 , saying [G5723] G2962 , Lord G4219 , when G1492 saw we [G5627] G4571 thee G3983 an hungred [G5723] G2228 , or G1372 athirst [G5723] G2228 , or G3581 a stranger G2228 , or G1131 naked G2228 , or G772 sick G2228 , or G1722 in G5438 prison G2532 , and G1247 did G3756 not G1247 minister [G5656] G4671 unto thee?

45 G5119 Then G611 shall he answer [G5700] G846 them G3004 , saying [G5723] G281 , Verily G3004 I say [G5719] G5213 unto you G1909 , Inasmuch G3745 as G4160 ye did [G5656] G3756 it not G1520 to one G1646 of the least G5130 of these G4160 , ye did [G5656] G3761 it not G1698 to me.

46 G2532 And G3778 these G565 shall go away [G5695] G1519 into G166 everlasting G2851 punishment G1161 : but G1342 the righteous G1519 into G2222 life G166 eternal.

G166 αἰώνιος - Strong's Greek Lexicon Number

Previous Strong's #G165 Next Strong's #G167

αἰώνιος

lasting for an age

αἰώνιος perpetual (also used of past time, or past and future as well)

Derivation: from G165;

KJV Usage: eternal, for ever, everlasting, world (began).

G165

1) without beginning and end, that which always has been and always will be

2) without beginning

3) without end, never to cease, everlasting

For Synonyms see entry G5801

G2851 κόλασις - Strong's Greek Lexicon Number

Previous Strong's #G2850 Next Strong's #G2852

κόλασις

chastisement, correction, punishment

κόλασις penal infliction

Derivation: from G2849;

KJV Usage: punishment, torment.

G2849

1) correction, punishment, penalty

2)

G2222 ζωή - Strong's Greek Lexicon Number

Previous Strong's #G2221 Next Strong's #G2223

ζωή

a living

ζωή life (literally or figuratively)

Derivation: from G2198;

KJV Usage: life(-time).

Compare G5590. G2198 G5590

1) life

1a) the state of one who is possessed of vitality or is animate

1b) every living soul

2) life

2a) of the absolute fulness of life, both essential and ethical, which belongs to God, and through him both to the hypostatic "logos" and to Christ in whom the "logos" put on human nature

2b) life real and genuine, a life active and vigorous, devoted to God, blessed, in the portion even in this world of those who put their trust in Christ, but after the resurrection to be consummated by new accessions (among them a more perfect body), and to last for ever.

For Synonyms see entry G5821

These two verses tell us that after Jesus was resurrected the graves opened, and the saints that were asleep arose. They didn't return from heaven or somewhere else. They came, resurrected from the dead, out of their graves.

Matthew 27:52-53 Strongs

52 G2532 And G3419 the graves G455 were opened [G5681] G2532 ; and G4183 many G4983 bodies G40 of the saints G3588 which G2837 slept [G5772] G1453 arose [G5681],

53 G2532 And G1831 came [G5631] G1537 out of G3419 the graves G3326 after G846 his G1454 resurrection G1525 , and went [G5627] G1519 into G40 the holy G4172 city G2532 , and G1718 appeared [G5681] G4183 unto many.

CHAPTER 18: BOOK OF MARK

TRANSFIGURATION PART TWO

This is another description of the transfiguration through Mark. It is clear the disciples were afraid and didn't understand what was going on. As in Mathew, God declares to them his relationship with Jesus which is the culmination of the event. The disciples remain oblivious of the true meaning of the transfiguration until after Jesus is resurrected and appears to them. Then their faith becomes strong and nothing frightens them. The vantage point of hind sight makes all of their experiences crystal clear. Was this event used by Jesus to teach them about the afterlife? If you think they saw the live version of Moses and Elias, can you reconcile your belief within the other scriptures that specifically talk about the afterlife and how it works? Or was the transfiguration a one off miracle, similar to turning water into wine. We don't expect to drink wine every time we open a bottle of water.

Mark 9:2-13 Strongs

2 G2532 And G3326 after G1803 six G2250 days G2424 Jesus G3880 taketh[G5719] G4074 with him Peter G2532 , and G2385 James G2532 , and G2491 John G2532 , and G399 leadeth G846 them G399 up [G5719] G1519 into G5308 an high G3735 mountain G2596 apart G2398 G3441 by themselves G2532 : and G3339 he was transfigured [G5681] G1715 before G846 them.

3 G2532 And G846 his G2440 raiment G1096 became [G5633] G4744 shining [G5723] G3029 , exceeding G3022 white G5613 as G5510 snow

G3634 ; so as G3756 no G1102 fuller G1909 on G1093 earth G1410 can [G5736] G3021 white [G5658] them.

4 G2532 And G3700 there appeared [G5681] G846 unto them G2243 Elias G4862 with G3475 Moses G2532 : and G2258 they were [G5713] G4814 talking [G5723] G2424 with Jesus.

5 G2532 And G4074 Peter G611 answered [G5679] G3004 and said [G5719] G2424 to Jesus G4461 , Master G2076 , it is [G5748] G2570 good G2248 for us G1511 to be [G5750] G5602 here G2532 : and G4160 let us make [G5661] G5140 three G4633 tabernacles G3391 ; one G4671 for thee G2532 , and G3391 one G3475 for Moses G2532 , and G3391 one G2243 for Elias.

6 G1063 For G1492 he wist [G5715] G3756 not G5101 what G2980 to say [G5661] G1063 ; for G2258 they were sore [G5713] G1630 afraid.

7 G2532 And G1096 there was [G5633] G3507 a cloud G1982 that overshadowed [G5723] G846 them G2532 : and G5456 a voice G2064 came [G5627] G1537 out of G3507 the cloud G3004 , saying [G5723] G3778 , This G2076 is [G5748] G3450 my G27 beloved G5207 Son G191 : hear [G5720] G846 him.

8 G2532 And G1819 suddenly G4017 , when they had looked round about [G5671] G1492 , they saw [G5627] G3762 no man G3765 any more G235 , save G2424 Jesus G3441 only G3326 with G1438 themselves.

9 G1161 And G846 as they G2597 came down [G5723] G575 from G3735 the mountain G1291 , he charged [G5668] G846 them G2443 that G1334 they should tell [G5657] G3367 no man G3739 what things G1492 they had seen [G5627] G1508 , till G3752 G5207 the Son G444 of man G450 were risen [G5632] G1537 from G3498 the dead.

10 G2532 And G2902 they kept [G5656] G3056 that saying G4314 with G1438 themselves G4802 , questioning one with another [G5723] G5101 what G450 the rising [G5629] G1537 from G3498 the dead G2076 should mean [G5748].

11 G2532 And G1905 they asked [G5707] G846 him G3004 , saying [G5723] G3754 , Why G3004 say [G5719] G1122 the scribes G3754 that G2243 Elias G1163 must [G5748] G4412 first G2064 come [G5629]?

12 G1161 And G611 he answered [G5679] G2036 and told [G5627] G846 them G2243 , Elias G3303 verily G2064 cometh [G5631] G4412 first G600 , and restoreth [G5719] G3956 all things G2532 ; and G4459 how G1125 it is written [G5769] G1909 of G5207 the Son G444 of man G2443 , that G3958 he must suffer [G5632] G4183 many things G2532 , and G1847 be set at nought [G5686].

13 G235 But G3004 I say [G5719] G5213 unto you G3754 , That G2243 Elias G2064 is G2532 indeed G2064 come [G5754] G2532 , and G4160 they have done [G5656] G846 unto him G3745 whatsoever G2309 they listed [G5656] G2531 , as G1125 it is written [G5769] G1909 of G846 him.

FIRES OF THE AFTERLIFE

Jesus gives us some insights into the fires of the afterlife here. It is important to note he is giving these insights in the context of instruction to the disciples about which one of them was the greatest. His main objective was not specifically to tell them what would happen to the evil people at the end times. We can glean some insight into what it might be like though. The fires that are mentioned are the ones in Gehenna, a valley just outside of Jerusalem that was used to burn carcases and the unwanted castoffs of society. He often uses this valley and its fires to represent the fires that will consume the wicked in the last days at his return. Jesus says in the passage, the fires will not be quenched. This is different than eternally burning. No one will put them out, but they could burn themselves out. Just a thought. What do you think they will be like?

Mark 9:33-50 Strongs

33 G2532 And G2064 he came [G5627] G1519 to G2584 Capernaum G2532 : and G1096 being [G5637] G1722 in G3614 the house G1905 he asked [G5707] G846 them G5101 , What G1260 was it that ye disputed

[G5711] G4314 among G1438 yourselves G1722 by G3598 the way?

34 G1161 But G4623 they held their peace [G5707] G1063 : for G1722 by G3598 the way G1256 they had disputed [G5675] G4314 among G240 themselves G5101 , who G3187 should be the greatest.

35 G2532 And G2523 he sat down [G5660] G5455 , and called [G5656] G1427 the twelve G2532 , and G3004 saith [G5719] G846 unto them G1536 , If any man G2309 desire [G5719] G1511 to be [G5750] G4413 first G2071 , the same shall be [G5704] G2078 last G3956 of all G2532 , and G1249 servant G3956 of all.

36 G2532 And G2983 he took [G5631] G3813 a child G2476 , and set [G5656] G846 him G1722 in G3319 the midst G846 of them G2532 : and G1723 when he had taken G846 him G1723 in his arms [G5666] G2036 , he said [G5627] G846 unto them,

37 G3739 Whosoever G1437 G1209 shall receive [G5667] G1520 one G5108 of such G3813 children G1909 in G3450 my G3686 name G1209 , receiveth [G5736] G1691 me G2532 : and G3739 whosoever G1437 G1209 shall receive [G5667] G1691 me G1209 , receiveth [G5736] G3756 not G1691 me G235 , but G649 him that sent [G5660] G3165 me.

38 G1161 And G2491 John G611 answered [G5662] G846 him G3004 , saying [G5723] G1320 , Master G1492 , we saw [G5627] G5100 one G1544 casting out [G5723] G1140 devils G4675 in thy G3686 name G3739 , and G190 he followeth [G5719] G3756 not G2254 us G2532 : and G2967 we forbad [G5656] G846 him G3754 , because G190 he followeth [G5719] G3756 not G2254 us.

39 G1161 But G2424 Jesus G2036 said [G5627] G2967 , Forbid [G5720] G846 him G3361 not G1063 : for G2076 there is [G5748] G3762 no man G3739 which G4160 shall do [G5692] G1411 a miracle G1909 in G3450 my G3686 name G2532 , that G1410 can [G5695] G5035 lightly G2551 speak evil [G5658] G3165 of me.

40 G1063 For G3739 he that G2076 is [G5748] G3756 not G2596 against

G2257 us G2076 is [G5748] G5228 on G2257 our G5228 part.

41 G1063 For G3739 whosoever G302 G4222 shall give G5209 you G4221
a cup G5204 of water G4222 to drink [G5661] G1722 in G3450 my G3686
name G3754 , because G2075 ye belong [G5748] G5547 to Christ G281 ,
verily G3004 I say [G5719] G5213 unto you G622 , he shall G3364 not
G622 lose [G5661] G846 his G3408 reward.

42 G2532 And G3739 whosoever G302 G4624 shall offend [G5661] G1520
one G3398 of these little ones G4100 that believe [G5723] G1519 in
G1691 me G2076 , it is [G5748] G2570 better G3123 G846 for him G1487
that G3037 a millstone G3457 G4029 were hanged [G5736] G4012 about
G846 his G5137 neck G2532 , and G906 he were cast [G5769] G1519 into
G2281 the sea.

43 G2532 And G1437 if G4675 thy G5495 hand G4624 offend [G5725]
G4571 thee G609 , cut G846 it G609 off [G5657] G2076 : it is [G5748]
G2570 better G4671 for thee G1525 to enter [G5629] G1519 into G2222
life G2948 maimed G2228 , than G2192 having [G5723] G1417 two G5495
hands G565 to go [G5629] G1519 into G1067 hell G1519 , into G4442 the
fire G762 that never shall be quenched:

44 G3699 Where G846 their G4663 worm G5053 dieth [G5719] G3756 not
G2532 , and G4442 the fire G4570 is G3756 not G4570 quenched [G5743].

45 G2532 And G1437 if G4675 thy G4228 foot G4624 offend [G5725]
G4571 thee G609 , cut G846 it G609 off [G5657] G2076 : it is [G5748]
G2570 better G4671 for thee G1525 to enter [G5629] G5560 halt G1519
into G2222 life G2228 , than G2192 having [G5723] G1417 two G4228 feet
G906 to be cast [G5683] G1519 into G1067 hell G1519 , into G4442 the
fire G762 that never shall be quenched:

46 G3699 Where G846 their G4663 worm G5053 dieth [G5719] G3756 not
G2532 , and G4442 the fire G4570 is G3756 not G4570 quenched [G5743].

47 G2532 And G1437 if G4675 thine G3788 eye G4624 offend [G5725]
G4571 thee G1544 , pluck G846 it G1544 out [G5628] G2076 : it is [G5748]

G2570 better G4671 for thee G1525 to enter [G5629] G1519 into G932 the kingdom G2316 of God G3442 with one eye G2228 , than G2192 having [G5723] G1417 two G3788 eyes G906 to be cast [G5683] G1519 into G1067 hell G4442 fire:

48 G3699 Where G846 their G4663 worm G5053 dieth [G5719] G3756 not G2532 , and G4442 the fire G4570 is G3756 not G4570 quenched [G5743].

49 G1063 For G3956 every one G233 shall be salted [G5701] G4442 with fire G2532 , and G3956 every G2378 sacrifice G233 shall be salted [G5701] G251 with salt.

50 G217 Salt G2570 is good G1161 : but G1437 if G217 the salt G1096 have lost [G5638] G358 his saltness G1722 , wherewith G5101 G741 will ye season [G5692] G846 it G2192 ? Have [G5720] G217 salt G1722 in G1438 yourselves G2532 , and G1514 have peace [G5720] G240 one G1722 with G240 another.

WHY ASK FOR WHAT YOU ALREADY POSSESS?

Similar to the account in Mathew here a rich young man comes to Jesus seeking the path to eternal life. Some people say, that the people from the Old Testament time had the law to make them acceptable to God. And that by keeping the law they would gain access to eternal life and heaven once they died. Apparently this doctrine wasn't one the young man believed in. He had kept all of the commandments from his youth. Jesus loved him. Jesus invited him to become one of his disciples. But he still didn't have eternal life, there was still something that he lacked. He had studied and had been faithful to the Old Testament scriptures, but still he thought he was lacking something in order to gain eternal life.

Verse 31 According to Jesus, those who lose worldly things for Jesus or the gospel will receive eternal life in the world to come. Remember the bible doesn't tell us what isn't, but what is. I believe we aren't to receive eternal life at the moment of death, nor is it something we already possess within ourselves. The believers will receive eternal life, in the world to come. What do you believe, and how do you support your belief scripturally?

Mark 10:17-31 Strongs

17 G2532 And G1607 when he was gone forth [G5740] G1519 into G846 the way G3598 G4370 , there came G1520 one G4370 running [G5631] G2532 , and G1120 kneeled [G5660] G846 to him G1905 , and asked [G5707] G846 him G18 , Good G1320 Master G5101 , what G4160 shall I do [G5661] G2443 that G2816 I may inherit [G5661] G166 eternal G2222 life?

18 G1161 And G2424 Jesus G2036 said [G5627] G846 unto him G5101 , Why G3004 callest thou [G5719] G3165 me G18 good G3762 ? there is none G18 good G1508 but G1520 one G2316 , that is, God.

19 G1492 Thou knowest [G5758] G1785 the commandments G3431 , Do G3361 not G3431 commit adultery [G5661] G5407 , Do G3361 not G5407 kill [G5661] G2813 , Do G3361 not G2813 steal [G5661] G5576 , Do G3361 not G5576 bear false witness [G5661] G650 , Defraud [G5661] G3361 not G5091 , Honour [G5720] G4675 thy G3962 father G2532 and G3384 mother.

20 G1161 And G611 he answered [G5679] G2036 and said [G5627] G846 unto him G1320 , Master G3956 , all G5023 these G5442 have I observed [G5668] G1537 from G3450 my G3503 youth.

21 G1161 Then G2424 Jesus G1689 beholding [G5660] G846 him G25 loved [G5656] G846 him G2532 , and G2036 said [G5627] G846 unto him G1520 , One thing G4671 thou G5302 lackest [G5719] G5217 : go thy way [G5720] G4453 , sell [G5657] G3745 whatsoever G2192 thou hast [G5719] G2532 , and G1325 give [G5628] G4434 to the poor G2532 , and G2192 thou shalt have [G5692] G2344 treasure G1722 in G3772 heaven G2532 : and G1204 come [G5773] G142 , take up [G5660] G4716 the cross G190 , and follow [G5720] G3427 me.

22 G1161 And G4768 he was sad [G5660] G1909 at G3056 that saying

G565 , and went away [G5627] G3076 grieved [G5746] G1063 : for G2192 he had [G5723] G2258 [G5713] G4183 great G2933 possessions.

23 G2532 And G2424 Jesus G4017 looked round about [G5671] G3004 , and saith [G5719] G846 unto his G3101 disciples G4459 , How G1423 hardly G2192 shall they that have [G5723] G5536 riches G1525 enter [G5695] G1519 into G932 the kingdom G2316 of God!

24 G1161 And G3101 the disciples G2284 were astonished [G5712] G1909 at G846 his G3056 words G1161 . But G2424 Jesus G611 answereth [G5679] G3825 again G3004 , and saith [G5719] G846 unto them G5043 , Children G4459 , how G1422 hard G2076 is it [G5748] G3982 for them that trust [G5756] G1909 in G5536 riches G1525 to enter [G5629] G1519 into G932 the kingdom G2316 of God!

25 G2076 It is [G5748] G2123 easier G2574 for a camel G1525 to go [G5629] [G5625] G1330 [G5629] G1223 through G5168 the eye G4476 of a needle G2228 , than G4145 for a rich man G1525 to enter [G5629] G1519 into G932 the kingdom G2316 of God.

26 G1161 And G1605 they were astonished [G5712] G4057 out of measure G3004 , saying [G5723] G4314 among G1438 themselves G2532 , G5101 Who G1410 then can [G5736] G4982 be saved [G5683]?

27 G1161 And G2424 Jesus G1689 looking upon [G5660] G846 them G3004 saith [G5719] G3844 , With G444 men G102 it is impossible G235 , but G3756 not G3844 with G2316 God G1063 : for G3844 with G2316 God G3956 all things G2076 are [G5748] G1415 possible.

28 G2532 Then G4074 Peter G756 began [G5662] G3004 to say [G5721] G846 unto him G2400 , Lo [G5628] G2249 , we G863 have left [G5656] G3956 all G2532 , and G190 have followed [G5656] G4671 thee.

29 G1161 And G2424 Jesus G611 answered [G5679] G2036 and said [G5627] G281 , Verily G3004 I say [G5719] G5213 unto you G2076 , There is [G5748] G3762 no man G3739 that G863 hath left [G5656] G3614 house G2228 , or G80 brethren G2228 , or G79 sisters G2228 , or G3962 father

G2228 , or G3384 mother G2228 , or G1135 wife G2228 , or G5043 children G2228 , or G68 lands G1700 , for my G1752 sake G2532 , and G2098 the gospel's,

30 G3362 But G2983 he shall receive [G5632] G1542 an hundredfold G3568 now G1722 in G5129 this G2540 time G3614 , houses G2532 , and G80 brethren G2532 , and G79 sisters G2532 , and G3384 mothers G2532 , and G5043 children G2532 , and G68 lands G3326 , with G1375 persecutions G2532 ; and G1722 in G165 the world G2064 to come [G5740] G166 eternal G2222 life.

31 G1161 But G4183 many G4413 that are first G2071 shall be [G5704] G2078 last G2532 ; and G2078 the last G4413 first.

WHEN GOD SAYS IT HE WILL DO IT

As in Mathew this passage tells us God is the God of the living not the dead. Again Jesus addresses the Sadducees who didn't believe in the resurrection. He reinforces the fact of a resurrection, and points out their lack of understanding of scriptures. Verse 25. When they rise. There is no discussion of when. A case could be made for anytime you want just using these verses. Prudently we should look to what other passages plainly tell us about the subject. We can say conclusively that the dead shall be raised.

Verse 26. God is committed to the resurrection of the dead. For when they rise. God is the God of the living, not the dead. They don't have a soul that is alive now and then the resurrection reunites them to a body. If they are alive by having an immortal soul, then why would they need a resurrection to make them alive? There is no mention of a resurrection of a body shell to house our immortal soul.

Mark 12:18-27 Strongs

18 G2532 Then G2064 come [G5736] G4314 unto G846 him G4523 the Sadducees G3748 , which G3004 say [G5719] G1511 there is [G5750]

G3361 no G386 resurrection G2532 ; and G1905 they asked [G5656] G846 him G3004 , saying [G5723],

19 G1320 Master G3475 , Moses G1125 wrote [G5656] G2254 unto us G3754 , If G1437 G5100 a man's G80 brother G599 die [G5632] G2532 , and G2641 leave [G5632] G1135 his wife G2532 behind him, and G863 leave [G5632] G3361 no G5043 children G2443 , that G846 his G80 brother G2983 should take [G5632] G846 his G1135 wife G2532 , and G1817 raise up [G5661] G4690 seed G846 unto his G80 brother.

20 G2258 Now there were [G5713] G2033 seven G80 brethren G2532 and G4413 the first G2983 took [G5627] G1135 a wife G2532 , and G599 dying [G5723] G863 left [G5656] G3756 no G4690 seed.

21 G2532 And G1208 the second G2983 took [G5627] G846 her G2532 , and G599 died [G5627] G2532 , G3761 neither G863 left [G5656] G846 he G4690 any seed G2532 : and G5154 the third G5615 likewise.

22 G2532 And G2033 the seven G2983 had [G5627] G846 her G2532 , and G863 left [G5656] G3756 no G4690 seed G2078 : last G3956 of all G1135 the woman G599 died [G5627] G2532 also.

23 G1722 In G386 the resurrection G3767 therefore G3752 , when G450 they shall rise [G5632] G5101 , whose G1135 wife G2071 shall she be [G5704] G846 of them G1063 ? for G2033 the seven G2192 had [G5627] G846 her G1135 to wife.

24 G2532 And G2424 Jesus G611 answering [G5679] G2036 said [G5627] G846 unto them G4105 , Do ye G3756 not G1223 therefore G5124 G4105 err [G5743] G1492 , because ye know [G5761] G3361 not G1124 the scriptures G3366 , neither G1411 the power G2316 of God?

25 G1063 For G3752 when G450 they shall rise [G5632] G1537 from G3498 the dead G3777 , they neither G1060 marry [G5719] G3777 , nor G1061 are given in marriage [G5743] G235 ; but G1526 are [G5748] G5613 as G32 the angels G3588 which G1722 are in G3772 heaven.

26 G1161 And G4012 as touching G3498 the dead G3754 , that G1453 they rise [G5743] G314 : have ye G3756 not G314 read [G5627] G1722 in G976 the book G3475 of Moses G5613 , how G1909 in G942 the bush G2316 God G2036 spake [G5627] G846 unto him G3004 , saying [G5723] G1473 , I G2316 am the God G11 of Abraham G2532 , and G2316 the God G2464 of Isaac G2532 , and G2316 the God G2384 of Jacob?

27 G2076 He is [G5748] G3756 not G2316 the God G3498 of the dead G235 , but G2316 the God G2198 of the living [G5723] G5210 : ye G3767 therefore G4105 do G4183 greatly G4105 err [G5743].

LIFE OR DEATH, CHOOSE WELL

Jesus tells us that if we believe and are baptized we will be saved. Those who are saved, as we have found, will receive eternal life. Those who don't believe will be dammed. The dammed will be thrown into the fires of hell. They will not receive eternal life. So they will die in the flames.

Mark 16:16 Strongs

16 G4100 He that believeth [G5660] G2532 and G907 is baptized [G5685] G4982 shall be saved [G5701] G1161 ; but G569 he that believeth not [G5660] G2632 shall be damned [G5701].

CHAPTER 19: BOOK OF LUKE

PUNNISHMENT OF THE WICKED

John the Baptist here describes the fire that Jesus will throw the chaff into, a metaphor for the wicked. It is said to be unquenchable. He is not talking about the fires of Ga-henna. But the fires of the end time when the wicked will be done away with. Notice that the fire isn't said to be eternal, but unquenchable. As no one will put them out, they may go out by themselves. Our sun for example could be said to be unquenchable, but over the course of time it may go out.

Luke 3:17 Strongs

17 G3739 Whose G4425 fan G1722 is in G846 his G5495 hand G2532 , and G1245 he will throughly purge [G5692] G846 his G257 floor G2532 , and G4863 will gather [G5692] G4621 the wheat G1519 into G846 his G596 garner G1161 ; but G892 the chaff G2618 he will burn [G5692] G4442 with fire G762 unquenchable.

RESURRECTION IN THE MOMENT

Here is an example of a resurrection that doesn't involve the end time, or the day of the Lord. Jesus brings a young man back to life in the present moment. Similar to Elija bringing the widows son back to life.

Luke 7:12-15 Strongs

12 G1161 Now G5613 when G1448 he came nigh [G5656] G4439 to the

gate G4172 of the city G2532 , behold G2400 [G5628] G1580 , there was G2348 a dead man [G5761] G1580 carried out [G5712] G3439 , the only G5207 son G846 of his G3384 mother G2532 , and G846 she G2258 was [G5713] G5503 a widow G2532 : and G2425 much G3793 people G4172 of the city G2258 was [G5713] G4862 with G846 her.

13 G2532 And G2962 when the Lord G1492 saw [G5631] G846 her G4697 , he had compassion [G5675] G1909 on G846 her G2532 , and G2036 said [G5627] G846 unto her G2799 , Weep [G5720] G3361 not.

14 G2532 And G4334 he came [G5631] G680 and touched [G5662] G4673 the bier G1161 : and G941 they that bare [G5723] G2476 him stood still [G5627] G2532 . And G2036 he said [G5627] G3495 , Young man G3004 , I say [G5719] G4671 unto thee G1453 , Arise [G5682].

15 G2532 And G3498 he that was dead G339 sat up [G5656] G2532 , and G756 began [G5662] G2980 to speak [G5721] G2532 . And G1325 he delivered [G5656] G846 him G846 to his G3384 mother.

As above, here is another resurrection that doesn't involve the end time. The person was brought back to life in the moment.

Luke 8:52-55 Strongs

52 G1161 And G3956 all G2799 wept [G5707] G2532 , and G2875 bewailed [G5710] G846 her G1161 : but G2036 he said [G5627] G2799 , Weep [G5720] G3361 not G599 ; she is G3756 not G599 dead [G5627] G235 , but G2518 sleepeth [G5719].

53 G2532 And G2606 they laughed G846 him G2606 to scorn [G5707] G1492 , knowing [G5761] G3754 that G599 she was dead [G5627].

54 G1161 And G846 he G1544 put [G5631] G3956 them all G1854 out G2532 , and G2902 took [G5660] G846 her G5495 by the hand G5455 , and called [G5656] G3004 , saying [G5723] G3816 , Maid G1453 , arise [G5728].

55 G2532 And G846 her G4151 spirit G1994 came again [G5656] G2532 , and G450 she arose [G5627] G3916 straightway G2532 : and G1299 he commanded [G5656] G1325 to give [G5683] G846 her G5315 meat [G5629] .

TRANSFIGURATION PART THREE

This version of the transfiguration seems to make it more clear that Moses and Elias were there talking to Jesus about his upcoming crucifixion. The word used for glory can be used in a literal or figurative sense, so there could still be some debate. The disciples who had just woken up from a deep sleep saw the three of them together. I get the impression that they didn't seem to fully comprehend what was going on.

I would hate to be the one trying to put God in a box or limit him in any way. If Moses and Elias were actually there in glory, or spirit, or in any form that God should desire, he is certainly capable of doing it. These scriptures however don't say humanity is immortal. There are many scriptures that plainly describe how and when the dead are raised to eternal life. The major point to the transfiguration seemed to be to bolster the will of Jesus, and his disciples before his crucifixion. The insights we can gain about the afterlife from these verses are circumstantial and speculative, as it was not the main subject being covered. We can draw conclusions, but should have conclusive proof from other scriptures in order to form a belief.

Luke 9:28-36 Strongs

28 G1161 And G1096 it came to pass [G5633] G5616 about G3638 an eight G2250 days G3326 after G5128 these G3056 sayings G2532 , G3880 he took [G5631] G4074 Peter G2532 and G2491 John G2532 and G2385 James G305 , and went up [G5627] G1519 into G3735 a mountain G4336 to pray [G5664].

29 G2532 And G1722 as G846 he G4336 prayed [G5738] G1491 , the fashion G846 of his G4383 countenance G1096 was [G5633] G2087

altered G2532 , and G846 his G2441 raiment G3022 was white G1823 and glistering [G5723].

30 G2532 And G2400 , behold [G5628] G4814 , there talked [G5707] G846 with him G1417 two G435 men G3748 , which G2258 were [G5713] G3475 Moses G2532 and G2243 Elias:

31 G3739 Who G3700 appeared [G5685] G1722 in G1391 glory G3004 , and spake [G5707] G846 of his G1841 decease G3739 which G3195 he should [G5707] G4137 accomplish [G5721] G1722 at G2419 Jerusalem.

32 G1161 But G4074 Peter G2532 and G4862 they that were with G846 him G2258 were [G5713] G916 heavy [G5772] G5258 with sleep G1161 : and G1235 when they were awake [G5660] G1492 , they saw [G5627] G846 his G1391 glory G2532 , and G1417 the two G435 men G4921 that stood with [G5761] G846 him.

33 G2532 And G1096 it came to pass [G5633] G1722 , as G846 they G1316 departed [G5738] G575 from G846 him G4074 , Peter G2036 said [G5627] G4314 unto G2424 Jesus G1988 , Master G2076 , it is [G5748] G2570 good G2248 for us G1511 to be [G5750] G5602 here G2532 : and G4160 let us make [G5661] G5140 three G4633 tabernacles G3391 ; one for G4671 thee G2532 , and G3391 one for G3475 Moses G2532 , and G3391 one for G2243 Elias G3361 : not G1492 knowing [G5761] G3739 what G3004 he said [G5719].

34 G1161 While G846 he G5023 thus G3004 spake [G5723] G1096 , there came [G5633] G3507 a cloud G2532 , and G1982 overshadowed [G5656] G846 them G1161 : and G5399 they feared [G5675] G1722 as G1565 they G1525 entered [G5629] G1519 into G3507 the cloud.

35 G2532 And G1096 there came [G5633] G5456 a voice G1537 out of G3507 the cloud G3004 , saying [G5723] G3778 , This G2076 is [G5748] G3450 my G27 beloved G5207 Son G191 : hear [G5720] G846 him.

36 G2532 And G5456 when the voice G1722 was past G1096 [G5635] G2424 , Jesus G2147 was found [G5681] G3441 alone G2532 . And G846

they G4601 kept it close [G5656] G2532 , and G518 told [G5656] G3762 no man G1722 in G1565 those G2250 days G3762 any G3739 of those things which G3708 they had seen [G5758].

G1391 δόξα - Strong's Greek Lexicon Number

Previous Strong's #G1390 Next Strong's #G1392

δόξα

a notion

δόξα glory (as very apparent), in a wide application (literal or figurative, objective or subjective)

Derivation: from the base of G1380;

SEAKING WHAT WE DON'T POSSES

This learned lawyer, would have known if he already had eternal life. He questioned Jesus on how to inherit it. The answer was to love God and others as himself. He didn't already have eternal life within himself.

Luke 10:25 Strongs

25 G2532 And G2400 , behold [G5628] G5100 , a certain G3544 lawyer G450 stood up [G5627] G2532 , and G1598 tempted [G5723] G846 him G3004 , saying [G5723] G1320 , Master G5101 , what G4160 shall I do [G5660] G2816 to inherit [G5692] G166 eternal G2222 life?

ETERNALY DEAD

Jesus tells us we should fear the one who can kill us and throw our dead bodies into Gehenna. Being dead, thrown into Gehenna. I think the KJV translators translate kill best in 2B, to deprive of spiritual life. This would mean that after being killed and thrown into the flames, they will not have spiritual life, those cast into the fire only had the physical life they just lost. To have eternal misery in the fires of hell would require eternal or spiritual life which they have been deprived of. So they, being mortal, will be dead.

Luke 12:5 Strongs

5 G1161 But G5263 I will forewarn [G5692] G5213 you G5101 whom G5399 ye shall fear [G5680] G5399 : Fear [G5676] G3326 him, which after G615 he hath killed [G5658] G2192 hath [G5723] G1849 power G1685 to cast [G5629] G1519 into G1067 hell G3483 ; yea G3004 , I say [G5719] G5213 unto you G5399 , Fear [G5676] G5126 him.

G615 ἀποκτείνω - Strong's Greek Lexicon Number

Previous Strong's #G614 Next Strong's #G616

ἀποκτείνω

to kill, slay

ἀποκτείνω to kill outright; figuratively, to destroy

Derivation: from G575 and κτείνω (to slay);

KJV Usage: put to death, kill, slay.

G575

1) to kill in any way whatever

1a) to destroy, to allow to perish

2) metaph. to extinguish, abolish

2a) to inflict mortal death

2b) to deprive of spiritual life and procure eternal misery in hell

MORE THAN ONE RESURRECTION

Do these verses suggest to you that there will be a different resurrection for the unjust?

Luke 14:13-14 Strongs

13 G235 But G3752 when G4160 thou makest [G5725] G1403 a feast G2564 , call [G5720] G4434 the poor G376 , the maimed G5560 , the lame G5185 , the blind:

14 G2532 And G2071 thou shalt be [G5704] G3107 blessed G3754 ; for G3756 they cannot G2192 [G5719] G467 recompense [G5629] G4671 thee G1063 : for G4671 thou G467 shalt be recompensed [G5701] G1722 at G386 the resurrection G1342 of the just.

ALLEGORY OF HOW THE HARD HEARTED WILL REJECT THE MIRACLES OF JESUS

This parable is often used to prove the dead are tortured in flames while in hell. Some will describe in gruesome detail how the demons will also join in, and add to the pain which will last for eternity. But is that the focus of this parable? Other parables have the story, setting the scenario, then the meaning comes at the end.

When I read this parable, I don't read it as a description of hell, but rather a description of the hard hearts the established religious leaders had. This parable was told at most only a few weeks before Jesus raised his friend Lazarus from the dead. The response by the religious leaders to this undeniable, the messiah could only do it miracle, was to plot how they could kill Jesus. I think the lesson can be found in verses 30-31.

Rather than being a verbal portrait of hell, this parable was told to the Pharisees as a precursor to one of Jesus' most undeniable, messianic miracles.

Luke 16:19-31 Strongs

19 G1161 G2258 There was [G5713] G5100 a certain G4145 rich G444 man G2532 , which G1737 was clothed [G5710] G4209 in purple G2532 and G1040 fine linen G2165 , and fared [G5746] G2988 sumptuously G2596 every G2250 day:

20 G1161 And G2258 there was [G5713] G5100 a certain G4434 beggar G3686 named G2976 Lazarus G3739 , which G906 was laid [G5718] G4314 at G846 his G4440 gate G1669 , full of sores [G5772],

21 G2532 And G1937 desiring [G5723] G5526 to be fed [G5683] G575 with G5589 the crumbs G3588 which G4098 fell [G5723] G575 from G4145 the rich man's G5132 table G235 : moreover G2532 G2965 the dogs G2064 came [G5740] G621 and licked [G5707] G846 his G1668 sores.

22 G1161 And G1096 it came to pass [G5633] G4434 , that the beggar G599 died [G5629] G2532 , and G667 was carried [G5683] G5259 by G32 the angels G1519 into G11 Abraham's G2859 bosom G4145 : the rich man G1161 also G2532 G599 died [G5627] G2532 , and G2290 was buried [G5648];

23 G2532 And G1722 in G86 hell G1869 he lift up [G5660] G846 his G3788 eyes G5225 , being [G5723] G1722 in G931 torments G3708 , and seeth [G5719] G11 Abraham G3113 afar G575 off G2532 , and G2976 Lazarus G1722 in G846 his G2859 bosom.

24 G2532 And G846 G5455 he cried [G5660] G2036 and said [G5627] G3962 , Father G11 Abraham G1653 , have mercy [G5657] G3165 on me G2532 , and G3992 send [G5657] G2976 Lazarus G2443 , that G911 he may dip [G5661] G206 the tip G846 of his G1147 finger G5204 in water G2532 , and G2711 cool [G5661] G3450 my G1100 tongue G3754 ; for G3600 I am tormented [G5743] G1722 in G5026 this G5395 flame.

25 G1161 But G11 Abraham G2036 said [G5627] G5043 , Son G3415 ,

remember [G5682] G3754 that G4771 thou G1722 in G4675 thy G2222 lifetime G618 receivedst [G5627] G4675 thy G18 good things G2532 , and G3668 likewise G2976 Lazarus G2556 evil things G1161 : but G3568 now G3592 G3870 he is comforted [G5743] G1161 , and G4771 thou G3600 art tormented [G5743].

26 G2532 And G1909 beside G3956 all G5125 this G3342 , between G2257 us G2532 and G5216 you G4741 there is G3173 a great G5490 gulf G4741 fixed [G5769] G3704 : so that G2309 they which would [G5723] G1224 pass [G5629] G1782 from hence G4314 to G5209 you G3361 cannot G1410 [G5741] G3366 ; neither G1276 can they pass [G5725] G4314 to G2248 us G1564 , that would come from thence.

27 G1161 Then G2036 he said [G5627] G2065 , I pray [G5719] G4571 thee G3767 therefore G3962 , father G2443 , that G3992 thou wouldest send [G5661] G846 him G1519 to G3450 my G3962 father's G3624 house:

28 G1063 For G2192 have [G5719] G4002 five G80 brethren G3704 ; that G1263 he may testify [G5741] G846 unto them G3363 , lest G846 they G2532 also G2064 come [G5632] G1519 into G5126 this G5117 place G931 of torment.

29 G11 Abraham G3004 saith [G5719] G846 unto him G2192 , They have [G5719] G3475 Moses G2532 and G4396 the prophets G191 ; let them hear [G5657] G846 them.

30 G1161 And G2036 he said [G5627] G3780 , Nay G3962 , father G11 Abraham G235 : but G1437 if G5100 one G4198 went [G5680] G4314 unto G846 them G575 from G3498 the dead G3340 , they will repent [G5692].

31 G1161 And G2036 he said [G5627] G846 unto him G1487 , If G191 they hear [G5719] G3756 not G3475 Moses G2532 and G4396 the prophets G3761 , neither G3982 will they be persuaded [G5701] G1437 , though G5100 one G450 rose [G5632] G1537 from G3498 the dead.

RAPTURE? I WANT TO BE LEFT BEHIND. PART TWO

People who believe in dispensational premillennialism believe these verses support the end time belief commonly called the rapture. I did a bit of research on Google and found a fairly in depth contrarian site you might like to look over. http://www.christdeaf.org/bible/rapture/ It's more in depth than I have time for. To finding sites supporting the belief, for subjective balance, isn't too hard to do with a Google search.

I think the key to understanding V. 30-36 is to understand the context in which they are given. The ones taken in V. 26-29 aren't the righteous, but the evil ones. Noe and his family were left behind to repopulate the earth. The wicked were taken away by the flood. Lot and his family were left behind, Sodom was destroyed, taken away with fire and brimstone. So in the stories Jesus used for his illustration the ones left behind were the ones who were righteous.

Setting the scene for V. 30-36. Those who are left behind will be the righteous not those who turn back and try to save their lives. The ones who are taken will be the ones who lose out on the Kingdom of God. They will be the evil ones.

Luke 17:26-37 Strongs

26 G2532 And G2531 as G1096 it was [G5633] G1722 in G2250 the days G3575 of Noe G3779 , so G2071 shall it be [G5704] G2532 also G1722 in G2250 the days G5207 of the Son G444 of man.

27 G2068 They did eat [G5707] G4095 , they drank [G5707] G1060 , they married wives [G5707] G1547 , they were given in marriage [G5712] G891 , until G2250 the day G3739 that G3575 Noe G1525 entered [G5627] G1519 into G2787 the ark G2532 , and G2627 the flood G2064 came [G5627] G2532 , and G622 destroyed [G5656] G537 them all.

28 G3668 Likewise G2532 also G5613 as G1096 it was [G5633] G1722 in G2250 the days G3091 of Lot G2068 ; they did eat [G5707] G4095 , they drank [G5707] G59 , they bought [G5707] G4453 , they sold [G5707] G5452 , they planted [G5707] G3618 , they builded [G5707];

29 G3739 But G1161 G2250 the same day G3091 that Lot G1831 went [G5627] G575 out of G4670 Sodom G1026 it rained [G5656] G4442 fire G2532 and G2303 brimstone G575 from G3772 heaven G2532 , and G622 destroyed [G5656] G537 them all.

30 G2596 Even G5024 thus G2071 shall it be [G5704] G3739 in the day G2250 G5207 when the Son G444 of man G601 is revealed [G5743].

31 G1722 In G1565 that G2250 day G3739 , he which G2071 shall be [G5704] G1909 upon G1430 the housetop G2532 , and G846 his G4632 stuff G1722 in G3614 the house G2597 , let G3361 him not G2597 come down [G5628] G142 to take G846 it G142 away [G5658] G2532 : and G1722 he that is in G68 the field G1994 , let him G3668 likewise G3361 not G1994 return [G5657] G1519 back G3694.

32 G3421 Remember [G5720] G3091 Lot's G1135 wife.

33 G3739 Whosoever G1437 G2212 shall seek [G5661] G4982 to save [G5658] G846 his G5590 life G622 shall lose [G5692] G846 it G2532 ; and G3739 whosoever G1437 G622 shall lose [G5661] G846 his G2225 life shall preserve [G5692] G846 it.

34 G3004 I tell [G5719] G5213 you G5026 , in that G3571 night G2071 there shall be [G5704] G1417 two G1909 men in G3391 one G2825 bed G1520 ; the one G3880 shall be taken [G5701] G2532 , and G2087 the other G863 shall be left [G5701].

35 G1417 Two G2071 women shall be [G5704] G229 grinding [G5723] G846 together G1909 G3391 ; the one G3880 shall be taken [G5701] G2532 , and G2087 the other G863 left [G5701].

36 G1417 Two G2071 men shall be [G5704] G1722 in G68 the field G1520 ; the one G3880 shall be taken [G5701] G2532 , and G2087 the other G863 left [G5701].

37 G2532 And G611 they answered [G5679] G3004 and said [G5719] G846 unto him G4226 , Where G2962 , Lord G1161 ? And G2036 he said

[G5627] G846 unto them G3699 , Wheresoever G4983 the body G1563 is, thither G4863 will G105 the eagles G4863 be gathered together [G5701].

CHILDLIKE FAITH

What do you think it means, to receive the kingdom as a little child? Historically there have been people who dressed like children their whole lives to try and fulfil this ideal. I think that it means we are to have a child like faith, and remain unjaded by the world.

Luke 18:17 Strongs

17 G281 Verily G3004 I say [G5719] G5213 unto you G3739 , Whosoever G1209 shall G3362 not G1209 receive [G5667] G932 the kingdom G2316 of God G5613 as G3813 a little child G1525 shall G3364 in no wise G1525 enter [G5632] G1519 therein G846.

SEEKING WHAT HE DIDN'T HAVE

This is a parallel story to the one in Mark. The ruler wants eternal life, has kept the commandments, but still knew he needed to do something more to inherit it. We receive life everlasting in the world to come, we don't possess it now.

Luke 18:18-30 Strongs

18 G2532 And G5100 a certain G758 ruler G1905 asked [G5656] G846 him G3004 , saying [G5723] G18 , Good G1320 Master G5101 , what G4160 shall I do [G5660] G2816 to inherit [G5692] G166 eternal G2222 life?

19 G1161 And G2424 Jesus G2036 said [G5627] G846 unto him G5101 , Why G3004 callest thou [G5719] G3165 me G18 good G3762 ? none G18 is good G1508 , save G1520 one G2316 , that is, God.

20 G1492 Thou knowest [G5758] G1785 the commandments G3431 , Do G3361 not G3431 commit adultery [G5661] G5407 , Do G3361 not G5407 kill [G5661] G2813 , Do G3361 not G2813 steal [G5661] G5576 , Do G3361

not G5576 bear false witness [G5661] G5091 , Honour [G5720] G4675 thy G3962 father G2532 and G4675 thy G3384 mother.

21 G1161 And G2036 he said [G5627] G3956 , All G5023 these G5442 have I kept [G5668] G1537 from G3450 my G3503 youth up.

22 G1161 Now G2424 when Jesus G191 heard [G5660] G5023 these things G2036 , he said [G5627] G846 unto him G2089 , Yet G3007 lackest [G5719] G4671 thou G1520 one G4453 thing: sell [G5657] G3956 all G3745 that G2192 thou hast [G5719] G2532 , and G1239 distribute [G5628] G4434 unto the poor G2532 , and G2192 thou shalt have [G5692] G2344 treasure G1722 in G3772 heaven G2532 : and G1204 come [G5773] G190 , follow [G5720] G3427 me.

23 G1161 And G191 when he heard [G5660] G5023 this G1096 , he was [G5633] G4036 very sorrowful G1063 : for G2258 he was [G5713] G4970 very G4145 rich.

24 G1161 And G2424 when Jesus G1492 saw [G5631] G846 that he G1096 was [G5637] G4036 very sorrowful G2036 , he said [G5627] G4459 , How G1423 hardly G1525 shall they G2192 that have [G5723] G5536 riches G1525 enter [G5695] G1519 into G932 the kingdom G2316 of God!

25 G1063 For G2076 it is [G5748] G2123 easier G2574 for a camel G1525 to go [G5629] G1223 through G4476 a needle's G5168 eye G2228 , than G4145 for a rich man G1525 to enter [G5629] G1519 into G932 the kingdom G2316 of God.

26 G1161 And G191 they that heard [G5660] G2036 it said [G5627] G5101 , Who G2532 then G1410 can be [G5736] G4982 saved [G5683]?

27 G1161 And G2036 he said [G5627] G102 , The things which are impossible G3844 with G444 men G2076 are [G5748] G1415 possible G3844 with G2316 God.

28 G1161 Then G4074 Peter G2036 said [G5627] G2400 , Lo [G5628] G2249 , we G863 have left [G5656] G3956 all G2532 , and G190 followed

[G5656] G4671 thee.

29 G1161 And G2036 he said [G5627] G846 unto them G281 , Verily G3004 I say [G5719] G5213 unto you G3754 , G2076 There is [G5748] G3762 no man G3739 that G863 hath left [G5656] G3614 house G2228 , or G1118 parents G2228 , or G80 brethren G2228 , or G1135 wife G2228 , or G5043 children G1752 , for G932 the kingdom G2316 of God's G1752 sake,

30 G3739 Who G618 shall G3364 not G618 receive [G5632] G4179 manifold more G1722 in G5129 this G2540 present time G2532 , and G1722 in G165 the world G2064 to come [G5740] G2222 life G166 everlasting.

GOD'S WORD IS TRUE

This version of the story makes it a bit clearer than others in that it talks more specifically about the resurrection. V. 38 now that the dead are raised, puts them in the context of the resurrection. God being the God of the living reinforces the fact that God will make the resurrection happen.

What will our new resurrected bodies be like? We get a view of it in V.36 we will be spirit, immortal like the angels, and in the family of God.

Luke 20:27-38 Strongs

27 G1161 Then G4334 came [G5631] G5100 to him certain G4523 of the Sadducees G3588 , which G483 deny [G5723] G1511 that there is [G5750] G3361 any G386 resurrection G1905 ; and they asked [G5656] G846 him,

28 G3004 Saying [G5723] G1320 , Master G3475 , Moses G1125 wrote [G5656] G2254 unto us G1437 , If G5100 any man's G80 brother G599 die [G5632] G2192 , having [G5723] G1135 a wife G2532 , and G3778 he G599 die [G5632] G815 without children G2443 , that G846 his G80 brother G2983 should take [G5632] G1135 his wife G2532 , and G1817 raise up [G5661] G4690 seed G846 unto his G80 brother.

29 G2258 There were [G5713] G3767 therefore G2033 seven G80 brethren G2532 : and G4413 the first G2983 took [G5631] G1135 a wife G599 , and died [G5627] G815 without children.

30 G2532 And G1208 the second G2983 took [G5627] G1135 her to wife G2532 , and G3778 he G599 died [G5627] G815 childless.

31 G2532 And G5154 the third G2983 took [G5627] G846 her G1161 ; and G5615 in like manner G2033 the seven G2532 also G2641 : and they left [G5627] G3756 no G5043 children G2532 , and G599 died [G5627].

32 G1161 G5305 Last G3956 of all G1135 the woman G599 died [G5627] G2532 also.

33 G3767 Therefore G1722 in G386 the resurrection G5101 whose G1135 wife G846 of them G1096 is she [G5736] G1063 ? for G2033 seven G2192 had [G5627] G846 her G1135 to wife.

34 G2532 And G2424 Jesus G611 answering [G5679] G2036 said [G5627] G846 unto them G5207 , The children G5127 of this G165 world G1060 marry [G5719] G2532 , and G1548 are given in marriage [G5743]:

35 G1161 But G2661 they which shall be accounted worthy [G5685] G5177 to obtain [G5629] G1565 that G165 world G2532 , and G386 the resurrection G1537 from G3498 the dead G3777 , neither G1060 marry [G5719] G3777 , nor G1548 are given in marriage [G5743]:

36 G3777 Neither G1063 G1410 can [G5736] G599 they die [G5629] G2089 any more G1063 : for G1526 they are [G5748] G2465 equal unto the angels G2532 ; and G1526 are [G5748] G5207 the children G2316 of God G5607 , being [G5752] G5207 the children G386 of the resurrection.

37 G1161 Now G3754 that G3498 the dead G1453 are raised [G5743] G2532 , even G3475 Moses G3377 shewed [G5656] G1909 at G942 the bush G5613 , when G3004 he calleth [G5719] G2962 the Lord G2316 the God G11 of Abraham G2532 , and G2316 the God G2464 of Isaac G2532 , and G2316 the God G2384 of Jacob.

38 G1161 For G2076 he is [G5748] G3756 not G2316 a God G3498 of the dead G235 , but G2198 of the living [G5723] G1063 : for G3956 all G2198 live [G5719] G846 unto him.

PUNCTUATION CAN BE MISLEADING

This next passage is often turned to in order to prove that when we die we go directly to heaven or conversely hell. V.43 After all, Jesus plainly tells the thief he would be with him that day in his kingdom. It is important to point out when writing in the Greek language of the day, punctuation wasn't used. The accounts and stories were one long run on sentence. It wasn't put into sentences until later translators did it along with chapter and verse. Often the verses and chapters will break up the flow and thoughts of a particular passage.

V.43 is an example of this. Ask yourself the following questions. Where did Jesus repeatedly say he was going to be after he was crucified? How long did he say he would be there? What was to be the ultimate proof he was the son of God to the nit-picky Pharisees? You possibly answered, in the grave for three days and three nights, then be resurrected. If you did, we wholeheartedly agree.

So, if Jesus was in the grave for the next three days to prove his Messiah-ship how could he have been in his kingdom on the same day he was crucified?The solution that I favour, is a misplaced comma. Read V.43 again. And Jesus said unto him, "Verily I say unto thee today, Shalt thou be with me in paradise." The today Jesus was talking about, was the day that he was speaking, not when they would be in paradise. He was giving assurance to the thief he would be with him in the future. I find this to be a scripturally accurate rendering of the verse. Otherwise the deity of Jesus could be questioned by those he gave the sign of Jonah to.

Luke 23:39-43 Strongs

39 G1161 And G1520 one G2557 of the malefactors G2910 which were hanged [G5685] G987 railed [G5707] G846 on him G3004 , saying [G5723]

G1487 , If G4771 thou G1488 be [G5748] G5547 Christ G4982 , save [G5657] G4572 thyself G2532 and G2248 us.

40 G1161 But G2087 the other G611 answering [G5679] G2008 rebuked [G5707] G846 him G3004 , saying [G5723] G5399 , Dost G3761 not G4771 thou G5399 fear [G5736] G2316 God G3754 , seeing G1488 thou art [G5748] G1722 in G846 the same G2917 condemnation?

41 G2532 And G2249 we G3303 indeed G1346 justly G1063 ; for G618 we receive [G5719] G514 the due reward G3739 of our G4238 deeds [G5656] G1161 : but G3778 this man G4238 hath done [G5656] G3762 nothing G824 amiss.

42 G2532 And G3004 he said [G5707] G2424 unto Jesus G2962 , Lord G3415 , remember [G5682] G3450 me G3752 when G2064 thou comest [G5632] G1722 into G4675 thy G932 kingdom.

43 G2532 And G2424 Jesus G2036 said [G5627] G846 unto him G281 , Verily G3004 I say [G5719] G4671 unto thee G4594 , To day G2071 shalt thou be [G5704] G3326 with G1700 me G1722 in G3857 paradise.

CHAPTER 20: BOOK OF JOHN

JESUS SAVES

Its Gods will, that we have the ability to become the children of God, by only believing in Jesus.

John 1:12-13 Strongs

12 G1161 But G3745 as many as G2983 received [G5627] G846 him G846 , to them G1325 gave he [G5656] G1849 power G1096 to become [G5635] G5043 the sons G2316 of God G4100 , even to them that believe [G5723] G1519 on G846 his G3686 name:

13 G3739 Which G1080 were born [G5681] G3756 , not G1537 of G129 blood G3761 , nor G1537 of G2307 the will G4561 of the flesh G3761 , nor G1537 of G2307 the will G435 of man G235 , but G1537 of G2316 God.

TO HEAVEN AND BACK?

The bible tells us what the truth is. No one has ever seen God, except for his son. This would eliminate anyone from being in heaven with him now.

John 1:18 Strongs

18 G3762 No man G3708 hath seen [G5758] G2316 God G4455 at any time G3439 ; the only begotten G5207 Son G3588 , which G5607 is [G5752] G1519 in G2859 the bosom G3962 of the Father G1565 , he G1834 hath declared [G5662] him .

G3762 οὐδείς - Strong s Greek Lexicon Number

οὐδείς

and not one

οὐδείς , including feminine οὐδεμία , and neuter οὐδέν not even one (man, woman or thing). i.e. none, nobody, nothing

G4455 πώποτε - Strong's Greek Lexicon Number

πώποτε

ever yet

πώποτε at any time, i.e. (with negative particle) at no time

NOT BORN OF THE SPIRIT, UNTILL WE BECOME SPIRIT

To get into the kingdom of God, we must be born again of the spirit, and water. Does this mean we need to be baptized as well? V.6 Can we be born of the spirit and be in this fleshly body at the same time? Or do we receive our spirit body at the resurrection?

John 3:1-12 Strongs

1 G1161 G2258 There was [G5713] G444 a man G1537 of G5330 the Pharisees G3686 , named G846 G3530 Nicodemus G758 , a ruler G2453 of the Jews:

2 G3778 The same G2064 came [G5627] G4314 to G2424 Jesus G3571 by night G2532 , and G2036 said [G5627] G846 unto him G4461 , Rabbi G1492 , we know [G5758] G3754 that G2064 thou art G1320 a teacher G2064 come [G5754] G575 from G2316 God G1063 : for G3762 no man G1410 can [G5736] G4160 do [G5721] G5023 these G4592 miracles G3739 that G4771 thou G4160 doest [G5719] G3362 , except G2316 God G5600 be [G5753] G3326 with G846 him.

3 G2424 Jesus G611 answered [G5662] G2532 and G2036 said [G5627] G846 unto him G281 , Verily G281 , verily G3004 , I say [G5719] G4671 unto thee G3362 , Except G5100 a man G1080 be born [G5686] G509 again G1410 , he cannot [G5736] G3756 G1492 see [G5629] G932 the kingdom G2316 of God.

4 G3530 Nicodemus G3004 saith [G5719] G4314 unto G846 him G4459 , How G1410 can [G5736] G444 a man G1080 be born [G5683] G5607 when he is [G5752] G1088 old G3361 ? can G1410 [G5736] G1525 he enter [G5629] G1208 the second time G1519 into G846 his G3384 mother's G2836 womb G2532 , and G1080 be born [G5683]?

5 G2424 Jesus G611 answered [G5662] G281 , Verily G281 , verily G3004 , I say [G5719] G4671 unto thee G3362 , Except G5100 a man G1080 be born [G5686] G1537 of G5204 water G2532 and G4151 of the Spirit G3756 , he cannot G1410 [G5736] G1525 enter [G5629] G1519 into G932 the kingdom G2316 of God.

6 G1080 That which is born [G5772] G1537 of G4561 the flesh G2076 is [G5748] G4561 flesh G2532 ; and G1080 that which is born [G5772] G1537 of G4151 the Spirit G2076 is [G5748] G4151 spirit.

7 G2296 Marvel [G5661] G3361 not G3754 that G2036 I said [G5627] G4671 unto thee G5209 , Ye G1163 must [G5748] G1080 be born [G5683] G509 again.

8 G4151 The wind G4154 bloweth [G5719] G3699 where G2309 it listeth [G5719] G2532 , and G191 thou hearest [G5719] G5456 the sound G846 thereof G235 , but G1492 canst G3756 not G1492 tell [G5758] G4159 whence G2064 it cometh [G5736] G2532 , and G4226 whither G5217 it goeth [G5719] G3779 : so G2076 is [G5748] G3956 every one G1080 that is born [G5772] G1537 of G4151 the Spirit.

9 G3530 Nicodemus G611 answered [G5662] G2532 and G2036 said [G5627] G846 unto him G4459 , How G1410 can [G5736] G5023 these things G1096 be [G5635]?

10 G2424 Jesus G611 answered [G5662] G2532 and G2036 said [G5627] G846 unto him G1488 , Art [G5748] G4771 thou G1320 a master G2474 of Israel G2532 , and G1097 knowest [G5719] G3756 not G5023 these things?

11 G281 Verily G281 , verily G3004 , I say [G5719] G4671 unto thee G2980 , We speak [G5719] G3754 that G3739 G1492 we do know [G5758] G2532 , and G3140 testify [G5719] G3739 that G3708 we have seen [G5758] G2532 ; and G2983 ye receive [G5719] G3756 not G2257 our G3141 witness.

12 G1487 If G2036 I have told [G5627] G5213 you G1919 earthly things G2532 , and G4100 ye believe [G5719] G3756 not G4459 , how G4100 shall ye believe [G5692] G1437 , if G2036 I tell [G5632] G5213 you G2032 of heavenly things?

TO HEAVEN AND BACK, WHO HAS DONE IT?

There are many different ideas about heaven, how and when we get there. I find this next verse to be very straight forward in its content and context. No man has ascended up to heaven except Jesus. I can't, nor would I want to argue with that. I haven't found any other verse more concise on the subject.

John 3:13 Strongs

13 G2532 And G3762 no man G305 hath ascended up [G5758] G1519 to G3772 heaven G1508 , but G2597 he that came down [G5631] G1537 from G3772 heaven G5207 , even the Son G444 of man G3588 which G5607 is [G5752] G1722 in G3772 heaven.

THE TRUTH

These verses foretell Jesus' crucifixion, and the fact that if we want to have eternal life we need to believe in him. No other way is mentioned to have eternal life. Conversely the opposite is true, those who don't believe in Jesus won't have eternal life, and will perish.

John 3:14-15 Strongs

14 G2532 And G2531 as G3475 Moses G5312 lifted up [G5656] G3789 the serpent G1722 in G2048 the wilderness G3779 , even so G1163 must [G5748] G5207 the Son G444 of man G5312 be lifted up [G5683]:

15 G3363 That G3956 whosoever G4100 believeth [G5723] G1519 in G846 him G622 should G3363 not G622 perish [G5643] G235 , but G2192 have [G5725] G166 eternal G2222 life.

THE WHOLE TRUTH

This is possibly the most memorized verse in the bible. Pretty straight forward. Believe in Jesus and have everlasting, eternal, spirit life. You will never die.

John 3:16 Strongs

16 G1063 For G2316 God G3779 so G25 loved [G5656] G2889 the world G5620 , that G1325 he gave [G5656] G846 his G3439 only begotten G5207 Son G2443 , that G3956 whosoever G4100 believeth [G5723] G1519 in G846 him G622 should G3361 not G622 perish [G5643] G235 , but G2192 have [G5725] G166 everlasting G2222 life.

AND NOTHING BUT THE TRUTH

The world is to be saved through the crucifixion of Jesus.

John 3:17 Strongs

17 G1063 For G2316 God G649 sent [G5656] G3756 not G846 his G5207 Son G1519 into G2889 the world G2443 to G2919 condemn [G5725] G2889 the world G235 ; but G2443 that G2889 the world G1223 through G846 him G4982 might be saved [G5686].

DEAD FOREVER

This plainly tells us those who don't believe in Jesus will be condemned. V. 16 -17 is a beautiful word picture of Gods' preferred plan for humanity. A photograph is developed from a negative image V.18 is the negative to the beautiful picture of V. 16-17. We receive eternal life by believing in Jesus. V.18 we receive eternal death by not believing in Jesus. Not eternal suffering, but eternal death.

John 3:18 Strongs

18 G4100 He that believeth [G5723] G1519 on G846 him G2919 is G3756 not G2919 condemned [G5743] G1161 : but G4100 he that believeth [G5723] G3361 not G2919 is condemned [G5769] G2235 already G3754 , because G4100 he hath G3361 not G4100 believed [G5758] G1519 in G3686 the name G3439 of the only begotten G5207 Son G2316 of God.

This verse sums up nicely what will happen to humanity, and the choice that we will have to face.

John 3:36 Strongs

36 G4100 He that believeth [G5723] G1519 on G5207 the Son G2192 hath [G5719] G166 everlasting G2222 life G1161 : and G544 he that believeth not [G5723] G5207 the Son G3700 shall G3756 not G3700 see [G5695] G2222 life G235 ; but G3709 the wrath G2316 of God G3306 abideth [G5719] G1909 on G846 him.

DESCRIBING A RESURRECTION

Here we are told God raises the dead, and quickens them. This sound to me like these are two separate things. Similar to Ezekiel 37:7-8 the bodies stood before him. V.9-10 then they were given the breath of life. What are your thoughts about it? What scriptures would you use to support your ideas? Jesus also has authority to raise the ones he wants.

John 5:21 Strongs

21 G1063 For G5618 as G3962 the Father G1453 raiseth up [G5719] G3498 the dead G2532 , and G2227 quickeneth [G5719] G2532 them; even G3779 so G5207 the Son G2227 quickeneth [G5719] G3739 whom G2309 he will [G5719].

JESUS IS THEJUDGE

Jesus is the one who will judge us at the end time.

John 5:22 Strongs

22 G1063 For G3761 G3962 the Father G2919 judgeth [G5719] G3762 no man G235 , but G1325 hath committed [G5758] G3956 all G2920 judgment G5207 unto the Son:

THE HOUR IS COMING. FUTURE TENSE

Here again we are told those who believe in Jesus will be saved. His place as the son of God is confirmed, as well as his role as judge of humanity, at the resurrection, when the dead are brought out of their graves to meet their destiny.

John 5:24-29 Strongs

24 G281 Verily G281 , verily G3004 , I say [G5719] G5213 unto you G3754 , G191 He that heareth [G5723] G3450 my G3056 word G2532 , and G4100 believeth [G5723] G3992 on him that sent [G5660] G3165 me G2192 , hath [G5719] G166 everlasting G2222 life G2532 , and G2064 shall G3756 not G2064 come [G5736] G1519 into G2920 condemnation G235 ; but G3327 is passed [G5758] G1537 from G2288 death G1519 unto G2222 life.

25 G281 Verily G281 , verily G3004 , I say [G5719] G5213 unto you G3754 ,

G5610 The hour G2064 is coming [G5736] G2532 , and G3568 now G2076 is [G5748] G3753 , when G3498 the dead G191 shall hear [G5695] G5456 the voice G5207 of the Son G2316 of God G2532 : and G191 they that hear [G5660] G2198 shall live [G5695].

26 G1063 For G5618 as G3962 the Father G2192 hath [G5719] G2222 life G1722 in G1438 himself G2532 ; so G3779 G1325 hath he given [G5656] G5207 to the Son G2192 to have [G5721] G2222 life G1722 in G1438 himself;

27 G2532 And G1325 hath given [G5656] G846 him G1849 authority G4160 to execute [G5721] G2920 judgment G2532 also G3754 , because G2076 he is [G5748] G5207 the Son G444 of man.

28 G2296 Marvel [G5720] G3361 not G5124 at this G3754 : for G5610 the hour G2064 is coming [G5736] G1722 , in G3739 the which G3956 all G1722 that are in G3419 the graves G191 shall hear [G5695] G846 his G5456 voice,

29 G2532 And G1607 shall come forth [G5695] G4160 ; they that have done [G5660] G18 good G1519 , unto G386 the resurrection G2222 of life G1161 ; and G4238 they that have done [G5660] G5337 evil G1519 , unto G386 the resurrection G2920 of damnation.

WHO HAS REJECTED ETERNAL LIFE

Speaking to the Jews from the synagogue Jesus tells them that the scriptures foretold his coming. He was the one they should believe because of the works he did. They thought the scriptures would lead them to eternal life. Rather they are told the scriptures were to lead them to Jesus, and the eternal life they sought could only be found through him. They rejected him and with that decision they rejected eternal life.

John 5:36-40 Strongs

36 G1161 But G1473 I G2192 have [G5719] G3187 greater G3141 witness

G2491 than that of John G1063 : for G2041 the works G3739 which G3962 the Father G1325 hath given [G5656] G3427 me G2443 to G5048 finish [G5661] G846 G846 , the same G2041 works G3739 that G1473 I G4160 do [G5719] G3140 , bear witness [G5719] G4012 of G1700 me G3754 , that G3962 the Father G649 hath sent [G5758] G3165 me.

37 G2532 And G3962 the Father G846 himself G3992 , which hath sent [G5660] G3165 me G3140 , hath borne witness [G5758] G4012 of G1700 me G191 . Ye have G3777 neither G191 heard [G5754] G846 his G5456 voice G4455 at any time G3777 , nor G3708 seen [G5758] G846 his G1491 shape.

38 G2532 And G2192 ye have [G5719] G3756 not G846 his G3056 word G3306 abiding [G5723] G1722 in G5213 you G3754 : for G3739 whom G1565 G649 he hath sent [G5656] G5129 , him G5210 ye G4100 believe [G5719] G3756 not.

39 G2045 Search [G5719] G1124 the scriptures G3754 ; for G1722 in G846 them G5210 ye G1380 think [G5719] G2192 ye have [G5721] G166 eternal G2222 life G2532 : and G1565 they G1526 are they [G5748] G3140 which testify [G5723] G4012 of G1700 me.

40 G2532 And G2309 ye will [G5719] G3756 not G2064 come [G5629] G4314 to G3165 me G2443 , that G2192 ye might have [G5725] G2222 life.

NEW LIFE, AT THE LAST DAY

Here Jesus plainly tells us he will raise those who the Father gives him, at the last day. It is quite straight forward as to when they will be raised. No other time is mentioned for a resurrection. In this verse, only the last day is mentioned for their resurrection.

John 6:39 Strongs

39 G1161 And G5124 this G2076 is [G5748] G3962 the Father's G2307 will

G3588 which G3992 hath sent [G5660] G3165 me G2443 , that G3956 of all G3739 which G1325 he hath given [G5758] G3427 me G622 I should lose [G5661] G3361 nothing G1537 G846 G235 , but G450 should raise G846 it G450 up again [G5692] G1722 at G2078 the last G2250 day.

Everlasting life for those who believe in Jesus is the will of God. They will be raised up to it, at the last day. Same as the verse above.

John 6:40 Strongs

40 G1161 And G5124 this G2076 is [G5748] G2307 the will G3992 of him that sent [G5660] G3165 me G2443 , that G3956 every one G3588 which G2334 seeth [G5723] G5207 the Son G2532 , and G4100 believeth [G5723] G1519 on G846 him G2192 , may have [G5725] G166 everlasting G2222 life G2532 : and G1473 I G450 will raise G846 him G450 up [G5692] G2078 at the last G2250 day.

IS GOD CALLING YOU

I find this to be an extremely important verse. In the beginning of this study I talked about how Christianity could be a stumbling block to some. As we have repeatedly read we can't be saved unless we believe in Jesus. This leaves a dark cloud over those who have died, and never had the opportunity to know Jesus. Or people who live their lives with plenty of opportunity, but have eyes that cannot see, and ears that cannot hear

This verse tells us no man can come to Jesus, unless God draws him. Is God drawing everyone now in this life? If he is, how did the people of North America get to learn of Jesus before Christian contact, but after Jesus died for them. They would have no opportunity to know about Jesus? God is no respecter of people. Wouldn't it make sense he would have a plan where they could learn about Jesus with open eyes and ears. A time without satanic influence. I believe the resurrections provide such a time. After we have looked at all the applicable scriptures, we can piece them together and look at one of the possibilities.

Here again Jesus tells us those who believe on him will be resurrected from the dead at the last day.

John 6:44 Strongs

44 G3762 No man G1410 can [G5736] G2064 come [G5629] G4314 to G3165 me G3362 , except G3962 the Father G3588 which G3992 hath sent [G5660] G3165 me G1670 draw [G5661] G846 him G2532 : and G1473 I G450 will raise G846 him G450 up [G5692] G2078 at the last G2250 day.

ALL WILL BE TAUGHT ABOUT GOD AND WILL HAVE A CHOICE

When will this teaching take place? Has it happened already, or is it yet to happen?

John 6:45 Strongs

45 G2076 It is [G5748] G1125 written [G5772] G1722 in G4396 the prophets G2532 , And G2071 they shall be [G5704] G3956 all G1318 taught G2316 of God G3956 . Every man G3767 therefore G191 that hath heard [G5660] G2532 , and G3129 hath learned [G5631] G3844 of G3962 the Father G2064 , cometh [G5736] G4314 unto G3165 me.

Again, if you believe, you will live.

John 6:47 Strongs

47 G281 Verily G281 , verily G3004 , I say [G5719] G5213 unto you G4100 , He that believeth [G5723] G1519 on G1691 me G2192 hath [G5719] G166 everlasting G2222 life.

NO ETERNAL LIFE BEFORE JESUS THE CHRIST

Those from the OT that knew God are dead. Not alive somewhere watching over us.

John 6:49 Strongs

49 G5216 Your G3962 fathers G5315 did eat [G5627] G3131 manna G1722 in G2048 the wilderness G2532 , and G599 are dead [G5627].

CONTEXT CAN BE EVERYTHING

With the 20-20 vision of hind sight we can easily see that Jesus was talking about the communion symbols and his crucifixion. It was harder for his audience to understand what he was talking about.

John 6:50-51 Strongs

50 G3778 This G2076 is [G5748] G740 the bread G3588 which G2597 cometh down [G5723] G1537 from G3772 heaven G3363 , that G5100 a man G5315 may eat [G5632] G1537 thereof G846 G2532 , and G3363 not G599 die [G5632].

51 G1473 I G1510 am [G5748] G2198 the living [G5723] G740 bread G3588 which G2597 came down [G5631] G1537 from G3772 heaven G1437 : if G5100 any man G5315 eat [G5632] G1537 of G5127 this G740 bread G2198 , he shall live [G5695] G1519 for G165 ever G1161 : and G2532 G740 the bread G3739 that G1473 I G1325 will give [G5692] G2076 is [G5748] G3450 my G4561 flesh G3739 , which G1473 I G1325 will give [G5692] G5228 for G2222 the life G2889 of the world.

REPETITION RE-ENFORCES THE POINT

For the fourth time in the same conversation, Jesus tells us that he will raise up the believers at the last day.

John 6:54 Strongs

54 G5176 Whoso eateth [G5723] G3450 my G4561 flesh G2532 , and G4095 drinketh [G5723] G3450 my G129 blood G2192 , hath [G5719] G166 eternal G2222 life G2532 ; and G1473 I G450 will raise G846 him G450 up [G5692] G2078 at the last G2250 day.

FORESHADOWING THE LAST SUPPER

Our forefathers are dead, even if they ate Gods manna. Knowing God and keeping the commandments won’t save us. We can only have eternal life if we accept and join with Jesus.

John 6:57-58 Strongs

57 G2531 As G2198 the living [G5723] G3962 Father G649 hath sent [G5656] G3165 me G2504 , and I G2198 live [G5719] G1223 by G3962 the Father G2532 : so G5176 he that eateth [G5723] G3165 me G2548 , even he G2198 shall live [G5695] G1223 by G1691 me.

58 G3778 This G2076 is [G5748] G740 that bread G3588 which G2597 came down [G5631] G1537 from G3772 heaven G3756 : not G2531 as G5216 your G3962 fathers G5315 did eat [G5627] G3131 manna G2532 , and G599 are dead [G5627] G5176 : he that eateth [G5723] G5126 of this G740 bread G2198 shall live [G5695] G1519 for G165 ever.

THE GIFT OF HIS CALLING

Once again Jesus explains that not everyone can come to him now. Only those who are called by God can come to Jesus. Those who aren't called have no chance to come to Jesus in this life. The word given used in V.65 can imply being given a gift.

John 6:65-66 Strongs

65 G2532 And G3004 he said [G5707] G1223 , Therefore G5124 G2046 said I [G5758] G5213 unto you G3754 , that G3762 no man G1410 can [G5736] G2064 come [G5629] G4314 unto G3165 me G3362 , except

G5600 it were [G5753] G1325 given [G5772] G846 unto him G1537 of G3450 my G3962 Father.

66 G1537 From G5127 that G4183 time many G846 of his G3101 disciples G565 went [G5627] G1519 back G3694 G2532 , and G4043 walked [G5707] G3765 no more G3326 with G846 him.

G1325 δίδωμι - Strong's Greek Lexicon Number

δίδωμι

to give

δίδωμι to give (used in a very wide application, properly, or by implication, literally or figuratively; greatly modified by the connection)

Derivation: a prolonged form of a primary verb (which is used as an alternative in most of the tenses);

KJV Usage: adventure, bestow, bring forth, commit, deliver (up), give, grant, hinder, make, minister, number, offer, have power, put, receive, set, shew, smite (+ with the hand), strike (+ with the palm of the hand), suffer, take, utter, yield.

1) to give

2) to give something to someone

2a) of one's own accord to give one something, to his advantage

2a1) to bestow a gift

2b) to grant, give to one asking, let have

2c) to supply, furnish, necessary things

2d) to give over, deliver

2d1) to reach out

JESUS IS THE WAY

The Pharisees needed to believe in Jesus to have their sins forgiven, we do too.

John 8:24 Strongs

24 G2036 I said [G5627] G3767 therefore G5213 unto you G3754 , that G599 ye shall die [G5695] G1722 in G5216 your G266 sins G1063 : for G3362 if G4100 ye believe [G5661] G3362 not G3754 that G1473 I G1510 am [G5748] G599 he, ye shall die [G5695] G1722 in G5216 your G266 sins.

DEAD MEANS DEAD, AND JESUS IS THE GREAT "I AM"

Abraham is dead, not taking care of the dead souls of mankind like Lazarus. V.58 Jesus tells the Jews he was the one talking to Abraham in scripture because he was the great "I Am" of the Old Testament. The Jews wanted to stone Jesus for saying he was the God of the patriarchs.

John 8:51-59 Strongs

51 G281 Verily G281 , verily G3004 , I say [G5719] G5213 unto you G1437 , If G5100 a man G5083 keep [G5661] G1699 my G3056 saying G2334 , he shall G3364 never G1519 G165 G2334 see [G5661] G2288 death.

52 G3767 Then G2036 said [G5627] G2453 the Jews G846 unto him G3568 , Now G1097 we know [G5758] G3754 that G2192 thou hast [G5719] G1140 a devil G11 . Abraham G599 is dead [G5627] G2532 , and G4396 the prophets G2532 ; and G4771 thou G3004 sayest [G5719] G1437 , If G5100 a man G5083 keep [G5661] G3450 my G3056 saying G1089 , he shall G3364 never G1519 G165 G1089 taste [G5695] G2288 of death.

53 G3361 Art G1488 [G5748] G4771 thou G3187 greater than G2257 our G3962 father G11 Abraham G3748 , which G599 is dead [G5627] G2532 ? and G4396 the prophets G599 are dead [G5627] G5101 : whom G4160 makest [G5719] G4771 thou G4572 thyself?

54 G2424 Jesus G611 answered [G5662] G1437 , If G1473 I G1392 honour [G5719] G1683 myself G3450 , my G1391 honour G2076 is [G5748] G3762 nothing G2076 : it is [G5748] G3450 my G3962 Father G1392 that honoureth [G5723] G3165 me G3739 ; of whom G5210 ye G3004 say [G5719] G3754 , that G2076 he is [G5748] G5216 your G2316 God:

55 G2532 Yet G1097 ye have G3756 not G1097 known [G5758] G846 him G1161 ; but G1473 I G1492 know [G5758] G846 him G2532 : and G1437 if G2036 I should say [G5632] G3754 , G1492 I know [G5758] G846 him G3756 not G2071 , I shall be [G5704] G5583 a liar G3664 like G5216 unto you G235 : but G1492 I know [G5758] G846 him G2532 , and G5083 keep [G5719] G846 his G3056 saying.

56 G5216 Your G3962 father G11 Abraham G21 rejoiced [G5662] G2443 to G1492 see [G5632] G1699 my G2250 day G2532 : and G1492 he saw [G5627] G2532 it, and G5463 was glad [G5644].

57 G3767 Then G2036 said [G5627] G2453 the Jews G4314 unto G846 him G2192 , Thou art [G5719] G3768 not yet G4004 fifty G2094 years old G2532 , and G3708 hast thou seen [G5758] G11 Abraham?

58 G2424 Jesus G2036 said [G5627] G846 unto them G281 , Verily G281 , verily G3004 , I say [G5719] G5213 unto you G4250 , Before G11 Abraham G1096 was [G5635] G1473 , I G1510 am [G5748].

59 G3767 Then G142 took they up [G5656] G3037 stones G2443 to G906 cast [G5632] G1909 at G846 him G1161 : but G2424 Jesus G2928 hid himself [G5648] G2532 , and G1831 went [G5627] G1537 out of G2411 the temple G1330 , going [G5631] G1223 through G3319 the midst G846 of them G2532 , and G3779 so G3855 passed by [G5707].

GIVEN TO JESUS

Jesus will give those who are his, eternal life, they are given to him by God. This idea parallels the thoughts in John. 6:65 where it says only those drawn by God can come to Jesus.

John 10:28-29 Strongs

28 G2504 And I G1325 give [G5719] G846 unto them G166 eternal G2222 life G2532 ; and G622 they shall G3364 never G1519 G165 G622 perish [G5643] G2532 , neither G3756 G726 shall G5100 any G726 man pluck [G5692] G846 them G1537 out of G3450 my G5495 hand.

29 G3450 My G3962 Father G3739 , which G1325 gave [G5758] G3427 them me G2076 , is [G5748] G3187 greater than G3956 all G2532 ; and G3762 no G1410 man is able [G5736] G726 to pluck [G5721] G1537 them out of G3450 my G3962 Father's G5495 hand.

MARTHA'S WISDOM

What does Martha tell us about the afterlife? Here she plainly describes her belief in when her brother will come back to life.

John 11:21-24 Strongs

21 G3767 Then G2036 said [G5627] G3136 Martha G4314 unto G2424 Jesus G2962 , Lord G1487 , if G2258 thou hadst been [G5713] G5602 here G3450 , my G80 brother G302 G2348 had G3756 not G2348 died [G5715].

22 G235 But G1492 I know [G5758] G2532 , that even G3568 now G3754 , whatsoever G3745 G302 G154 thou wilt ask [G5672] G2316 of God G2316 , God G1325 will give [G5692] G4671 it thee.

23 G2424 Jesus G3004 saith [G5719] G846 unto her G4675 , Thy G80 brother G450 shall rise again [G5698].

24 G3136 Martha G3004 saith [G5719] G846 unto him G1492 , I know [G5758] G3754 that G450 he shall rise again [G5698] G1722 in G386 the resurrection G1722 at G2078 the last G2250 day.

COULDN'T BE SAVED TILL JESUS CAME

Jesus doesn't correct Martha about her understanding of the resurrection.

Instead he expands on the concept and tells her, belief in him is the only way to eternal life. She expresses her belief in Jesus and his divinity.

John 11:25-27 Strongs

25 G2424 Jesus G2036 said [G5627] G846 unto her G1473 , I G1510 am [G5748] G386 the resurrection G2532 , and G2222 the life G4100 : he that believeth [G5723] G1519 in G1691 me G2579 , though G599 he were dead [G5632] G2198 , yet shall he live [G5695]:

26 G2532 And G3956 whosoever G2198 liveth [G5723] G2532 and G4100 believeth [G5723] G1519 in G1691 me G599 shall G3364 never G1519 G165 G599 die [G5632] G4100 . Believest thou [G5719] G5124 this?

27 G3004 She saith [G5719] G846 unto him G3483 , Yea G2962 , Lord G1473 : I G4100 believe [G5758] G3754 that G4771 thou G1488 art [G5748] G5547 the Christ G5207 , the Son G2316 of God G3588 , which G2064 should come [G5740] G1519 into G2889 the world.

JESUS LET HIM DIE JUST TO PROVE A POINT

Jesus called Lazarus out from the grave. He brought him back to life. He did this to fulfil one of the proofs the Jews had about what only the coming Messiah could do. They knew people could be brought back to life, if they hadn't been dead too long. But after three days dead, and starting to stink, then that would be a miracle worthy only of the Messiah. Notice that Lazarus was in the grave, not anywhere else. And that he was dead, not alive somewhere else looking down at what was going on.

John 11:38-44 Strongs

38 G2424 Jesus G3767 therefore G3825 again G1690 groaning [G5740] G1722 in G1438 himself G2064 cometh [G5736] G1519 to G3419 the grave G1161 . G2258 It was [G5713] G4693 a cave G2532 , and G3037 a stone G1945 lay [G5711] G1909 upon G846 it.

39 G2424 Jesus G3004 said [G5719] G142 , Take ye away [G5657] G3037

the stone G3136 . Martha G79 , the sister G2348 of him that was dead [G5761] G3004 , saith [G5719] G846 unto him G2962 , Lord G2235 , by this time G3605 he stinketh [G5719] G1063 : for G2076 he hath been [G5748] G5066 dead four days.

40 G2424 Jesus G3004 saith [G5719] G846 unto her G2036 , Said I [G5627] G3756 not G4671 unto thee G3754 , that G1437 , if G4100 thou wouldest believe [G5661] G3700 , thou shouldest see [G5695] G1391 the glory G2316 of God?

41 G3767 Then G142 they took away [G5656] G3037 the stone G3757 from the place where G2348 the dead [G5761] G2258 was [G5713] G2749 laid [G5740] G1161 . And G2424 Jesus G142 lifted [G5656] G507 up G3788 his eyes G2532 , and G2036 said [G5627] G3962 , Father G2168 , I thank [G5719] G4671 thee G3754 that G191 thou hast heard [G5656] G3450 me.

42 G1161 And G1473 I G1492 knew [G5715] G3754 that G191 thou hearest [G5719] G3450 me G3842 always G235 : but G1223 because G3793 of the people G3588 which G4026 stand by [G5761] G2036 I said [G5627] G2443 it, that G4100 they may believe [G5661] G3754 that G4771 thou G649 hast sent [G5656] G3165 me.

43 G2532 And G5023 when he thus G2036 had spoken [G5631] G2905 , he cried [G5656] G3173 with a loud G5456 voice G2976 , Lazarus G1204 , come [G5773] G1854 forth.

44 G2532 And G2348 he that was dead [G5761] G1831 came forth [G5627] G1210 , bound [G5772] G5495 hand G2532 and G4228 foot G2750 with graveclothes G2532 : and G846 his G3799 face G4019 was bound about [G5718] G4676 with a napkin G2424 . Jesus G3004 saith [G5719] G846 unto them G3089 , Loose [G5657] G846 him G2532 , and G863 let him [G5628] G5217 go [G5721].

Even though Jesus fulfilled all of the test miracles the religious leaders had set out for the Messiah to accomplish, they still wouldn't believe in him. Just as he had predicted in the parable found in Luke 16:19-31. They wouldn't be persuaded by someone who returned from the dead. V.30-31.

Jesus performs a miracle like no one had ever seen before. And rather than recognizing him as their Messiah, the religious leaders seek to kill him because they are afraid of losing their status and position in society.

John 11:45-53 Strongs

45 G3767 Then G4183 many G1537 of G2453 the Jews G3588 which G2064 came [G5631] G4314 to G3137 Mary G2532 , and G2300 had seen [G5666] G3739 the things which G2424 Jesus G4160 did [G5656] G4100 , believed [G5656] G1519 on G846 him.

46 G1161 But G5100 some G1537 of G846 them G565 went their ways [G5627] G4314 to G5330 the Pharisees G2532 , and G2036 told [G5627] G846 them G3739 what things G2424 Jesus G4160 had done [G5656].

47 G3767 Then G4863 gathered [G5627] G749 the chief priests G2532 and G5330 the Pharisees G4892 a council G2532 , and G3004 said [G5707] G5101 , What G4160 do we [G5719] G3754 ? for G3778 this G444 man G4160 doeth [G5719] G4183 many G4592 miracles.

48 G1437 If G863 we let G846 him G3779 thus G863 alone [G5632] G3956 , all G4100 men will believe [G5692] G1519 on G846 him G2532 : and G4514 the Romans G2064 shall come [G5695] G2532 and G142 take away [G5692] G2532 both G2257 our G5117 place G2532 and G1484 nation.

49 G1161 And G1520 one G5100 G1537 of G846 them G2533 , named Caiaphas G5607 , being [G5752] G749 the high priest G1565 that same G1763 year G2036 , said [G5627] G846 unto them G5210 , Ye G1492 know [G5758] G3756 nothing at all G3762,

50 G3761 Nor G1260 consider [G5736] G3754 that G4851 it is expedient

[G5719] G2254 for us G2443 , that G1520 one G444 man G599 should die [G5632] G5228 for G2992 the people G2532 , and G3650 that the whole G1484 nation G622 perish [G5643] G3361 not.

51 G1161 And G5124 this G2036 spake he [G5627] G3756 not G575 of G1438 himself G235 : but G5607 being [G5752] G749 high priest G1565 that G1763 year G4395 , he prophesied [G5656] G3754 that G2424 Jesus G3195 should [G5707] G599 die [G5721] G5228 for that G1484 nation;

52 G2532 And G3756 not G5228 for that G1484 nation G3440 only G235 , but G2443 that G2532 also G4863 he should gather together [G5632] G1519 in G1520 one G5043 the children G2316 of God G1287 that were scattered abroad [G5772].

53 G3767 Then G575 from G1565 that G2250 day G4823 forth they took counsel together [G5668] G2443 for to G615 put G846 him G615 to death [G5725].

RESURRECTIONS, THE HOPE FOR THE LOST

This verse tells us God had made it so that some people couldn't understand the message Jesus brought. If this life is their only opportunity to know and accept Jesus, then God would be condemning them to eternal death. He would be blinding them to their only chance to obtain eternal life. This is what Oprah found so unfair. When you limit the afterlife to going to heaven or hell immediately after dieing, there is no chance for people blinded by God, to have any opportunity for eternal life in heaven. If God is to be fair to his children born into humanity, then he will need to give everyone a chance to come to Jesus. I have found only through the promises found in the resurrections, doe's all humanity have a chance to be saved. The truth that everyone will get their opportunity, at their God ordained time, is humanities salvation.

John 12:39-40 Strongs

39 G5124 Therefore G1223 G1410 they could [G5711] G3756 not G4100

believe [G5721] G3754 , because G2268 that Esaias G2036 said [G5627] G3825 again,

40 G5186 He hath blinded [G5758] G846 their G3788 eyes G2532 , and G4456 hardened [G5758] G846 their G2588 heart G3363 ; that G1492 they should G3363 not G1492 see [G5632] G3788 with their eyes G2532 , nor G3539 understand [G5661] G2588 with their heart G2532 , and G1994 be converted [G5652] G2532 , and G2390 I should heal [G5667] G846 them.

IF GOD CALLS YOU, YOUR CHOICE IS NOW

Some people receive their calling during this life but lose out on it by loving the world more than God. All humanity will receive a chance to come to God. But not multiple chances.

John 12:42-43 Strongs

42 G3676 Nevertheless G3305 G1537 among G758 the chief rulers G2532 also G4183 many G4100 believed [G5656] G1519 on G846 him G235 ; but G1223 because G5330 of the Pharisees G3670 they did G3756 not G3670 confess [G5707] G3363 him, lest G1096 they should be [G5638] G656 put out of the synagogue:

43 G1063 For G25 they loved [G5656] G1391 the praise G444 of men G3123 more G2260 than G1391 the praise G2316 of God.

Mathew 10: 32-33

32 Whosoever therefore shall confess me before men, him will I confess also before my Father which is in heaven.

33 But whosoever shall deny me before men, him will I also deny before my Father which is in heaven.

NOT WITH HIM TILL HE COMES AGAIN

We will be received by Jesus into his fathers house, when he comes again.

John 14:2-3 Strongs

2 G1722 In G3450 my G3962 Father's G3614 house G1526 are [G5748] G4183 many G3438 mansions G1490 : if it were not G302 so, I would have told G2036 [G5627] G5213 you G4198 . I go [G5736] G2090 to prepare [G5658] G5117 a place G5213 for you.

3 G2532 And G1437 if G4198 I go [G5680] G2532 and G2090 prepare [G5661] G5117 a place G5213 for you G2064 , I will come [G5736] G3825 again G2532 , and G3880 receive [G5695] G5209 you G4314 unto G1683 myself G2443 ; that G3699 where G1473 I G1510 am [G5748] G5210 , there ye G5600 may be [G5753] G2532 also.

NOT WITH GOD UNTIL AFTER SALVATION

No one can get to God unless they go through Jesus. This is just as true for those that lived before Jesus, as it is for those that lived after he died. No one could be with God before Jesus came. Everyone must go through Jesus.

John 14:6 Strongs

6 G2424 Jesus G3004 saith [G5719] G846 unto him G1473 , I G1510 am [G5748] G3598 the way G2532 , G225 the truth G2532 , and G2222 the life G3762 : no man G2064 cometh [G5736] G4314 unto G3962 the Father G1508 , but G1223 by G1700 me.

WE ARE THE FAMILY OF GOD

This teaching of Jesus puts us in Gods family if we are his followers. We are destined to be the children of God, reborn with new bodies at the resurrection.

John 14:20 Strongs

20 G1722 At G1565 that G2250 day G5210 ye G1097 shall know [G5695] G3754 that G1473 I G1722 am in G3450 my G3962 Father G2532 , and G5210 ye G1722 in G1698 me G2504 , and I G1722 in G5213 you.

Jesus is talking to his disciples here, but I think it can apply to us as wel . God has chosen the ones he wants to follow him at this time. We are not to be doing the things the world does. Not letting the world tell us what's important in life. We need to be counter cultural and become who God leads us to be, following his command to love one another.

John 15:16-19 Strongs

16 G5210 Ye G1586 have G3756 not G1586 chosen [G5668] G3165 me G235 , but G1473 I G1586 have chosen [G5668] G5209 you G2532 , and G5087 ordained [G5656] G5209 you G2443 , that G5210 ye G5217 should go [G5725] G2532 and G5342 bring forth [G5725] G2590 fruit G2532 , and G5216 that your G2590 fruit G3306 should remain [G5725] G2443 : that G3739 whatsoever G302 G3748 G154 ye shall ask [G5661] G3962 of the Father G1722 in G3450 my G3686 name G1325 , he may give it [G5632] G5213 you.

17 G5023 These things G1781 I command [G5736] G5213 you G2443 , that G25 ye love [G5725] G240 one another.

18 G1487 If G2889 the world G3404 hate [G5719] G5209 you G1097 , ye know [G5719] [G5720] G3754 that G3404 it hated [G5758] G1691 me G4412 before G5216 it hated you.

19 G1487 If G2258 ye were [G5713] G1537 of G2889 the world G2889 , the world G302 would G5368 love [G5707] G2398 his own G1161 : but G3754 because G2075 ye are [G5748] G3756 not G1537 of G2889 the world G235 , but G1473 I G1586 have chosen [G5668] G5209 you G1537

out of G2889 the world G5124 , therefore G1223 G2889 the world G3404 hateth [G5719] G5209 you.

BLINDED SO THAT OTHERS MAY BE SAVED

Did the religious leaders have any excuse for their sin and hatred? They hated Jesus even though he passed all the tests they had set out for the Messiah to do to prove his authenticity. They showed themselves enemies of God.

John 15:21-25 Strongs

21 G235 But G3956 all G5023 these things G4160 will they do [G5692] G5213 unto you G1223 for G3450 my G3686 name's G3450 sake G3754 , because G1492 they know [G5758] G3756 not G3992 him that sent [G5660] G3165 me.

22 G1508 If G2064 I had G1508 not G2064 come [G5627] G2532 and G2980 spoken [G5656] G846 unto them G2192 , they had G3756 not G2192 had [G5707] G266 sin G1161 : but G3568 now G2192 they have [G5719] G3756 no G4392 cloke G4012 for G846 their G266 sin.

23 G3404 He that hateth [G5723] G1691 me G3404 hateth [G5719] G3450 my G3962 Father G2532 also.

24 G1508 If G4160 I had G1508 not G4160 done [G5656] G1722 among G846 them G2041 the works G3739 which G3762 none G243 other man G4160 did [G5758] G2192 , they had G3756 not G2192 had [G5707] G266 sin G1161 : but G3568 now G3708 have they G2532 both G3708 seen [G5758] G2532 and G3404 hated [G5758] G2532 both G1691 me G2532 and G3450 my G3962 Father.

25 G235 But G2443 this cometh to pass, that G3056 the word G4137 might be fulfilled [G5686] G1125 that is written [G5772] G1722 in G846 their G3551 law G3754 , G3404 They hated [G5656] G3165 me G1432 without a cause.

JESUS TAUGHT SO MOST WOULDN'T UNDERSTAND

These next two verses show us Jesus deliberately used proverbs when teaching about God to cloud the meaning of what he was saying. His proverbs weren't to be taken literally in every point. But to convey an overall point by means of a story.

John 16:25 Strongs

25 G5023 These things G2980 have I spoken [G5758] G5213 unto you G1722 in G3942 proverbs G235 : but G5610 the time G2064 cometh [G5736] G3753 , when G2980 I shall G3765 no more G2980 speak [G5692] G5213 unto you G1722 in G3942 proverbs G235 , but G312 I shall shew [G5692] G5213 you G3954 plainly G4012 of G3962 the Father.

John 16:29 Strongs

29 G846 His G3101 disciples G3004 said [G5719] G846 unto him G2396 , Lo G3568 , now G2980 speakest thou [G5719] G3954 plainly G2532 , and G3004 speakest [G5719] G3762 no G3942 proverb.

FOLLOWING JESUS IS,"A MISSION FROM GOD"

Eternal life comes through Jesus. But only to those that God gives him. Again reinforcing the fact we need to be called by God to come to Jesus.

John 17:2-3 Strongs

2 G2531 As G1325 thou hast given [G5656] G846 him G1849 power G3956 over all G4561 flesh G2443 , that G1325 he should give [G5661] G166 eternal G2222 life G3739 to G3956 as many as G846 G1325 thou hast given [G5758] G846 him.

3 G1161 And G3778 this G2076 is [G5748] G2222 life G166 eternal G2443 , that G1097 they might know [G5725] G4571 thee G3441 the only G228

true G2316 God G2532 , and G2424 Jesus G5547 Christ G3739 , whom G649 thou hast sent [G5656].

SANCTIFIED. BEING ONE WITH GOD

As in John:14:20 we are told here that we are to be one with each other, as Jesus is one with the father. God in Jesus, Jesus in us, we will all be one together. Giving us a hint of our future potential as children of God.

John 17:16-23 Strongs

16 G1526 They are [G5748] G3756 not G1537 of G2889 the world G2531 , even as G1473 I G1510 am [G5748] G3756 not G1537 of G2889 the world.

17 G37 Sanctify [G5657] G846 them G1722 through G4675 thy G225 truth G4674 : thy G3056 word G2076 is [G5748] G225 truth.

18 G2531 As G649 thou hast sent [G5656] G1691 me G1519 into G2889 the world G2504 , even so G649 have G2504 I also G649 sent [G5656] G846 them G1519 into G2889 the world.

19 G2532 And G5228 for G846 their G5228 sakes G1473 I G37 sanctify [G5719] G1683 myself G2443 , that G846 they G2532 also G5600 might [G5753] G37 be sanctified [G5772] G1722 through G225 the truth.

20 G1161 Neither G3756 G2065 pray I [G5719] G4012 for G5130 these G3440 alone G235 , but G4012 for G2532 them also G4100 which shall believe [G5694] G1519 on G1691 me G1223 through G846 their G3056 word;

21 G2443 That G3956 they all G5600 may be [G5753] G1520 one G2531 ; as G4771 thou G3962 , Father G1722 , art in G1698 me G2504 , and I G1722 in G4671 thee G2443 , that G846 they G2532 also G5600 may be [G5753] G1520 one G1722 in G2254 us G2443 : that G2889 the world G4100 may believe [G5661] G3754 that G4771 thou G649 hast sent [G5656] G3165 me.

22 G2532 And G1391 the glory G3739 which G1325 thou gavest [G5758] G3427 me G1473 I G1325 have given [G5758] G846 them G2443 ; that G5600 they may be [G5753] G1520 one G2531 , even as G2249 we G2070 are [G5748] G1520 one:

23 G1473 I G1722 in G846 them G2532 , and G4771 thou G1722 in G1698 me G2443 , that G5600 they may be [G5753] G5048 made perfect [G5772] G1519 in G1520 one G2532 ; and G2443 that G2889 the world G1097 may know [G5725] G3754 that G4771 thou G649 hast sent [G5656] G3165 me G2532 , and G25 hast loved [G5656] G846 them G2531 , as G25 thou hast loved [G5656] G1691 me.

SOME ATRIBUTES OF A SPIRIT BODY

Here we see what Jesus' spirit body was like. He could appear before them in a closed room. Going through solid objects wasn't a problem, yet Thomas was able to feel him as a solid person. Putting his finger into the holes in his hands, and reaching his hand into his side. It is also interesting that Jesus didn't come back healed of these wounds but there is no mention of him leaving a bloody trail behind. I wonder if the wounds from the scourging were healed. I would think he would have been easier to recognize if they weren't. There probably wouldn't have been people walking around in such bad condition. His resurrected body had attributes that his old physical one didn't have.

John 20:26-27 Strongs

26 G2532 And G3326 after G3638 eight G2250 days G3825 again G846 his G3101 disciples G2258 were [G5713] G2080 within G2532 , and G2381 Thomas G3326 with G846 them G2064 : then came [G5736] G2424 Jesus G2374 , the doors G2808 being shut [G5772] G2532 , and G2476 stood [G5627] G1519 in G3319 the midst G2532 , and G2036 said [G5627] G1515 , Peace G5213 be unto you.

27 G1534 Then G3004 saith he [G5719] G2381 to Thomas G5342 , Reach [G5720] G5602 hither G4675 thy G1147 finger G2532 , and G1492 behold

[G5657] G3450 my G5495 hands G2532 ; and G5342 reach hither [G5720] G4675 thy G5495 hand G2532 , and G906 thrust [G5628] G1519 it into G3450 my G4125 side G2532 : and G1096 be [G5737] G3361 not G571 faithless G235 , but G4103 believing.

THE KEY TO ETERNAL LIFE

Again it is emphasized that we have life through his name when we believe.

John 20:31 Strongs

31 G1161 But G5023 these G1125 are written [G5769] G2443 , that G4100 ye might believe [G5661] G3754 that G2424 Jesus G2076 is [G5748] G5547 the Christ G5207 , the Son G2316 of God G2532 ; and G2443 that G4100 believing [G5723] G2192 ye might have [G5725] G2222 life G1722 through G846 his G3686 name.

Chapter 21: THE BOOK OF ACTS

THE SECOND COMMING OF JESUS

Jesus returns on the day of the Lord. Those that call upon his name shall be saved.

Acts 2:20-21 Strongs

20 G2246 The sun G3344 shall be turned [G5691] G1519 into G4655 darkness G2532 , and G4582 the moon G1519 into G129 blood G2228 , before G4250 G3173 that great G2532 and G2016 notable G2250 day G2962 of the Lord G2064 come [G5629]:

21 G2532 And G2071 it shall come to pass [G5704] G3739 , that whosoever G3956 G302 G1941 shall call on [G5672] G3686 the name G2962 of the Lord G4982 shall be saved [G5701].

DEAD THE OPPOSITE OF ALIVE

David is dead and buried, his grave is still here. He isn't anywhere else. He isn't conscious looking down on us, which would by definition make him alive.

Acts 2:29 Strongs

29 G435 Men G80 and brethren G2036 , let G1832 me [G5752] G3326 freely G3954 G2036 speak [G5629] G4314 unto G5209 you G4012 of G3966 the patriarch G1138 David G3754 , that G5053 he is G2532 both G5053 dead [G5656] G2532 and G2290 buried [G5648] G2532 , and G846

his G3418 sepulchre G2076 is [G5748] G1722 with G2254 us G891 unto G5026 this G2250 day.

DAVID PROPHESIES ABOUT JESUS

This verse tells us that David knew Jesus would be resurrected.

Acts 2:31 Strongs

31 G4275 He seeing this before [G5631] G2980 spake [G5656] G4012 of G386 the resurrection G5547 of Christ G3754 , that G846 his G5590 soul G2641 was G3756 not G2641 left [G5681] G1519 in G86 hell G3761 , neither G846 his G4561 flesh G1492 did see [G5627] G1312 corruption.

It can be misleading to use pagan inspired Greek words to define the Hebrew words of God's truth. The Greek word used here for soul G5590, has one definition stating the soul is immortal. Then it goes on to say that this exactly corresponds to the Hebrew words used for soul. When you look up the Hebrew words none of them talk of immortality related to the soul.

The Greek language came out of a heathen society. One that believed in a large panacea of Gods. So the very act of writing in Greek using words developed by a religiously pagan society would corrupt the exact meaning of the Hebrew thoughts. They could only approximate the desired meaning.

Similarly the word Hell in its definitions in the Greek are corrupted by the heathen teachings the Greek language came from. Using all the Greek definitions of a word to identify the meaning that the authors intended, could be misleading. As with most of the world's religions, the Greeks believed immortal life was something that mankind had within themselves. They didn't believe there was a creator God that loved them and would bring them back to life, like we find in the Old Testament.

The language that was spoken in most of the New Testament was Hebrew or Aramaic. It was written in Greek by God led people, however they sti l were using the Greek words to convey the message. In Canada, Christians might wish you good luck before you go on a trip, or have a job interview. They may say it was fortunate that your toddler wasn't hit by a car when they ventured out onto a busy street. This doesn't mean they have renounced Jesus and now hold to pagan gods for salvation. They are just using commonly understood phrases that is part of their culture. English is an eclectic language. Definitions we are intending aren't necessarily all of the ones that the word could be used to represent.

Using a word like G86 ᾅδης which means the place of the dead or the grave, would be the normal word to use to refer to someone's grave, even though it may have other meanings that you didn't intend. How biblically accurate would it be to say that Hades or Pluto are the gods in charge there? Doesn't the bible teach us the pagan gods are nothing but human imagination? We would be prudent to balance the definitions used in the Greek against what the Hebrew definitions say about a subject.

Jeremiah 10:1-15

King James Version

10 Hear ye the word which the LORD speaketh unto you, O house of Israel:

2 Thus saith the LORD, Learn not the way of the heathen, and be not dismayed at the signs of heaven; for the heathen are dismayed at them.

3 For the customs of the people are vain: for one cutteth a tree out of the forest, the work of the hands of the workman, with the axe.

4 They deck it with silver and with gold; they fasten it with nails and with hammers, that it move not.

5 They are upright as the palm tree, but speak not: they must needs be borne, because they cannot go. Be not afraid of them; for they cannot do

evil, neither also is it in them to do good.

6 Forasmuch as there is none like unto thee, O LORD; thou art great, and thy name is great in might.

7 Who would not fear thee, O King of nations? for to thee doth it appertain: forasmuch as among all the wise men of the nations, and in all their kingdoms, there is none like unto thee.

8 But they are altogether brutish and foolish: the stock is a doctrine of vanities.

9 Silver spread into plates is brought from Tarshish, and gold from Uphaz, the work of the workman, and of the hands of the founder: blue and purple is their clothing: they are all the work of cunning men.

10 But the LORD is the true God, he is the living God, and an everlasting king: at his wrath the earth shall tremble, and the nations shall not be able to abide his indignation.

11 Thus shall ye say unto them, The gods that have not made the heavens and the earth, even they shall perish from the earth, and from under these heavens.

12 He hath made the earth by his power, he hath established the world by his wisdom, and hath stretched out the heavens by his discretion.

13 When he uttereth his voice, there is a multitude of waters in the heavens, and he causeth the vapours to ascend from the ends of the earth; he maketh lightnings with rain, and bringeth forth the wind out of his treasures.

14 Every man is brutish in his knowledge: every founder is confounded by the graven image: for his molten image is falsehood, and there is no breath in them.

15 They are vanity, and the work of errors: in the time of their visitation they shall perish.

G5590 ψυχή - Strong's Greek Lexicon Number

ψυχή

breath

ψυχή breath, i.e. (by implication) spirit, abstractly or concretely (the animal sentient principle only; thus distinguished on the one hand from G4151, which is the rational and immortal soul; and on the other from G2222, which is mere vitality, even of plants: these terms thus exactly correspond respectively to the Hebrew H5315, H7307 and H2416)

Derivation: from G5594;

KJV Usage: heart (+ -ily), life, mind, soul, + us, + you.

G5594 G4151 G2222 H5315 H7307 H2416

1) breath

1a) the breath of life

1a1) the vital force which animates the body and shows itself in breathing

1a1a) of animals

1a12) of men

1b) life

1c) that in which there is life

1c1) a living being, a living soul

2) the soul

2a) the seat of the feelings, desires, affections, aversions (our heart, scul etc.)

2b) the (human) soul in so far as it is constituted that by the right use of the aids offered it by God it can attain its highest end and secure eternal blessedness, the soul regarded as a moral being designed for everlasting life

2c) the soul as an essence which differs from the body and is not dissolved by death (distinguished from other parts of the body)

G86 ᾅδης - Strong's Greek Lexicon Number

ᾅδης properly, unseen, i.e. "Hades" or the place (state) of departed souls

Derivation: from G1 (as negative particle) and G1492;

KJV Usage: grave, hell.

G1 G1492

1) name Hades or Pluto, the god of the lower regions

2) Orcus, the nether world, the realm of the dead

3) later use of this word: the grave, death, hellIn Biblical Greek it is associated with Orcus, the infernal regions, a dark and dismal place in the very depths of the earth, the common receptacle of disembodied spirits. Usually Hades is just the abode of the wicked, Lu. 16:23, Rev. 20:13,14; a very uncomfortable place. TDNT.

- Hades

ᾅδης

hadēs

hah'-dace

From G1 (as a negative particle) and G1492; properly unseen, that is,

"Hades" or the place (state) of departed souls.

DAVID DEAD IN HIS GRAVE

Just in case we miss understood the first time Peter again explains about David and heaven.

Acts 2:34-35 Strongs

34 G1063 For G1138 David G3756 is not G305 ascended [G5627] G1519 into G3772 the heavens G1161 : but G3004 he saith [G5719] G846 himself G2962 , The LORD G2036 said [G5627] G3450 unto my G2962 Lord G2521 , Sit thou [G5737] G1537 on G3450 my G1188 right hand,

35 G2193 Until G302 I make G5087 [G5632] G4675 thy G2190 foes G4675 thy G4228 footstool G5286.

ONLY SAVED BY JESUS

There is no other name for salvation, it only comes through Jesus. No Jesus, no salvation. Fairly straight forward. So how do those who never got to know Jesus get the opportunity to be saved? If no way is available for them how can God say he wants all people to know him? It is his will that all should be able to become his children. Read on to learn about their time for salvation.

Acts 4:12 Strongs

12 G2532 Neither G3756 G2076 is there [G5748] G4991 salvation G1722 in G3762 any G243 other G1063 : for G2076 there is [G5748] G3777 none G2087 other G3686 name G5259 under G3772 heaven G1325 given [G5772] G1722 among G444 men G1722 , whereby G3739 G2248 we G1163 must [G5748] G4982 be saved [G5683].

This is a good example of how people learn about Jesus. V31. How can they know unless someone guides them, in person, or through some type of a recording? God usually teaches people about Jesus, by using other people to tell them. Philip was directed by an angel to talk to the eunuch. The eunuch was receptive to Gods' calling in his life. It was a divine appointment for both of them.

Acts 8:26-39 Strongs

26 G1161 And G32 the angel G2962 of the Lord G2980 spake [G5656] G4314 unto G5376 Philip G3004 , saying [G5723] G450 , Arise [G5628] G2532 , and G4198 go [G5737] G2596 toward G3314 the south G1909 unto G3598 the way G2597 that goeth down [G5723] G575 from G2419 Jerusalem G1519 unto G1048 Gaza G3778 , which G2076 is [G5748] G2048 desert.

27 G2532 And G450 he arose [G5631] G4198 and went [G5675] G2532 : and G2400 , behold [G5628] G435 , a man G128 of Ethiopia G2135 , an eunuch G1413 of great authority G2582 under Candace G938 queen G128 of the Ethiopians G3739 , who G2258 had [G5713] G1909 the charge of G3956 all G846 her G1047 treasure G3739 , and G2064 had come [G5715] G1519 to G2419 Jerusalem G4352 for to worship [G5694],

28 G5037 G2258 Was [G5713] G5290 returning [G5723] G2532 , and G2521 sitting [G5740] G1909 in G846 his G716 chariot G2532 G314 read [G5707] G2268 Esaias G4396 the prophet.

29 G1161 Then G4151 the Spirit G2036 said [G5627] G5376 unto Philip G4334 , Go near [G5628] G2532 , and G2853 join thyself to [G5682] G5129 this G716 chariot.

30 G1161 And G5376 Philip G4370 ran [G5631] G191 thither to him, and heard [G5656] G846 him G314 read [G5723] G4396 the prophet G2268 Esaias G2532 , and G2036 said [G5627] G687 , Understandest thou G1065 G1097 [G5719] G3739 what G314 thou readest [G5719]?

31 G1161 And G2036 he said [G5627] G1063 , How G4459 G302 can I

G1410 [G5739] G3362 , except G5100 some man G3594 should guide [G5661] G3165 me G5037 ? And G3870 he desired [G5656] G5376 Philip G305 that he would come up [G5631] G2523 and sit [G5658] G4862 with G846 him.

32 G1161 G4042 The place G1124 of the scripture G3739 which G314 he read [G5707] G2258 was [G5713] G3778 this G71 , He was led [G5681] G5613 as G4263 a sheep G1909 to G4967 the slaughter G2532 ; and G5613 like G286 a lamb G880 dumb G1726 before G846 his G2751 shearer [G5723] G3779 , so G455 opened he [G5719] G3756 not G846 his G4750 mouth:

33 G1722 In G846 his G5014 humiliation G846 his G2920 judgment G142 was taken away [G5681] G1161 : and G5101 who G1334 shall declare [G5695] G846 his G1074 generation G3754 ? for G846 his G2222 life G142 is taken [G5743] G575 from G1093 the earth.

34 G1161 And G2135 the eunuch G611 answered [G5679] G5376 Philip G2036 , and said [G5627] G1189 , I pray [G5736] G4675 thee G4012 , of G5101 whom G3004 speaketh [G5719] G4396 the prophet G5124 this G4012 ? of G1438 himself G2228 , or G4012 of G5100 some G2087 other man?

35 G1161 Then G5376 Philip G455 opened [G5660] G846 his G4750 mouth G2532 , and G756 began [G5671] G575 at G5026 the same G1124 scripture G2097 , and preached [G5668] G846 unto him G2424 Jesus.

36 G1161 And G5613 as G4198 they went [G5711] G2596 on G3598 their way G2064 , they came [G5627] G1909 unto G5100 a certain G5204 water G2532 : and G2135 the eunuch G5346 said [G5748] G2400 , See [G5628] G5204 , here is water G5101 ; what G2967 doth hinder [G5719] G3165 me G907 to be baptized [G5683]?

37 G1161 And G5376 Philip G2036 said [G5627] G1487 , If G4100 thou believest [G5719] G1537 with G3650 all thine G2588 heart G1832 , thou mayest [G5748] G1161 . And G611 he answered [G5679] G2036 and said

[G5627] G4100 , I believe [G5719] G2424 that Jesus G5547 Christ G1511 is [G5750] G5207 the Son G2316 of God.

38 G2532 And G2753 he commanded [G5656] G716 the chariot G2476 to stand still [G5629] G2532 : and G2597 they went down [G5627] G297 both G1519 into G5204 the water G5037 , both G5376 Philip G2532 and G2135 the eunuch G2532 ; and G907 he baptized [G5656] G846 him.

39 G1161 And G3753 when G305 they were come up [G5627] G1537 out of G5204 the water G4151 , the Spirit G2962 of the Lord G726 caught away [G5656] G5376 Philip G2532 , G2135 that the eunuch G1492 saw [G5627] G3756 G846 him G3765 no more G1063 : and G4198 he went [G5711] G846 on his G3598 way G5463 rejoicing [G5723].

GOD WORKS WITH THOSE FROM EVERY NATION THAT RESPECT HIM

Here we are told God is not a respecter of persons, he will accept people regardless of background or lineage.

Acts 10:34-36 Strongs

34 G1161 Then G4074 Peter G455 opened [G5660] G4750 his mouth G2036 , and said [G5627] G1909 , Of G225 a truth G2638 I perceive [G5731] G3754 that G2316 God G2076 is [G5748] G3756 no G4381 respecter of persons:

35 G235 But G1722 in G3956 every G1484 nation G5399 he that feareth [G5740] G846 him G2532 , and G2038 worketh [G5740] G1343 righteousness G2076 , is [G5748] G1184 accepted G846 with him.

36 G3056 The word G3739 which G649 God sent [G5656] G5207 unto the children G2474 of Israel G2097 , preaching [G5734] G1515 peace G1223 by G2424 Jesus G5547 Christ G3778 : (he G2076 is [G5748] G2962 Lord G3956 of all:)

SALVATION CAME AFTER THE TEMPLE VAIL WAS TORN

It is important to be sin free if we are to live with God. Sin wasn't removed until Jesus was crucified for us. So any one that died before Jesus, would have had to wait till after Jesus died to have their sins blotted out.

Acts 10:43 Strongs

43 G5129 To him G3140 give G3956 all G4396 the prophets G3140 witness [G5719] G1223 , that through G846 his G3686 name G3956 whosoever G4100 believeth [G5723] G1519 in G846 him G2983 shall receive [G5629] G859 remission G266 of sins.

THROUGH BELIEVING WE CAN BE SAVED

They were saved by hearing the word.

Acts 11:14 Strongs

14 G3739 Who G2980 shall tell [G5692] G4314 thee G4571 G4487 words G1722 , whereby G3739 G4771 thou G2532 and G3956 all G4675 thy G3624 house G4982 shall be saved [G5701].

DEAD AND DECAYED

David died and turned back to the dust mankind was made from. He sleeps with his fathers.

Acts 13:36 Strongs

36 G1063 For G3303 G1138 David G5256 , after he had served [G5660] G2398 his own G1074 generation G1012 by the will G2316 of God G2837 , fell on sleep [G5681] G2532 , and G4369 was laid [G5681] G4314 unto G846 his G3962 fathers G2532 , and G1492 saw [G5627] G1312 corruption:

NO JESUS NO LIFE KNOW JESUS KNOW LIFE

I have heard it said that people from the Old Testament times are saved and now in heaven through keeping the law of God. However we have read mankind is only saved by the sacrifice of Jesus. Only those justified by him can be saved. This is what is being taught here. The law of Moses saved no one. The only way to gain eternal life is through belief in Jesus and his redemptive sacrifice. That fact eliminates any possibility of there being anyone in heaven before Jesus completed mankind's salvation. If there were a waiting room for conscious dead people they would all be there together, good and bad. For all have sinned and come short of the glory of God.

Acts 13:38-39 Strongs

38 G2077 Be it [G5749] G1110 known G5213 unto you G3767 therefore G435 , men G80 and brethren G3754 , that G1223 through G5127 this man G2605 is preached [G5743] G5213 unto you G859 the forgiveness G266 of sins:

39 G2532 And G1722 by G5129 him G3956 all G4100 that believe [G5723] G1344 are justified [G5743] G575 from G3956 all things G3739 , from which G1410 ye could [G5675] G3756 not G1344 be justified [G5683] G1722 by G3551 the law G3475 of Moses.

EVERYONE GETS A CHANCE TO ACCEPT GOD

The traditional teaching about hell is, you are tormented there for all eternity, forever, never ending. Sounds like eternal life in misery, and pain. But here Paul and Barnabas tell us that the Jews judged themselves unworthy of everlasting life. They wouldn't receive eternal life because of their hard hearts. If they aren't to receive eternal life how is it that they will be tormented in hell for all eternity? If they possessed an immortal soul already then they would be immortal. Unworthy or not, they would have everlasting life. Here we are told they gave up their opportunity to receive everlasting life. Which means they didn't already have it and will not receive it.

Acts 13:46 Strongs

46 G1161 Then G3972 Paul G2532 and G921 Barnabas G3955 waxed bold [G5666] G2036 , and said [G5627] G2258 , It was [G5713] G316 necessary G3056 that the word G2316 of God G2980 should G4412 first G2980 have been spoken [G5683] G5213 to you G1161 : but G1894 seeing G683 ye put G846 it G683 from you [G5736] G2532 , and G2919 judge [G5719] G1438 yourselves G3756 unworthy G514 G166 of everlasting G2222 life G2400 , lo [G5628] G4762 , we turn [G5743] G1519 to G1484 the Gentiles.

GOD HAS YOU IN HIS PLAN

Those who are ordained to eternal life become believers. This verse tells me that you need to be drawn to Jesus by God. The meaning for the word ordained is, to arrange, put in order. Those who are drawn to Jesus in this life are being arranged in order by God, for his purposes. Scripture will show us the order God has arranged for mankind to make their choice of life or death.

Acts 13:48 Strongs

48 G1161 And G1484 when the Gentiles G191 heard this [G5723] G5463 , they were glad [G5707] G2532 , and G1392 glorified [G5707] G3056 the word G2962 of the Lord G2532 : and G3745 as many as G2258 were [G5713] G5021 ordained [G5772] G1519 to G166 eternal G2222 life G4100 believed [G5656].

G5021 τάσσω - Strong's Greek Lexicon Number

τάσσω

to arrange, put in order

τάσσω to arrange in an orderly manner, i.e. assign or dispose (to a certain position or lot)

Derivation: a prolonged form of a primary verb (which latter appears only in certain tenses);

KJV Usage: addict, appoint, determine, ordain, set.

1) to put in order, to station

1a) to place in a certain order, to arrange, to assign a place, to appoint

1a1) to assign (appoint) a thing to one

1b) to appoint, ordain, order

1b1) to appoint on one's own responsibility or authority

1b2) to appoint mutually, i.e. agree upon

For Synonyms see entry G5844

- Modest
- Appoint, Appointed
- Determine, Determinate
- Ordain
- Set

τάσσω

tassō

tas'-so

A prolonged form of a primary verb (which latter appears only in certain tenses); to arrange in an orderly manner, that is, assign or dispose (to a certain position or lot)

JESUS IS THE ONLY WAY

Some churches put a lot of emphasis on law. Doing certain things in a particular way, or at a particular time. The Law of Moses could be understood as all of the laws from the first five books of the bible that Moses wrote.

Acts 15:5 Strongs

5 G1161 But G1817 there rose up [G5627] G5100 certain G575 of G139 the sect G5330 of the Pharisees G4100 which believed [G5761] G3004 , saying [G5723] G3754 , That G1163 it was needful [G5748] G4059 to circumcise [G5721] G846 them G5037 , and G3853 to command [G5721] G5083 them to keep [G5721] G3551 the law G3475 of Moses.

The first century church leaders didn't see the need for new converts to follow the Law of Moses, or be circumcised. This is not only a good verse to demonstrate that we are saved by our faith in Jesus alone and not by works, but can also help free people from the bondage of legalism. Having external rules, and laws can be helpful in keeping us from sinning, but it's the internal limits we place on ourselves that show our true character.

Acts 15:28-29 Strongs

28 G1063 For G1380 it seemed good [G5656] G40 to the Holy G4151 Ghost G2532 , and G2254 to us G2007 , to lay upon [G5733] G5213 you G3367 no G4119 greater G922 burden G4133 than G5130 these G1876 necessary things;

29 G567 That ye abstain [G5733] G1494 from meats offered to idols G2532 , and G129 from blood G2532 , and G4156 from things strangled

G2532 , and G4202 from fornication G1537 : from G3739 which G1301 if ye keep [G5723] G1438 yourselves G4238 , ye shall do [G5692] G2095 well G4517 . Fare ye well [G5770].

GOD DRAWS, JESUS SAVES

This verse tells us the Lord opened the heart of Lydia. Would this be an example of being drawn to Jesus?

Acts 16:14 Strongs

14 G2532 And G5100 a certain G1135 woman G3686 named G3070 Lydia G4211 , a seller of purple G4172 , of the city G2363 of Thyatira G4576 , which worshipped [G5740] G2316 God G191 , heard [G5707] G3739 us : whose G2588 heart G2962 the Lord G1272 opened [G5656]G4337 , that she attended [G5721] G2980 unto the things which were spoken [G5746] G5259 of G3972 Paul.

FAITH. NOT WORKS

This is the minimum we must do to be saved.

Acts 16:31 Strongs

31 G1161 And G2036 they said [G5627] G4100 , Believe [G5657] G1909 on G2962 the Lord G2424 Jesus G5547 Christ G2532 , and G4771 thou G4982 shalt be saved [G5701] G2532 , and G4675 thy G3624 house.

IF I HAVE NOT LOVE, I HAVE NOTHING

This is a good lesson about peripheral topics. We might get very passionate about some biblical teachings, and feel they are crucial. Baptism can be one of these divisive topics. How it's done, to who, when, how often. All of these aspects can divide Christians and even lead to murder. Just look at church history from the reformation. God used

Apollos to teach others in a big way, being fervent in the spirit, even though his knowledge of baptism was limited. God uses those that love him and willingly follow where he leads. God doesn't destroy us because of what we don't know. We should treat other Christians the same way God treats us. With loving patience.

Acts 18:24-26 Strongs

24 G1161 And G5100 a certain G2453 Jew G3686 named G625 Apollos G1085 , born G221 at Alexandria G3052 , an eloquent G435 man G5607 , and mighty [G5752] G1415 G1722 in G1124 the scriptures G2658 , came [G5656] G1519 to G2181 Ephesus.

25 G3778 This man G2258 was [G5713] G2727 instructed in [G5772] G3598 the way G2962 of the Lord G2532 ; and G2204 being fervent [G5723] G4151 in the spirit G2980 , he spake [G5707] G2532 and G1321 taught [G5707] G199 diligently G4012 the things of G2962 the Lord G1987 , knowing [G5740] G3440 only G908 the baptism G2491 of John.

26 G5037 And G3778 he G756 began [G5662] G3955 to speak boldly [G5738] G1722 in G4864 the synagogue G846 : whom G1161 when G207 Aquila G2532 and G4252 Priscilla G191 had heard [G5660] G4355 , they took [G5639] G846 him G2532 unto them, and G1620 expounded [G5639] G846 unto him G3598 the way G2316 of God G197 more perfectly.

When these disciples learned more about baptism they accepted where God was leading them with open hearts. How long God left them not knowing the full story, we can only speculate. But we do know God used these men in spite of their lack of understanding. And in time God led the twelve into a fuller knowledge of him.

Acts 19:1-7 Strongs

1 G1161 And G1096 it came to pass [G5633] G625 , that, while Apollos G1511 was [G5750] G1722 G1722 at G2882 Corinth G3972 , Paul G1330

having passed [G5631] G510 through the upper G3313 coasts G2064 came [G5629] G1519 to G2181 Ephesus G2532 : and G2147 finding [G5631] G5100 certain G3101 disciples,

2 G2036 He said [G5627] G4314 unto G846 them G1487 , G2983 Have ye received [G5627] G40 the Holy G4151 Ghost G4100 since ye believed [G5660] G1161 ? And G2036 they said [G5627] G4314 unto G846 him G235 , G191 We have G3761 not so much as G191 heard [G5656] G1487 whether G2076 there be any [G5748] G40 Holy G4151 Ghost.

3 G5037 And G2036 he said [G5627] G4314 unto G846 them G1519 , Unto G5101 what G3767 then G907 were ye baptized [G5681] G1161 ? And G2036 they said [G5627] G1519 , Unto G2491 John's G908 baptism.

4 G1161 Then G2036 said [G5627] G3972 Paul G2491 , John G3303 verily G907 baptized [G5656] G908 with the baptism G3341 of repentance G3004 , saying [G5723] G2992 unto the people G2443 , that G4100 they should believe [G5661] G1519 on G2064 him which should come [G5740] G3326 after G846 him G5123 , that is [G5748] G1519 , on G5547 Christ G2424 Jesus.

5 G1161 When G191 they heard [G5660] G907 this, they were baptized [G5681] G1519 in G3686 the name G2962 of the Lord G2424 Jesus.

6 G2532 And G3972 when Paul G2007 had laid G5495 his hands G2007 upon [G5631] G846 them G40 , the Holy G4151 Ghost G2064 came [G5627] G1909 on G846 them G5037 ; and G2980 they spake [G5707] G1100 with tongues G2532 , and G4395 prophesied [G5707].

7 G1161 And G3956 all G435 the men G2258 were [G5713] G5616 about G1177 twelve.

BROUGHT BACK TO LIFE

Here after teaching late into the night Paul brings a young man that fell from a high window ledge back to life. It is a resurrection that took place pretty much immediately after the person died. This is not the way the majority of people will be resurrected.

Acts 20:9-12 Strongs

9 G1161 And G2521 there sat [G5740] G1909 in G2376 a window G5100 a certain G3494 young man G3686 named G2161 Eutychus G2702 , being fallen [G5746] G901 into a deep G5258 sleep G3972 : and as Paul G1909 was long G4119 G1256 preaching [G5740] G2702 , he sunk down [G5685] G575 with G5258 sleep G2736 , and fell down G4098 [G5627] G575 from G5152 the third loft G2532 , and G142 was taken up [G5681] G3498 dead.

10 G1161 And G3972 Paul G2597 went down [G5631] G1968 , and fell on [G5627] G846 him G2532 , and G4843 embracing [G5631] G2036 him said [G5627] G2350 , Trouble G3361 not G2350 yourselves [G5744] G1063 ; for G846 his G5590 life G2076 is [G5748] G1722 in G846 him.

11 G1161 When G305 he G305 therefore was come up again [G5631] G2532 , and G2806 had broken [G5660] G740 bread G2532 , and G1089 eaten [G5666] G5037 , and G3656 talked [G5660] G1909 G2425 a long while G891 , even till G827 break of day G3779 , so G1831 he departed [G5627].

12 G1161 And G71 they brought [G5627] G3816 the young man G2198 alive [G5723] G2532 , and G3870 were G3756 not G3357 a little G3870 comforted [G5681].

TRADITIONS DON'T SAVE

Paul taught the gentiles not to follow the customs of Moses.

Acts 21:21 Strongs

21 G1161 And G2727 they are informed [G5681] G4012 of G4675 thee G3754 , that G1321 thou teachest [G5719] G3956 all G2453 the Jews G2596 which are among G1484 the Gentiles G575 to G646 forsake G3475 Moses G3004 , saying [G5723] G846 that they G4059 ought G3361 not G4059 to circumcise [G5721] G5043 their children G3366 , neither G4043

to walk [G5721] G1485 after the customs.

THE HOPE THAT IS WITHIN US

Paul believed in, and had a hope of, a resurrection.

Acts 23:6 Strongs

6 G1161 But G3972 when Paul G1097 perceived [G5631] G3754 that G1520 the one G3313 part G2076 were [G5748] G4523 Sadducees G1161 , and G2087 the other G5330 Pharisees G2896 , he cried out [G5656] G1722 in G4892 the council G435 , Men G80 and brethren G1473 , I G1510 am [G5748] G5330 a Pharisee G5207 , the son G5330 of a Pharisee G4012 : of G1680 the hope G2532 and G386 resurrection G3498 of the dead G1473 I G2919 am called in question [G5743].

Paul said of himself, that he was a Pharisee of Pharisees. He knew and was a believer of the prophets and Gods law. He studied them for most of his life. He would know if the resurrection was taught in the Old Testament. Those who say the Old Testament doesn't teach the resurrection would be arguing with Paul who clearly believed in a resurrection of all of the dead.

Acts 24:14-15 Strongs

14 G1161 But G5124 this G3670 I confess [G5719] G4671 unto thee G3754 , that G2596 after G3598 the way G3739 which G3004 they call [G5719] G139 heresy G3779 , so G3000 worship I [G5719] G2316 the God G3971 of my fathers G4100 , believing [G5723] G3956 all things G3588 which G1125 are written [G5772] G2596 in G3551 the law G2532 and G1722 in G4396 the prophets:

15 G2192 And have [G5723] G1680 hope G1519 toward G2316 God G3739 , which G3778 they G846 themselves G2532 also G4327 allow [G5736] G3195 , that there shall be [G5721] G1510 [G5705] G386 a

resurrection G3498 of the dead G5037 , both G1342 of the just G2532 and G94 unjust.

Chapter 22: BOOK OF ROMANS

CALLED TO ACCEPT JESUS

We are called, to come to Jesus. Called can also be understood as, divinely selected and appointed. God has invited us to come to Jesus that we may be saved now in this life. This is our time to choose Jesus. Those who aren't called cannot come to Jesus at this time.

Romans 1:6-7 Strongs

6 G1722 Among G3739 whom G2075 are [G5748] G5210 ye G2532 also G2822 the called G2424 of Jesus G5547 Christ:

7 G3956 To all G5607 that be [G5752] G1722 in G4516 Rome G27 , beloved G2316 of God G2822 , called G40 to be saints G5485 : Grace G5213 to you G2532 and G1515 peace G575 from G2316 God G2257 our G3962 Father G2532 , and G2962 the Lord G2424 Jesus G5547 Christ.

G2822 κλητός - Strong's Greek Lexicon Number

κλητός

called, invited, welcome

κλητός invited, i.e. appointed, or (specially), a saint

Derivation: from the same as G2821;

KJV Usage: called.

G2821

1)called, invited (to a banquet)

1a) invited (by God in the proclamation of the Gospel) to obtain eterna salvation in the kingdom through Christ

1b) called to (the discharge of) some office

1b1) divinely selected and appointed

THERE IS NO ETERNAL LIFE WITHOUT JESUS

No one can be saved without Jesus to cover their sins. No one in all of humanity could be with God without the sacrifice of Jesus to purge them of their sins.

Romans 3:9-12 Strongs

9 G5101 What G3767 then G4284 ? are we better [G5736] G3756 than they ? No G3843 , in no wise G1063 : for G4256 we have before proved [G5662] G5037 both G2453 Jews G2532 and G1672 Gentiles G1511 , that they are [G5750] G3956 all G5259 under G266 sin;

10 G2531 As G1125 it is written [G5769] G3754 , G2076 There is [G5748] G3756 none G1342 righteous G3761 , no, not G1520 one:

11 G2076 There is [G5748] G3756 none G4920 that understandeth [G5723] G2076 , there is [G5748] G3756 none G1567 that seeketh after [G5723] G2316 God.

12 G1578 They are G3956 all G1578 gone out of the way [G5656] G889 , they are G260 together G889 become unprofitable [G5681] G2076 ; there is [G5748] G3756 none G4160 that doeth [G5723] G5544 good G3756 , no, not G2076 one [G5748] G2193 G1520.

GOD IS NOT A LIAR

In case you were not sure what was meant when God refers to the faithful dead patriarchs as being alive, this verse should help clear things up. God is faithful to his promises. What he has said he will do, that he will do. Since it is a certainty they will live again, he speaks as if it has already happened. As though they were alive.

Romans 4:17 Strongs

17 G2531 (As G1125 it is written [G5769] G3754 , G5087 I have made [G5758] G4571 thee G3962 a father G4183 of many G1484 nations G2713 ,) before G3739 him whom G4100 he believed [G5656] G2316 , even God G2227 , who quickeneth [G5723] G3498 the dead G2532 , and G2564 calleth [G5723] G5607 those things which be [G5752] G3361 not G5613 as though G5607 they were [G5752].

BY FAITH WE ARE SAVED

Some will say because Abraham had faith in God, and as these verses say, "that therefore it was imputed to him for righteousness" that he is now in heaven with God. Imputed to him for righteousness doesn't give him eternal life in heaven immediately. V. 24 makes him the same as those who accept Jesus now. Jesus told his disciples repeatedly in John 6 that he would raise them up to be with him on the last day. On the last day is when Abraham will also receive the rest of his promises

Romans 4:20-25 Strongs

20 G1161 G1252 He staggered [G5681] G3756 not G1519 at G1860 the promise G2316 of God G570 through unbelief G235 ; but G1743 was strong [G5681] G4102 in faith G1325 , giving [G5631] G1391 glory G2316 to God;

21 G2532 And G4135 being fully persuaded [G5685] G3754 that G3739 , what G1861 he had promised [G5766] G2076 , he was [G5748] G1415

able G2532 also G4160 to perform [G5658].

22 G2532 And G1352 therefore G3049 it was imputed [G5681] G846 to him G1519 for G1343 righteousness.

23 G1161 Now G1125 it was G3756 not G1125 written [G5648] G1223 for his sake G846 G3440 alone G3754 , that G3049 it was imputed [G5681] G846 to him;

24 G235 But G1223 for G2248 us G2532 also G3739 , to whom G3195 it shall be [G5719] G3049 imputed [G5745] G4100 , if we believe [G5723] G1909 on G1453 him that raised up [G5660] G2424 Jesus G2257 our G2962 Lord G1537 from G3498 the dead;

25 G3739 Who G3860 was delivered [G5681] G1223 for G2257 our G3900 offences G2532 , and G1453 was raised again [G5681] G1223 for G2257 our G1347 justification.

ONE DOOR AND ONLY ONE

Only through Jesus can anyone be saved and have eternal life. If it wasn't for the free gift of his perfect life as a sacrifice for us, we couldn't be justified and reconciled to God. His sacrifice covers all of humanity, but justification didn't take effect until after Jesus actually lived that perfect life. It didn't take effect until after Jesus was sacrificed for us. Not until after Jesus lived and died could humanity be saved.

Romans 5:1-21 Strongs

1 G3767 Therefore G1344 being justified [G5685] G1537 by G4102 faith G2192 , we have [G5719] G1515 peace G4314 with G2316 God G1223 through G2257 our G2962 Lord G2424 Jesus G5547 Christ:

2 G1223 By G3739 whom G2532 also G2192 we have [G5758] G4318 access G4102 by faith G1519 into G5026 this G5485 grace G1722 wherein G3739 G2476 we stand [G5758] G2532 , and G2744 rejoice [G5736] G1909 in G1680 hope G1391 of the glory G2316 of God.

3 G1161 And G3756 not G3440 only G235 so, but G2744 we glory [G5736] G1722 in G2347 tribulations G2532 also G1492 : knowing [G5761] G3754 that G2347 tribulation G2716 worketh [G5736] G5281 patience;

4 G1161 And G5281 patience G1382 , experience G1161 ; and G1382 experience G1680 , hope:

5 G1161 And G1680 hope G2617 maketh G3756 not G2617 ashamed [G5719] G3754 ; because G26 the love G2316 of God G1632 is shed abroad [G5769] G1722 in G2257 our G2588 hearts G1223 by G40 the Holy G4151 Ghost G3588 which G1325 is given [G5685] G2254 unto us.

6 G1063 For G2257 when we G5607 were [G5752] G2089 yet G772 without strength G2596 , in due G2540 time G5547 Christ G599 died [G5627] G5228 for G765 the ungodly.

7 G1063 For G3433 scarcely G5228 for G1342 a righteous man G599 will G5100 one G599 die [G5695] G1063 : yet G5029 peradventure G5228 for G18 a good man G5100 some G5111 would G2532 even G5111 dare [G5719] G599 to die [G5629].

8 G1161 But G2316 God G4921 commendeth [G5719] G1438 his G26 love G1519 toward G2248 us G3754 , in that G2257 , while we G5607 were [G5752] G2089 yet G268 sinners G5547 , Christ G599 died [G5627] G5228 for G2257 us.

9 G4183 Much G3123 more G3767 then G1344 , being G3568 now G1344 justified [G5685] G1722 by G846 his G129 blood G4982 , we shall be saved [G5701] G575 from G3709 wrath G1223 through G846 him.

10 G1063 For G1487 if G5607 , when we were [G5752] G2190 enemies G2644 , we were reconciled [G5648] G2316 to God G1223 by G2288 the death G846 of his G5207 Son G4183 , much G3123 more G2644 , being reconciled [G5651] G4982 , we shall be saved [G5701] G1722 by G846 his G2222 life.

11 G1161 And G3756 not G3440 only G235 so, but G2532 we also G2744

joy [G5740] G1722 in G2316 God G1223 through G2257 our G2962 Lord G2424 Jesus G5547 Christ G1223 , by G3739 whom G2983 we have G3568 now G2983 received [G5627] G2643 the atonement.

12 G1223 Wherefore G5124 G5618 , as G1223 by G1520 one G444 man G266 sin G1525 entered [G5627] G1519 into G2889 the world G2532 , and G2288 death G1223 by G266 sin G2532 ; and G3779 so G2288 death G1330 passed [G5627] G1519 upon G3956 all G444 men G1909 , for G3739 that G3956 all G264 have sinned [G5627]:

13 G1063 (For G891 until G3551 the law G266 sin G2258 was [G5713] G1722 in G2889 the world G1161 : but G266 sin G1677 is G3756 not G1677 imputed [G5743] G5607 when there is [G5752] G3361 no G3551 law.

14 G235 Nevertheless G2288 death G936 reigned [G5656] G575 from G76 Adam G3360 to G3475 Moses G2532 , even G1909 over G264 them that had G3361 not G264 sinned [G5660] G1909 after G3667 the similitude G76 of Adam's G3847 transgression G3739 , who G2076 is [G5748] G5179 the figure G3195 of him that was to come [G5723].

15 G235 But G3756 not G5613 as G3900 the offence G3779 , so G2532 also G5486 is the free gift G1063 . For G1487 if G3900 through the offence G1520 of one G4183 many G599 be dead [G5627] G4183 , much G3123 more G5485 the grace G2316 of God G2532 , and G1431 the gift G1722 by G5485 grace G3588 , which is G1520 by one G444 man G2424 , Jesus G5547 Christ G4052 , hath abounded [G5656] G1519 unto G4183 many.

16 G2532 And G3756 not G5613 as G1223 it was by G1520 one G264 that sinned [G5660] G1434 , so is the gift G1063 : for G3303 G2917 the judgment G1537 was by G1520 one G1519 to G2631 condemnation G1161 , but G5486 the free gift G1537 is of G4183 many G3900 offences G1519 unto G1345 justification.

17 G1063 For G1487 if G1520 by one man's G3900 offence G2288 death G936 reigned [G5656] G1223 by G1520 one G4183 ; much G3123 more

G2983 they which receive [G5723] G4050 abundance G5485 of grace G2532 and G1431 of the gift G1343 of righteousness G936 shall reign [G5692] G1722 in G2222 life G1223 by G1520 one G2424 , Jesus G5547 Christ.)

18 G686 Therefore G3767 G5613 as G1223 by G3900 the offence G1520 of one G1519 judgment came upon G3956 all G444 men G1519 to G2631 condemnation G2532 ; even G3779 so G1223 by G1345 the righteousness G1520 of one G1519 the free gift came upon G3956 all G444 men G1519 unto G1347 justification G2222 of life.

19 G1063 For G5618 as G1223 by G1520 one G444 man's G3876 disobedience G4183 many G2525 were made [G5681] G268 sinners G3779 , so G2532 G1223 by G5218 the obedience G1520 of one G2525 shall G4183 many G2525 be made [G5701] G1342 righteous.

20 G1161 Moreover G3551 the law G3922 entered [G5627] G2443 , that G3900 the offence G4121 might abound [G5661] G1161 . But G3757 where G266 sin G4121 abounded [G5656] G5485 , grace G5248 did much more abound [G5656]:

21 G2443 That G5618 as G266 sin G936 hath reigned [G5656] G1722 unto G2288 death G2532 , even G3779 so G936 might G5485 grace G936 reign [G5661] G1223 through G1343 righteousness G1519 unto G166 eternal G2222 life G1223 by G2424 Jesus G5547 Christ G2257 our G2962 Lord.

FREE GIFT OF GREAT VALUE

We should produce good fruit in our lives. And in the end everlasting life will be ours, as a free gift through Jesus. I think the end is not referring to our lives, but to the end of this age. When God will complete the work he has started with mankind.

The wages of sin is death, the opposite of life. The gift of God is eternal life. Does he give us what we already possess? No that wouldn't be a gift. We don't have eternal life until he gives it to us after we accept Jesus as our Lord and Savior.

Romans 6:22-23 Strongs

22 G1161 But G3570 now G1659 being made free [G5685] G575 from G266 sin G1161 , and G1402 become servants [G5685] G2316 to God G2192 , ye have [G5719] G5216 your G2590 fruit G1519 unto G38 holiness G1161 , and G5056 the end G166 everlasting G2222 life.

23 G1063 For G3800 the wages G266 of sin G2288 is death G1161 ; but G5486 the gift G2316 of God G166 is eternal G2222 life G1722 through G2424 Jesus G5547 Christ G2257 our G2962 Lord.

G5056 τέλος - Strong's Greek Lexicon Number

τέλος

the fulfilment

τέλος properly, the point aimed at as a limit, i.e. (by implication) the conclusion of an act or state (termination (literally, figuratively or indefinitely), result (immediate, ultimate or prophetic), purpose); specially, an impost or levy (as paid)

Derivation: from a primary τέλλω (to set out for a definite point or goal);

KJV Usage: + continual, custom, end(-ing), finally, uttermost.

Compare G5411. G5411

1) end

1a) termination, the limit at which a thing ceases to be (always of the end of some act or state, but not of the end of a period of time)

1b) the end

1b1) the last in any succession or series

1b2) eternal

1c) that by which a thing is finished, its close, issue

1d) the end to which all things relate, the aim, purpose

2) toll, custom (i.e. indirect tax on goods)

- Tax
- Form
- Perfect
- Custom (toll)
- End, Ending
- Final, Finally
- Uttermost

τέλος

telos

tel'-os

From a primary word τέλλω tellō (to set out for a definite point or goal); properly the point aimed at as a limit, that is, (by implication) the conclusion of an act or state (termination [literally, figuratively or indefinitely], result [immediate, ultimate or prophetic], purpose); specifically an impost or levy (as paid)

OH HAPPY DAY

This quickening by his spirit will take place after death at the return of Jesus.

Romans 8:11 Strongs

11 G1161 But G1487 if G4151 the Spirit G1453 of him that raised up [G5660] G2424 Jesus G1537 from G3498 the dead G3611 dwell [G5719] G1722 in G5213 you G1453 , he that raised up [G5660] G5547 Christ G1537 from G3498 the dead G2227 shall G2532 also G2227 quicken [G5692] G5216 your G2349 mortal G4983 bodies G1223 by G846 his G4151 Spirit G1774 that dwelleth [G5723] [G5625] G1774 [G5723] G1722 in G5213 you.

ADOPTED INTO GODS FAMILY

We are the children of God. We will be joint-heirs with Jesus, and glorified as he is glorified.

Romans 8:14-23 Strongs

14 G1063 For G3745 as many as G71 are led [G5743] G4151 by the Spirit G2316 of God G3778 , they G1526 are [G5748] G5207 the sons G2316 of God.

15 G1063 For G2983 ye have G3756 not G2983 received [G5627] G4151 the spirit G1397 of bondage G3825 again G1519 to G5401 fear G235 ; but G2983 ye have received [G5627] G4151 the Spirit G5206 of adoption G1722 , whereby G3739 G2896 we cry [G5719] G5 , Abba G3962 , Father.

16 G4151 The Spirit G846 itself G4828 beareth witness [G5719] G2257 with our G4151 spirit G3754 , that G2070 we are [G5748] G5043 the children G2316 of God:

17 G1161 And G1487 if G5043 children G2532 , then G2818 heirs G2818 ; heirs G3303 of God G2316 G1161 , and G4789 joint-heirs G5547 with Christ G1512 ; if so be G4841 that we suffer with [G5719] G2443 him, that G4888 we may be G2532 also G4888 glorified together [G5686].

18 G1063 For G3049 I reckon [G5736] G3754 that G3804 the sufferings G3568 of this present G2540 time G3756 are not G514 worthy G4314 to

be compared with G1391 the glory G3195 which shall [G5723] G601 be revealed [G5683] G1519 in G2248 us.

19 G1063 For G603 the earnest expectation G2937 of the creature G553 waiteth [G5736] G602 for the manifestation G5207 of the sons G2316 of God.

20 G1063 For G2937 the creature G5293 was made subject [G5648] G3153 to vanity G3756 , not G1635 willingly G235 , but G1223 by reason G5293 of him who hath subjected [G5660] G1909 the same in G1680 hope,

21 G3754 Because G2937 the creature G846 itself G2532 also G1659 shall be delivered [G5701] G575 from G1397 the bondage G5356 of corruption G1519 into G1391 the glorious G1657 liberty G5043 of the children G2316 of God.

22 G1063 For G1492 we know [G5758] G3754 that G3956 the whole G2937 creation G4959 groaneth [G5719] G2532 and G4944 travaileth in pain together [G5719] G891 until G3568 now.

23 G1161 And G3756 not G3440 only G235 they, but G846 ourselves G2532 also G2192 , which have [G5723] G536 the firstfruits G4151 of the Spirit G2532 , even G2249 we G846 ourselves G4727 groan [G5719] G1722 within G1438 ourselves G553 , waiting [G5740] G5206 for the adoption G629 , to wit, the redemption G2257 of our G4983 body.

GOD IS FOR THOSE HE HAS CHOSEN ACCORDING TO HIS PURPOSE

We are called by God according to his purpose, we are his elect. He has plans for us as part of his family.

Romans 8:28-34 Strongs

28 G1161 And G1492 we know [G5758] G3956 that all things G4903 work together [G5719] G1519 for G18 good G3754 to them that G25 love

[G5723] G2316 God G5607 , to them who are [G5752] G2822 the called G2596 according G4286 to his purpose.

29 G3754 For G3739 whom G4267 he did foreknow [G5656] G4309 , he G2532 also G4309 did predestinate [G5656] G4832 to be conformed G1504 to the image G846 of his G5207 Son G1519 , that G846 he G1511 might be [G5750] G4416 the firstborn G1722 among G4183 many G80 brethren.

30 G1161 Moreover G3739 whom G4309 he did predestinate [G5656] G5128 , them G2564 he G2532 also G2564 called [G5656] G2532 : and G3739 whom G2564 he called [G5656] G5128 , them G1344 he G2532 also G1344 justified [G5656] G1161 : and G3739 whom G1344 he justified [G5656] G5128 , them G1392 he G2532 also G1392 glorified [G5656].

31 G5101 What G2046 shall we G3767 then G2046 say [G5692] G4314 to G5023 these things G1487 ? If G2316 God G5228 be for G2257 us G5101 , who G2596 can be against G2257 us?

32 G3739 He that G1065 G5339 spared [G5662] G3756 not G2398 his own G5207 Son G235 , but G3860 delivered G846 him G3860 up [G5656] G5228 for G2257 us G3956 all G4459 , how G5483 shall he G3780 not G4862 with G846 him G2532 also G5483 freely give [G5695] G2254 us G3956 all things?

33 G5101 Who G1458 shall lay any thing [G5692] G2596 to the charge G2316 of God's G1588 elect G2316 ? It is God G1344 that justifieth [G5723].

34 G5101 Who G2632 is he that condemneth [G5723] [G5694] G5547 ? It is Christ G599 that died [G5631] G1161 , yea G3123 rather G2532 G1453 , that is risen again [G5685] G3739 , who G2076 is [G5748] G2532 even G1722 at G1188 the right hand G2316 of God G3739 , who G2532 also G1793 maketh intercession [G5719] G5228 for G2257 us.

THE BARE NECESSITIES OF LIFE

The very basic necessities for spiritual life are stated here. The other things we discuss are peripheral.

Romans 10:9-10 Strongs

9 G3754 That G1437 if G3670 thou shalt confess [G5661] G1722 with G4675 thy G4750 mouth G2962 the Lord G2424 Jesus G2532 , and G4100 shalt believe [G5661] G1722 in G4675 thine G2588 heart G3754 that G2316 God G1453 hath raised [G5656] G846 him G1537 from G3498 the dead G4982 , thou shalt be saved [G5701].

10 G1063 For G2588 with the heart G4100 man believeth [G5743] G1519 unto G1343 righteousness G1161 ; and G4750 with the mouth G3670 confession is made [G5743] G1519 unto G4991 salvation.

WE DON'T KNOW WHO GOD WILL CALL SO TEACH ALL

The primary process God uses to call and teach mankind about Jesus, is to teach people through other people, using the scriptures and stories.

Romans 10:13-17 Strongs

13 G3956 For G1063 G3739 whosoever G302 G1941 shall call upon [G5672] G3686 the name G2962 of the Lord G4982 shall be saved [G5701].

14 G4459 How G3767 then G1941 shall they call on [G5698] G1519 him in G3739 whom G4100 they have G3756 not G4100 believed [G5656] G1161 ? and G4459 how G4100 shall they believe in [G5692] G3739 him of whom G191 they have G3756 not G191 heard [G5656] G1161 ? and G4459 how G191 shall they hear [G5692] G5565 without G2784 a preacher [G5723]?

15 G1161 And G4459 how G2784 shall they preach [G5692] G3362 , except G649 they be sent [G5652] G2531 ? as G1125 it is written [G5769] G5613 , How G5611 beautiful G4228 are the feet of them G2097 that

preach the gospel [G5734] G1515 of peace G2097 , and bring glad tidings [G5734] G18 of good things!

16 G235 But G5219 they have G3756 not G3956 all G5219 obeyed [G5656] G2098 the gospel G1063 . For G2268 Esaias G3004 saith [G5719] G2962 , Lord G5101 , who G4100 hath believed [G5656] G2257 our G189 report?

17 G686 So then G4102 faith G1537 cometh by G189 hearing G1161 , and G189 hearing G1223 by G4487 the word G2316 of God.

OUR HEALING GOD WILL OPEN THE EYES OF THE BLIND

Paul is teaching us in this chapter about the people of Israel. How God hasn't cast them all away, but has only called a remnant to himself. The rest of them were blinded to God on purpose.

Romans 11:1-7 Strongs

1 G3004 I say [G5719] G3767 then G3361 , G683 Hath G2316 God G683 cast away [G5662] G846 his G2992 people G3361 ? God forbid G1096 [G5636] G1063 . For G1473 I G2532 also G1510 am [G5748] G2475 an Israelite G1537 , of G4690 the seed G11 of Abraham G5443 , of the tribe G958 of Benjamin.

2 G2316 God G683 hath G3756 not G683 cast away [G5662] G846 his G2992 people G3739 which G4267 he foreknew [G5656] G2228 . G1492 Wot ye [G5758] G3756 not G5101 what G1124 the scripture G3004 saith [G5719] G1722 of G2243 Elias G5613 ? how G1793 he maketh intercession [G5719] G2316 to God G2596 against G2474 Israel G3004 , saying [G5723],

3 G2962 Lord G615 , they have killed [G5656] G4675 thy G4396 prophets G2532 , and G2679 digged down [G5656] G4675 thine G2379 altars G2504 ; and I G5275 am left [G5681] G3441 alone G2532 , and G2212 they seek [G5719] G3450 my G5590 life.

4 G235 But G5101 what G3004 saith [G5719] G5538 the answer of God G846 unto him G2641 ? I have reserved [G5627] G1683 to myself G2035 seven thousand G435 men G3748 , who G2578 have G3756 not G2578 bowed [G5656] G1119 the knee G896 to the image of Baal.

5 G3779 Even so G3767 then G1722 at G3568 this present G2540 time G2532 also G1096 there is [G5754] G3005 a remnant G2596 according G1589 to the election G5485 of grace.

6 G1161 And G1487 if G5485 by grace G2089 , then is it no more G3765 G1537 of G2041 works G1893 : otherwise G5485 grace G1096 is [G5736] G2089 no more G3765 G5485 grace G1161 . But G1487 if G1537 it be of G2041 works G2076 , then is it [G5748] G2089 no more G3765 G5485 grace G1893 : otherwise G2041 work G2076 is [G5748] G2089 no more G3765 G2041 work.

7 G5101 What G3767 then G2474 ? Israel G2013 hath G3756 not G2013 obtained [G5627] G5127 that G3739 which G1934 he seeketh for [G5719] G1161 ; but G1589 the election G2013 hath obtained it [G5627] G1161 , and G3062 the rest G4456 were blinded [G5681]

God prevented them from coming to understand him so that salvation could come to the Gentiles. V12. If through their blindness the whole world has salvation, then it is a good thing they are a stubborn and stiff necked people. They played the part that God gave them very well. They will have their eyes and hearts opened to God at a time God has ordained for their fullness to be realised.

Romans 11:8-12 Strongs

8 G2531 (According as G1125 it is written [G5769] G2316 , God G1325 hath given [G5656] G846 them G4151 the spirit G2659 of slumber G3788 , eyes G991 that they should G3361 not G991 see [G5721] G2532 , and G3775 ears G191 that they should G3361 not G191 hear [G5721] G2193 ;) unto G4594 this G2250 day.

9 G2532 And G1138 David G3004 saith [G5719] G1096 , Let G846 their G5132 table G1096 be made [G5676] G1519 a snare G3803 G2532 , and G1519 a trap G2339 G2532 , and G1519 a stumblingblock G4625 G2532 , and G1519 a recompence G468 G846 unto them:

10 G4654 Let G846 their G3788 eyes G4654 be darkened [G5682] G991 , that they may G3361 not G991 see [G5721] G2532 , and G4781 bow down [G5657] G846 their G3577 back G1275 alway.

11 G3004 I say [G5719] G3767 then G3361 , G4417 Have they stumbled [G5656] G2443 that G4098 they should fall [G5632] G3361 ? God forbid G1096 [G5636] G235 : but G846 rather through their G3900 fall G4991 salvation G1484 is come unto the Gentiles G1519 , for to G3863 provoke G846 them G3863 to jealousy [G5658].

12 G1161 Now G1487 if G3900 the fall G846 of them G4149 be the riches G2889 of the world G2532 , and G2275 the diminishing G846 of them G4149 the riches G1484 of the Gentiles G4214 ; how G3123 much more G846 their G4138 fulness?

GOD CALLS PEOPLE AS IT FITS HIS PLAN OF REDEMTION

Paul was the apostle to the Gentiles but he would still preach to those from Israel because he never knew who the remnant would be.

Romans 11:13-15 Strongs

13 G1063 For G3004 I speak [G5719] G5213 to you G1484 Gentiles G1909 , inasmuch as G3745 G3303 G1473 I G1510 am [G5748] G652 the apostle G1484 of the Gentiles G1392 , I magnify [G5719] G3450 mine G1248 office:

14 G1513 If by any means G4458 G3863 I may provoke to emulation [G5661] G3450 them which are my G4561 flesh G2532 , and G4982 might save [G5661] G5100 some G1537 of G846 them.

15 G1063 For G1487 if G580 the casting away G846 of them G2643 be the

reconciling G2889 of the world G5101 , what G4356 shall the receiving G1508 of them be, but G2222 life G1537 from G3498 the dead?

Paul tells the Gentiles not to feel superior to Israel because they know Jesus. But to be thankful to God for the opportunity. V.22 if we don't continue in our belief then we can also be cut off from God, if repentant they can come back to him.

Romans 11:16-24 Strongs

16 G1161 For G1487 if G536 the firstfruit G40 be holy G5445 , the lump G2532 is also G2532 holy : and G1487 if G4491 the root G40 be holy G2532 , so G2798 are the branches.

17 G1161 And G1536 if some G2798 of the branches G1575 be broken off [G5681] G1161 , and G4771 thou G5607 , being [G5752] G65 a wild olive tree G1461 , wert graffed in [G5681] G1722 among G846 them G2532 , and G4791 with G1096 them [G5633] G4791 partakest G4491 of the root G2532 and G4096 fatness G1636 of the olive tree;

18 G2620 Boast G3361 not G2620 against [G5737] G2798 the branches G1161 . But G1487 if G2620 thou boast [G5736] G4771 , thou G941 bearest [G5719] G3756 not G4491 the root G235 , but G4491 the root G4571 thee.

19 G2046 Thou wilt say [G5692] G3767 then G2798 , The branches G1575 were broken off [G5681] G2443 , that G1473 I G1461 might be graffed in [G5686].

20 G2573 Well G570 ; because of unbelief G1575 they were broken off [G5681] G1161 , and G4771 thou G2476 standest [G5758] G4102 by faith G5309 . Be G3361 not G5309 highminded [G5720] G235 , but G5399 fear [G5737]:

21 G1063 For G1487 if G2316 God G5339 spared [G5662] G3756 not G5449 the natural G2798 branches G2596 G4458 , take heed lest G3381

G5339 he G3381 also G5339 spare [G5667] G3761 not G4675 thee.

22 G1492 Behold [G5657] G3767 therefore G5544 the goodness G2532 and G663 severity G2316 of God G1909 : on G4098 them which fell [G5631] G3303 G663 , severity G1161 ; but G1909 toward G4571 thee G5544 , goodness G1437 , if G1961 thou continue [G5661] G5544 in his goodness G1893 : otherwise G4771 thou G2532 also G1581 shalt be cut off [G5691].

23 G1161 And G1565 they G2532 also G3362 , if G1961 they abide [G5661] G3362 not G570 still in unbelief G1461 , shall be graffed in [G5701] G1063 : for G2316 God G2076 is [G5748] G1415 able G1461 to graff G846 them G1461 in [G5658] G3825 again.

24 G1063 For G1487 if G4771 thou G1581 wert cut [G5648] G1537 out of G65 the olive tree which is wild G2596 by G5449 nature G2532 , and G1461 wert graffed [G5681] G3844 contrary to G5449 nature G1519 into G2565 a good olive tree G4214 : how much G3123 more G3778 shall these G2596 , which be the natural G5449 G1461 branches, be graffed into [G5701] G2398 their own G1636 olive tree?

Israel for the most part, is to be blind to God until all the Gentiles that are called by God respond to him. Then Israel as a whole will have their eyes opened to God and be drawn to him. Israel is still waiting for this future time of deliverance. God say's that it will happen. He says that all Israel is to be saved. How is that possible, if this present life is all there is, if this present life is mankind's only chance to accept the salvation only Jesus can bring?

For salvation to come to people who are already dead. When the only way to be saved is to believe in the name of Jesus. Then those that are dead must have the chance to believe in Jesus and be saved. As we have already read from previous scriptures the only mechanism the bible gives us so they can come back to life, is by the resurrection from the dead.

Then they will have their opportunity for salvation. Through the resurrection of the dead, all of mankind can have their chance to know God.

Romans 11:25-36 Strongs

25 G1063 For G2309 I would [G5719] G3756 not G80 , brethren G5209 , that ye G50 should be ignorant [G5721] G5124 of this G3466 mystery G3363 , lest G5600 ye should be [G5753] G5429 wise G3844 in G1438 your own conceits G3754 ; that G4457 blindness G575 in G3313 part G1096 is happened [G5754] G2474 to Israel G891 , until G3739 G4138 the fulness G1484 of the Gentiles G1525 be come in [G5632].

26 G2532 And G3779 so G3956 all G2474 Israel G4982 shall be saved [G5701] G2531 : as G1125 it is written [G5769] G2240 , There shall come [G5692] G1537 out of G4622 Sion G4506 the Deliverer [G5740] G2532 , and G654 shall turn away [G5692] G763 ungodliness G575 from G2384 Jacob:

27 G2532 For G3778 this G3844 is my G1700 G1242 covenant G846 unto them G3752 , when G851 I shall take away [G5643] G846 their G266 sins.

28 G2596 As concerning G3303 G2098 the gospel G2190 , they are enemies G1223 for your sakes G5209 G1161 : but G2596 as touching G1589 the election G27 , they are beloved G1223 for G3962 the fathers G1223 ' sakes.

29 G1063 For G5486 the gifts G2532 and G2821 calling G2316 of God G278 are without repentance.

30 G1063 For G5618 as G2532 G5210 ye G4218 in times past G544 have not believed [G5656] G2316 God G1161 , yet G1653 have G3568 now G1653 obtained mercy [G5681] G5130 through G543 their unbelief:

31 G3779 Even so G544 have G3778 these G2532 also G3568 now G544 not believed [G5656] G2443 , that G5212 through your G1656 mercy G846 they G2532 also G1653 may obtain mercy [G5686].

32 G1063 For G2316 God G4788 hath concluded [G5656] G3956 them all G1519 in G543 unbelief G2443 , that G1653 he might have mercy [G5661] G3956 upon all.

33 G5599 O G899 the depth G4149 of the riches G2532 both G4678 of the wisdom G2532 and G1108 knowledge G2316 of God G5613 ! how G419 unsearchable G846 are his G2917 judgments G2532 , and G846 his G3598 ways G421 past finding out!

34 G1063 For G5101 who G1097 hath known [G5627] G3563 the mind G2962 of the Lord G2228 ? or G5101 who G1096 hath been [G5633] G846 his G4825 counsellor?

35 G2228 Or G5101 who G4272 hath first given [G5656] G846 to him G2532 , and G467 it shall be recompensed G846 unto him G467 again [G5701]?

36 G3754 For G1537 of G846 him G2532 , and G1223 through G846 him G2532 , and G1519 to G846 him G3956 , are all things G846 : to whom G1391 be glory G1519 for G165 ever G281 . Amen.

Chapter 23: BOOKS OF 1&2 CORINTHIANS

DRAFTED BY GOD BUT WE CHOOSE TO GO

We are called by God to know Jesus.

1 Corinthians 1:9 Strongs

9 G2316 God G4103 is faithful G1223 , by G3739 whom G2564 ye were called [G5681] G1519 unto G2842 the fellowship G846 of his G5207 Son G2424 Jesus G5547 Christ G2257 our G2962 Lord.

THE WEAK AND FOOLISH DISPLAY GODS POWER

Not for everyone, but unto them which are called for Gods' purpose. By our weakness he is made strong. All glory belongs to God. The wise will get their opportunity in time.

1 Corinthians 1:24-29 KJV Strongs

24 G1161 But G846 unto them G3588 which G2822 are called G5037 , both G2453 Jews G2532 and G1672 Greeks G5547 , Christ G1411 the power G2316 of God G2532 , and G4678 the wisdom G2316 of God.

25 G3754 Because G3474 the foolishness G2316 of God G2076 is [G5748] G4680 wiser than G444 men G2532 ; and G772 the weakness G2316 of God G2076 is [G5748] G2478 stronger than G444 men.

26 G1063 For G991 ye see [G5719] G5216 your G2821 calling G80 , brethren G3754 , how that G3756 not G4183 many G4680 wise men G2596 after G4561 the flesh G3756 , not G4183 many G1415 mighty

G3756 , not G4183 many G2104 noble, are called :

27 G235 But G2316 God G1586 hath chosen [G5668] G3474 the foolish things G2889 of the world G2443 to G2617 confound [G5725] G4680 the wise G2532 ; and G2316 God G1586 hath chosen [G5668] G772 the weak things G2889 of the world G2443 to G2617 confound [G5725] G2478 the things which are mighty;

28 G2532 And G36 base things G2889 of the world G2532 , and G1848 things which are despised [G5772] G1586 , hath G2316 God G1586 chosen [G5668] G2532 , yea, and G3588 things which G5607 are [G5752] G3361 not G2443 , to G2673 bring to nought [G5661] G5607 things that are [G5752]:

29 G3704 That G3361 no G3956 G4561 flesh G2744 should glory [G5667] G1799 in his presence G846.

SAVED IS DIFFERENT THAN REWARD

We will become immortal if we believe in Jesus. But if that's all we have right, then our reward in the kingdom will be small. The more we follow where the spirit leads us the greater our rewards in the kingdom will be.

1 Corinthians 3:8-15 KJV Strongs

8 G1161 Now G5452 he that planteth [G5723] G2532 and G4222 he that watereth [G5723] G1526 are [G5748] G1520 one G1161 : and G1538 every man G2983 shall receive [G5695] G2398 his own G3408 reward G2596 according G2398 to his own G2873 labour.

9 G1063 For G2070 we are [G5748] G4904 labourers together G2316 with God G2075 : ye are [G5748] G2316 God's G1091 husbandry G2316 , ye are God's G3619 building.

10 G2596 According G5485 to the grace G2316 of God G3588 which G1325 is given [G5685] G3427 unto me G5613 , as G4680 a wise G753 masterbuilder G5087 , I have laid [G5758] G2310 the foundation G1161 ,

and G243 another G2026 buildeth [G5719] G1161 thereon. But G991 let G1538 every man G991 take heed [G5720] G4459 how G2026 he buildeth [G5719] thereupon.

11 G1063 For G243 other G2310 foundation G1410 can [G5736] G3762 no man G5087 lay [G5629] G3844 than G2749 that is laid [G5740] G3739 , which G2076 is [G5748] G2424 Jesus G5547 Christ.

12 G1161 Now G1536 if any man G2026 build [G5719] G1909 upon G5126 this G2310 foundation G5557 gold G696 , silver G5093 , precious G3037 stones G3586 , wood G5528 , hay G2562 , stubble;

13 G1538 Every man's G2041 work G1096 shall be made [G5695] G5318 manifest G1063 : for G2250 the day G1213 shall declare [G5692] G3754 it, because G601 it shall be revealed [G5743] G1722 by G4442 fire G2532 ; and G4442 the fire G1381 shall try [G5692] G1538 every man's G2041 work G3697 of what sort G2076 it is [G5748].

14 G1536 If any man's G2041 work G3306 abide [G5719] G3739 which G2026 he hath built [G5656] G2983 thereupon, he shall receive [G5695] G3408 a reward.

15 G1536 If any man's G2041 work G2618 shall be burned [G5691] G2210 , he shall suffer loss [G5701] G1161 : but G846 he himself G4982 shall be saved [G5701] G1161 ; yet G3779 so G5613 as G1223 by G4442 fire.

SALVATION COMES NOT AT DEATH BUT AT THE RETURN OF JESUS

The unrepentant sinner is to be put out of the church so their sin won't influence others to sin and so they might repent and stop sinning. Notice they will be saved in the day of the Lord Jesus. Which is when Jesus returns to earth. There is no salvation for the backslider at the time of their death, but is available at Christ's return to earth, on the day of the Lord.

1 Corinthians 5:5 KJV Strongs

5 G3860 To deliver [G5629] G5108 such an one G4567 unto Satan G1519 for G3639 the destruction G4561 of the flesh G2443 , that G4151 the spirit G4982 may be saved [G5686] G1722 in G2250 the day G2962 of the Lord G2424 Jesus.

HERE COME THE JUDGE

This is to be part of our jobs in the Kingdom of God. Judgement day is coming and we will be active participants in it.

1 Corinthians 6:2-3 Strongs

2 G1492 Do ye G3756 not G1492 know [G5758] G3754 that G40 the saints G2919 shall judge [G5692] G2889 the world G2532 ? and G1487 if G2889 the world G2919 shall be judged [G5743] G1722 by G5213 you G2075 , are ye [G5748] G370 unworthy G2922 to judge G1646 the smallest matters?

3 G1492 Know ye [G5758] G3756 not G3754 that G2919 we shall judge [G5692] G32 angels G3386 ? how much more G1065 G982 things that pertain to this life?

ASLEEP NOT AWAKE

They fell asleep, or died. They didn't go on to become disembodied spirits, they died.

1 Corinthians 15:6 Strongs

6 G1899 After that G3700 , he was seen [G5681] G1883 of above G4001 five hundred G80 brethren G2178 at once G1537 ; of G3739 whom G4119 the greater part G3306 remain [G5719] G2193 unto G737 this present G1161 , but G5100 some G2532 G2837 are fallen asleep [G5681].

RESURECTION OF THE DEAD IN THIER ORDER

Paul is a great defender of the resurrection in this passage, not only the resurrection of Jesus, but of the future resurrection of the believers V.23 at Christ's coming. Everyone in their own order. Then Christ will rule till all enemies are defeated, the last one to be defeated is death.

1 Corinthians 15:12-26 Strongs

12 G1161 Now G1487 if G5547 Christ G2784 be preached [G5743] G3754 that G1453 he rose [G5769] G1537 from G3498 the dead G4459 , how G3004 say [G5719] G5100 some G1722 among G5213 you G3754 that G2076 there is [G5748] G3756 no G386 resurrection G3498 of the dead?

13 G1161 But G1487 if G2076 there be [G5748] G3756 no G386 resurrection G3498 of the dead G3761 , then G1453 is G5547 Christ G3761 not G1453 risen [G5769]:

14 G1161 And G1487 if G5547 Christ G1453 be G3756 not G1453 risen [G5769] G686 , then G2257 is our G2782 preaching G2756 vain G2532 , and G5216 your G4102 faith G1161 is G2532 also G2756 vain.

15 G1161 Yea G2532 , and G2147 we are found [G5743] G5575 false witnesses G2316 of God G3754 ; because G3140 we have testified [G5656] G2596 of G2316 God G3754 that G1453 he raised up [G5656] G5547 Christ G3739 : whom G1453 he raised G3756 not G1453 up [G5656] G1512 , if G686 so be G3498 that the dead G1453 rise [G5743] G3756 not.

16 G1063 For G1487 if G3498 the dead G1453 rise [G5743] G3756 not G1453 , then is G3761 not G5547 Christ G1453 raised [G5769]:

17 G1161 And G1487 if G5547 Christ G1453 be G3756 not G1453 raised [G5769] G5216 , your G4102 faith G3152 is vain G2075 ; ye are [G5748] G2089 yet G1722 in G5216 your G266 sins.

18 G686 Then G2532 they also G2837 which are fallen asleep [G5685] G1722 in G5547 Christ G622 are perished [G5639].

19 G1487 If G1722 in G5026 this G2222 life G3440 only G1679 we have hope [G5761] G2070 [G5748] G1722 in G5547 Christ G2070 , we are [G5748] G3956 of all G444 men G1652 most miserable.

20 G1161 But G3570 now G1453 is G5547 Christ G1453 risen [G5769] G1537 from G3498 the dead G1096 , and become [G5633] G536 the firstfruits G2837 of them that slept [G5772].

21 G1063 For G1894 since G1223 by G444 man G2288 came death G1223 , by G444 man G2532 came also G386 the resurrection G3498 of the dead.

22 G1063 For G5618 as G1722 in G76 Adam G3956 all G599 die [G5719] G2532 , even G3779 so G1722 in G5547 Christ G2227 shall G3956 all G2227 be made alive [G5701].

23 G1161 But G1538 every man G1722 in G2398 his own G5001 order G5547 : Christ G536 the firstfruits G1899 ; afterward G3588 they that are G5547 Christ's G1722 at G846 his G3952 coming.

24 G1534 Then G5056 cometh the end G3752 , when G3860 he shall have delivered up [G5632] G932 the kingdom G2316 to God G2532 , even G3962 the Father G3752 ; when G2673 he shall have put down [G5661] G3956 all G746 rule G2532 and G3956 all G1849 authority G2532 and G1411 power.

25 G1063 For G846 he G1163 must [G5748] G936 reign [G5721] G891 , till G3739 G302 he hath put G5087 [G5632] G3956 all G2190 enemies G5259 under G846 his G4228 feet.

26 G2078 The last G2190 enemy G2673 that shall be destroyed [G5743] G2288 is death.

GOD IS OUR LEADER

Then the victorious Christ will hand everything over to God so that he may be all in all.

1 Corinthians 15:27-28 Strongs

27 G1063 For G5293 he hath put [G5656] G3956 all things G5259 under G846 his G4228 feet G1161 . But G3752 when G2036 he saith [G5632] G3754 G3956 all things G5293 are put under [G5769] G1212 him, it is manifest G3754 that G1622 he is excepted G5293 , which did put G3956 all things G5293 under [G5660] G846 him.

28 G1161 And G3752 when G3956 all things G5293 shall be subdued [G5652] G846 unto him G5119 , then G5293 shall G5207 the Son G2532 also G846 himself G5293 be subject [G5691] G5293 unto him that put G3956 all things G5293 under [G5660] G846 him G2443 , that G2316 God G5600 may be [G5753] G3956 all G1722 in G3956 all.

LOCAL PAGAN CUSTOM

This is a controversial verse. If you Google it there are many in depth articles that are very good in explaining the differing opinions. Whichever opinion you hold to on baptism, it doesn't negate the fact of a resurrection from the dead.

1 Corinthians 15:29 Strongs

29 G1893 Else G5101 what G4160 shall they do [G5692] G907 which are baptized [G5746] G5228 for G3498 the dead G1487 , if G3498 the dead G1453 rise [G5743] G3756 not G3654 at all G5101 ? why G2532 G907 are they then baptized [G5743] G5228 for G3498 the dead?

GO DEEPER IN YOUR PERSONAL KNOWLEDGE OF GOD

Paul exhorts them to awake to righteousness and learn the knowledge of God. He states categorically there is a resurrection, and that they needed to know about it, as do we.

1 Corinthians 15:30-34 Strongs

30 G2532 And G5101 why G2793 stand G2249 we G2793 in jeopardy [G5719] G3956 every G5610 hour?

31 G3513 I protest by G5212 your G2251 rejoicing G2746 G3739 which G2192 I have [G5719] G1722 in G5547 Christ G2424 Jesus G2257 our G2962 Lord G599 , I die [G5719] G2596 daily G2250.

32 G1487 If G2596 after the manner G444 of men G2341 I have fought with beasts [G5656] G1722 at G2181 Ephesus G5101 , what G3786 advantageth it G3427 me G1487 , if G3498 the dead G1453 rise [G5743] G3756 not G5315 ? let us eat [G5632] G2532 and G4095 drink [G5632] G1063 ; for G839 to morrow G599 we die [G5719].

33 G4105 Be G3361 not G4105 deceived [G5744] G2556 : evil G3657 communications G5351 corrupt [G5719] G5543 good G2239 manners.

34 G1594 Awake [G5657] G1346 to righteousness G2532 , and G264 sin [G5720] G3361 not G1063 ; for G5100 some G2192 have [G5719] G56 not the knowledge G2316 of God G3004 : I speak [G5719] G4314 this to G5213 your G1791 shame.

A SEED DOESN'T LOOK LIKE THE PLANT

We will have a spiritual body when we are resurrected. We won't be constrained by our physical limitations anymore.

1 Corinthians 15:35-44 Strongs

35 G235 But G5100 some G2046 man will say [G5692] G4459 , How G1453 are G3498 the dead G1453 raised up [G5743] G1161 ? and G4169 with what G4983 body G2064 do they come [G5736]?

36 G878 Thou fool G3739 , that which G4771 thou G4687 sowest [G5719] G2227 is G3756 not G2227 quickened [G5743] G3362 , except G599 it die [G5632]:

37 G2532 And G3739 that which G4687 thou sowest [G5719] G4687 ,

thou sowest [G5719] G3756 not G4983 that body G1096 that shall be [G5697] G235 , but G1131 bare G2848 grain G1487 , it may chance G5177 [G5630] G4621 of wheat G2228 , or G5100 of some G3062 other grain :

38 G1161 But G2316 God G1325 giveth [G5719] G846 it G4983 a body G2531 as G2309 it hath pleased him [G5656] G2532 , and G1538 to every G4690 seed G2398 his own G4983 body.

39 G3956 All G4561 flesh G3756 is not G846 the same G4561 flesh G235 : but G3303 G243 there is one G4561 kind of flesh G444 of men G1161 , G243 another G4561 flesh G2934 of beasts G1161 , G243 another G2486 of fishes G1161 , and G243 another G4421 of birds.

40 G2532 There are also G2032 celestial G4983 bodies G2532 , and G4983 bodies G1919 terrestrial G235 : but G3303 G1391 the glory G2032 of the celestial G2087 is one G1161 , and G1919 the glory of the terrestrial G2087 is another.

41 G243 There is one G1391 glory G2246 of the sun G2532 , and G243 another G1391 glory G4582 of the moon G2532 , and G243 another G1391 glory G792 of the stars G1063 : for G792 one star G1308 differeth from [G5719] G792 another star G1722 in G1391 glory.

42 G3779 So G2532 also G386 is the resurrection G3498 of the dead G4687 . It is sown [G5743] G1722 in G5356 corruption G1453 ; it is raised [G5743] G1722 in G861 incorruption:

43 G4687 It is sown [G5743] G1722 in G819 dishonour G1453 ; it is raised [G5743] G1722 in G1391 glory G4687 : it is sown [G5743] G1722 in G769 weakness G1453 ; it is raised [G5743] G1722 in G1411 power:

44 G4687 It is sown [G5743] G5591 a natural G4983 body G1453 ; it is raised [G5743] G4152 a spiritual G4983 body G2076 . There is [G5748] G5591 a natural G4983 body G2532 , and G2076 there is [G5748] G4152 a spiritual G4983 body.

Here we are told the spiritual body is different than the physical one. V.46 and how the natural will turn into the spiritual. The spiritual body doesn't dwell inside us. It is born later after we die.

1 Corinthians 15:45-47 Strongs

45 G2532 And G3779 so G1125 it is written [G5769] G4413 , The first G444 man G76 Adam G1096 was made [G5633] G1519 G2198 a living [G5723] G5590 soul G2078 ; the last G76 Adam G1519 was made G2227 a quickening [G5723] G4151 spirit.

46 G235 Howbeit G3756 that was not G4412 first G4152 which is spiritual G235 , but G5591 that which is natural G1899 ; and afterward G4152 that which is spiritual.

47 G4413 The first G444 man G1537 is of G1093 the earth G5517 , earthy G1208 : the second G444 man G2962 is the Lord G1537 from G3772 heaven.

SPIRIT WITH SPIRIT

Earthly mortal bodies can't inherit the Kingdom of God, only spiritual bodies.

1 Corinthians 15:48-50 Strongs

48 G3634 As G5517 is the earthy G5108 , such G2532 are they also G5517 that are earthy G2532 : and G3634 as is G2032 the heavenly G5108 , such G2032 are they G2532 also G2032 that are heavenly.

49 G2532 And G2531 as G5409 we have borne [G5656] G1504 the image G5517 of the earthy G5409 , we shall G2532 also G5409 bear [G5692] G1504 the image G2032 of the heavenly.

50 G1161 Now G5124 this G5346 I say [G5748] G80 , brethren G3754 , that G4561 flesh G2532 and G129 blood G3756 cannot G1410 [G5736] G2816 inherit [G5658] G932 the kingdom G2316 of God G3761 ; neither

G2816 doth G5356 corruption G2816 inherit [G5719] G861 incorruption.

THE ANSWER IS CLEAR

So the answer to the big question is told to us again. When will we be changed into our spiritual bodies? The answer is plain and straight forward. We shall all be changed quickly, at the last trump. The last trump is when Jesus returns to earth. Like Jesus repeatedly said in John.6: we will be changed when he returns. That's when the dead shall be raised incorruptible. Until then they shall all be asleep in their graves.

1 Corinthians 15:51-52 Strongs

51 G2400 Behold [G5628] G3004 , I shew [G5719] G5213 you G3466 a mystery G2837 ; We shall G3756 not G3956 all G3303 G2837 sleep [G5701] G1161 , but G236 we shall G3956 all G236 be changed [G5691],

52 G1722 In G823 a moment G1722 , in G4493 the twinkling G3788 of an eye G1722 , at G2078 the last G4536 trump G1063 : for G4537 the trumpet shall sound [G5692] G2532 , and G3498 the dead G1453 shall be raised [G5701] G862 incorruptible G2532 , and G2249 we G236 shall be changed [G5691].

VICTORY THROUGH JESUS

We must be changed into our new spiritual bodies for us to be in the kingdom of God, and for the victory over death to be won. Our victory only comes to us through our Lord and Savior Jesus Christ

1 Corinthians 15:53-58 Strongs

53 G1063 For G5124 this G5349 corruptible G1163 must [G5748] G1746 put on [G5670] G861 incorruption G2532 , and G5124 this G2349 mortal G1746 must put on [G5670] G110 immortality.

54 G1161 So G3752 when G5124 this G5349 corruptible G1746 shall have

put on [G5672] G861 incorruption G2532 , and G5124 this G2349 mortal G1746 shall have put on [G5672] G110 immortality G5119 , then G1096 shall be brought to pass [G5695] G3056 the saying G1125 that is written [G5772] G2288 , Death G2666 is swallowed up [G5681] G1519 in G3534 victory.

55 G2288 O death G4226 , where G4675 is thy G2759 sting G86 ? O grave G4226 , where G4675 is thy G3534 victory?

56 G1161 G2759 The sting G2288 of death G266 is sin G1161 ; and G1411 the strength G266 of sin G3551 is the law.

57 G1161 But G5485 thanks G2316 be to God G3588 , which G1325 giveth [G5723] G2254 us G3534 the victory G1223 through G2257 our G2962 Lord G2424 Jesus G5547 Christ.

58 G5620 Therefore G3450 , my G27 beloved G80 brethren G1096 , be ye [G5737] G1476 stedfast G277 , unmoveable G3842 , always G4052 abounding [G5723] G1722 in G2041 the work G2962 of the Lord G1492 , forasmuch as ye know [G5761] G3754 that G5216 your G2873 labour G2076 is [G5748] G3756 not G2756 in vain G1722 in G2962 the Lord.

BY OURSELVES WE CAN DO NOTHING

Without Jesus our nature is to die, but God is trustworthy to deliver us.

2 Corinthians 1:9-10 Strongs

9 G235 But G846 G2192 we had [G5758] G610 the sentence G2288 of death G1722 in G1438 ourselves G3363 , that G3982 we should G3363 not G3982 trust [G5756] G1909 in G1438 ourselves G5600 [G5753] G235 , but G1909 in G2316 God G3588 which G1453 raiseth [G5723] G3498 the dead:

10 G3739 Who G4506 delivered [G5673] G2248 us G1537 from G5082 so great G2288 a death G2532 , and G4506 doth deliver [G5736] G1519 : in G3739 whom G1679 we trust [G5758] G3754 that G4506 he will G2532

G2089 yet G4506 deliver [G5695] us;

ALL PRESENTED TOGETHER

The believers in Jesus are to all be raised together at the same time.

2 Corinthians 4:14 Strongs

14 G1492 Knowing [G5761] G3754 that G1453 he which raised up [G5660] G2962 the Lord G2424 Jesus G1453 shall raise up [G5692] G2248 us G2532 also G1223 by G2424 Jesus G2532 , and G3936 shall present [G5692] G4862 us with G5213 you.

LISTEN WHEN GOD CALLS YOU

Some people say this verse demonstrates that now is the time for the world to be saved. That all people must accept Jesus now in this life if they miss the opportunity to know Jesus now in this life then they are lost, and will not be able to live with God in paradise.

If we put this verse in context, we will see that Paul is writing to the church in Corinth. 1:1. He is not addressing a non-believing audience, but rather believers that have been called by God to know Jesus. For these believers now is their time to make their election sure. The same holds true for all those God draws to himself now, in this life. Now is our time to be approved, we will have no other chance. Anyone who puts their hand to the plough and then looks back is not worthy of the kingdom. Luke.9:62

2 Corinthians 6:2 Strongs

2 G1063 (For G3004 he saith [G5719] G1873 , I have heard [G5656] G4675 thee G2540 in a time G1184 accepted G2532 , and G1722 in G2250 the day G4991 of salvation G997 have I succoured [G5656] G4671 thee G2400 : behold [G5628] G3568 , now G2144 is the accepted G2540 time G2400 ; behold [G5628] G3568 , now G2250 is the day G4991 of salvation.)

EVEN STILL PAUL TAUGHT THE RESURRECTION

Paul couldn't tell if the man was real or a vision. That is how real a vision can be perceived by someone.This person was taken up to paradise and herd unspeakable words. Again not sure if it was real, or in the spirit, or a vision that was very realistic. I think this still happens today to some people. They will tell of being in heaven after a near death experience. I don't discount they're experience but I can't rely on their experiences to form my belief of an afterlife. I need to form my beliefs about spiritual matters from the word of God, and what it reveals. God hasn't left us in the dark, he gives us instruction and knowledge through his word if we will listen to him.

2 Corinthians 12:2-6 Strongs

2 G1492 I knew [G5758] G444 a man G1722 in G5547 Christ G4253 above G1180 fourteen G2094 years G4253 ago G1535 , (whether G1722 in G4983 the body G3756 , I cannot G1492 tell [G5758] G1535 ; or whether G1622 out G4983 of the body G3756 , I cannot G1492 tell [G5758] G2316 : God G1492 knoweth [G5758] G5108 ;) such an one G726 caught up [G5651] G2193 to G5154 the third G3772 heaven.

3 G2532 And G1492 I knew [G5758] G5108 such G444 a man G1535 , (whether G1722 in G4983 the body G1535 , or G1622 out G4983 of the body G3756 , I cannot G1492 tell [G5758] G2316 : God G1492 knoweth [G5758];)

4 G3754 How that G726 he was caught up [G5648] G1519 into G3857 paradise G2532 , and G191 heard [G5656] G731 unspeakable G4487 words G3739 , which G1832 it is G3756 not G1832 lawful [G5752] G444 for a man G2980 to utter [G5658].

5 G5228 Of G5108 such an one G2744 will I glory [G5695] G1161 : yet G5228 of G1683 myself G2744 I will G3756 not G2744 glory [G5695] G1508 , but G1722 in G3450 mine G769 infirmities.

6 G1063 For G1437 though G2309 I would desire [G5661] G2744 to glory [G5664] G2071 , I shall G3756 not G2071 be [G5704] G878 a fool G1063 ; for G2046 I will say [G5692] G225 the truth G1161 : but G5339 now I forbear [G5736] G3361 , lest G5100 any man G3049 should think [G5667] G1519 of G1691 me G5228 above G3739 that which G991 he seeth [G5719] G3165 me G2228 to be, or G191 that he heareth [G5719] G5100 of G1537 G1700 me.

Chapter 24: BOOK OF GALATIANS

NO SALVATION WITHOUT JESUS; NO SALVATION BEFORE JESUS

Our works or the keeping of the law can't save us. We can only be saved through Christ. Those who were dead before Jesus came and died for them, couldn't be in paradise with God once they died, because they at best only had the law to follow with the hope and faith that God would save them.

Galatians 2:16-21 Strongs

16 G1492 Knowing [G5761] G3754 that G444 a man G1344 is G3756 not G1344 justified [G5743] G1537 by G2041 the works G3551 of the law G3362 , but G1223 by G4102 the faith G2424 of Jesus G5547 Christ G2532 , even G2249 we G4100 have believed [G5656] G1519 in G2424 Jesus G5547 Christ G2443 , that G1344 we might be justified [G5686] G1537 by G4102 the faith G5547 of Christ G2532 , and G3756 not G1537 by G2041 the works G3551 of the law G1360 : for G1537 by G2041 the works G3551 of the law G1344 shall G3756 no G3956 G4561 flesh G1344 be justified [G5701].

17 G1161 But G1487 if G2212 , while we seek [G5723] G1344 to be justified [G5683] G1722 by G5547 Christ G2147 , we G846 ourselves G2532 also G2147 are found [G5681] G268 sinners G687 , is therefore G5547 Christ G1249 the minister G266 of sin G3361 ? God forbid G1096 [G5636].

18 G1063 For G1487 if G3618 I build [G5719] G3825 again G5023 the

things G3739 which G2647 I destroyed [G5656] G4921 , I make [G5719] G1683 myself G3848 a transgressor.

19 G1063 For G1473 I G1223 through G3551 the law G599 am dead [G5627] G3551 to the law G2443 , that G2198 I might live [G5661] G2316 unto God.

20 G4957 I am crucified [G5769] G5547 with Christ G1161 : nevertheless G2198 I live [G5719] G3765 ; yet not G1473 I G1161 , but G5547 Christ G2198 liveth [G5719] G1722 in G1698 me G1161 : and G3739 the life which G2198 I G3568 now G2198 live [G5719] G1722 in G4561 the flesh G2198 I live [G5719] G1722 by G4102 the faith G5207 of the Son G2316 of God G3588 , who G25 loved [G5660] G3165 me G2532 , and G3860 gave [G5631] G1438 himself G5228 for G1700 me.

21 G114 I do G3756 not G114 frustrate [G5719] G5485 the grace G2316 of God G1063 : for G1487 if G1343 righteousness G1223 come by G3551 the law G686 , then G5547 Christ G599 is dead [G5627] G1432 in vain.

RIGHTEOUSNESS IS NOT THE SAME AS IMMORTALITY

Abraham's belief and faith in God was accounted to him for righteousness. People say this put Abraham in heaven when he died. Is that for sure, or is this what people assume to be true? Righteousness as shown by the lexicon doesn't give you immortality. It makes you acceptable to God, he will resurrect you to life when he is ready to do so. These verses show how the gentiles are able to become acceptable to God, and how it was prophesied to come about. There is a verse in Hebrews which we will see later showing Abraham is waiting for us. So we can all enter into God's kingdom at the same time. When we get to it we will refer back to this verse and see how the two go together.

Galatians 3:6-8 Strongs

6 G2531 Even as G11 Abraham G4100 believed [G5656] G2316 God G2532 , and G3049 it was accounted [G5681] G846 to him G1519 for

G1343 righteousness.

7 G1097 Know ye [G5719] [G5720] G686 therefore G3754 that G1537 they which are of G4102 faith G3778 , the same G1526 are [G5748] G5207 the children G11 of Abraham.

8 G1161 And G1124 the scripture G4275 , foreseeing [G5631] G3754 that G2316 God G1344 would justify [G5719] G1484 the heathen G1537 through G4102 faith G4283 , preached before the gospel [G5662] G11 unto Abraham G3754 , saying, G1722 In G4671 thee G1757 shall G3956 all G1484 nations G1757 be blessed [G5701].

G1343 δικαιοσύνη - Strong's Greek Lexicon Number

δικαιοσύνη

righteousness, justice

δικαιοσύνη equity (of character or act); specially (Christian) justification

Derivation: from G1342;

KJV Usage: righteousness.

G1342

1) in a broad sense: state of him who is as he ought to be, righteousness, the condition acceptable to God

1a) the doctrine concerning the way in which man may attain a state approved of God

1b) integrity, virtue, purity of life, rightness, correctness of thinking feeling, and acting

2) in a narrower sense, justice or the virtue which gives each his due

We are Abraham's seed and heirs according to the promise. An heir to a fortune doesn't possess the fortune, but has to wait until it is given to them. When they have the fortune, they are no longer heirs, but the possessors of the fortune. We receive the promise of eternal life and son-ship to god, according to the way God has promised in his word.

Galatians 3:29 KJV Strongs

29 G1161 And G1487 if G5210 ye G5547 be Christ's G686 , then G2075 are ye [G5748] G11 Abraham's G4690 seed G2532 , and G2818 heirs G2596 according G1860 to the promise.

TO EVERYTHING THERE IS A SEASON

We will reap what we sow. If we want to reap blessings in God's kingdom then we need to set aside treasures for ourselves there. We store up those treasures when we do good to others.

Galatians 6:7-10

Strongs

7 G4105 Be G3361 not G4105 deceived [G5744] G2316 ; God G3456 is G3756 not G3456 mocked [G5743] G1063 : for G3739 whatsoever G1437 G444 a man G4687 soweth [G5725] G5124 , that G2325 shall he G2532 also G2325 reap [G5692].

8 G3754 For G4687 he that soweth [G5723] G1519 to G1438 his G4561 flesh G2325 shall G1537 of G4561 the flesh G2325 reap [G5692] G5356 corruption G1161 ; but G4687 he that soweth [G5723] G1519 to G4151 the Spirit G2325 shall G1537 of G4151 the Spirit G2325 reap [G5692] G2222 life G166 everlasting.

9 G1161 And G1573 let us G3361 not G1573 be weary [G5725] G2570 in well G4160 doing [G5723] G1063 : for G2398 in due G2540 season G2325 we shall reap [G5692] G1590 , if we faint [G5746] G3361 not.

10 G5613 As G2192 we have [G5719] G686 therefore G3767 G2540 opportunity G2038 , let us do [G5741] G18 good G4314 unto G3956 all G1161 men, especially G3122 G4314 unto G3609 them who are of the household G4102 of faith.

Chapter 25: BOOK OF EPHESIANS

CALLED TO BE FAMILY

God has called us to Christ. He knew he would call us before we were born, before he created the world.

Ephesians 1:4-5 Strongs

4 G2531 According as G1586 he hath chosen [G5668] G2248 us G1722 in G846 him G4253 before G2602 the foundation G2889 of the world G2248 , that we G1511 should be [G5750] G40 holy G2532 and G299 without blame G2714 before G846 him G1722 in G26 love:

5 G4309 Having predestinated [G5660] G2248 us G1519 unto G5206 the adoption of children G1223 by G2424 Jesus G5547 Christ G1519 to G846 himself G2596 , according G2107 to the good pleasure G846 of his G2307 will,

HE IS IN US WE ARE IN HIM

Through Jesus we are saved. We are part of him, and he is part of us. We sit in heavenly places vicariously through Jesus.

Ephesians 2:6-7 Strongs

6 G2532 And G4891 hath raised us up together [G5656] G2532 , and G4776 made us sit together [G5656] G1722 in G2032 heavenly G1722 places in G5547 Christ G2424 Jesus:

7 G2443 That G1722 in G165 the ages G1904 to come [G5740] G1731 he might shew [G5672] G5235 the exceeding [G5723] G4149 riches G846 of his G5485 grace G1722 in G5544 his kindness G1909 toward G2248 us G1722 through G5547 Christ G2424 Jesus.

ARE WE THE ONLY MEMBERS IN GODS FAMILY

The whole family in heaven and earth. Does this say that there are dead believers in heaven now? If it does, it doesn't seem to me to be very explicit. Could there be spirit beings that live in heaven with God now that will be part of the family of God later?

Ephesians 3:15 Strongs

15 G1537 Of G3739 whom G3956 the whole G3965 family G1722 in G3772 heaven G2532 and G1909 earth G1093 G3687 is named [G5743],

DAY OF REDEMPTION IS THE DAY OF THE LORD

Now it may be the day of redemption is the day of our death, but then each of us would be redeemed at different days. This passage puts the day of redemption in a singular form, not a plural form. Otherwise it should say days of redemption. I think this shows us there is only one day of redemption, and we are sealed until that day comes.

Ephesians 4:30 Strongs

30 G2532 And G3076 grieve [G5720] G3361 not G40 the holy G4151 Spirit G2316 of God G1722 , whereby G3739 G4972 ye are sealed [G5681] G1519 unto G2250 the day G629 of redemption.

GOD IS CALLING US OUT OF THIS WORLD

This could be talking metaphorically about waking up and knowing God in this life. Or it could be telling us about the resurrection.

Ephesians 5:14 Strongs

14 G1352 Wherefore G3004 he saith [G5719] G1453 , Awake thou [G5669] G2518 that sleepest [G5723] G2532 , and G450 arise [G5628] G1537 from G3498 the dead G2532 , and G5547 Christ G2017 shall give G4671 thee G2017 light [G5692].

Chapter 26: BOOK OF PHILIPPIANS

DO OUR TRADITIONAL BELIEFS CONTRADICT THE BIBLE

Now here is a verse that seems to support the thought that when you die you go directly to be with Jesus and God. Having the desire to depart (die) and be with Christ. It seems like Paul wouldn't mind dieing and going to be with Christ instantly. Or he could also be meaning that after he died he would be with Christ at his next thought, but he would have to wait for the resurrection of the saints asleep in his grave. How do you understand this passage? How does your understanding fit with the verses we have looked at so far? Is it contradictory to other scriptures, or does it blend with them? If challenged, what verses covered so far would you use to support your opinion? Remember the early church didn't have the New Testament to prove the validity of their opinions, they needed to use Old Testament scriptures.

Philippians 1:20-24 Strongs

20 G2596 According G3450 to my G603 earnest expectation G2532 and G1680 my hope G3754 , that G1722 in G3762 nothing G153 I shall be ashamed [G5701] G235 , but G1722 that with G3956 all G3954 boldness G5613 , as G3842 always G3568 , so now G2532 also G5547 Christ G3170 shall be magnified [G5701] G1722 in G3450 my G4983 body G1535 , whether G1223 it be by G2222 life G1535 , or G1223 by G2288 death.

21 G1063 For G1698 to me G2198 to live [G5721] G5547 is Christ G2532 , and G599 to die [G5629] G2771 is gain.

22 G1161 But G1487 if G2198 I live [G5721] G1722 in G4561 the flesh G5124 , this G2590 is the fruit G2041 of my labour G3427 G2532 : yet G5101 what G138 I shall choose [G5698] G1107 I wot [G5719] G3756 not.

23 G1063 For G4912 I am in a strait [G5743] G1537 betwixt G1417 two G2192 , having [G5723] G1939 a desire G1519 to G360 depart [G5658] G2532 , and G1511 to be [G5750] G4862 with G5547 Christ G4183 ; which is far G3123 G2908 better:

24 G1161 Nevertheless G1961 to abide [G5721] G1722 in G4561 the flesh G316 is more needful G1223 for G5209 you.

WE ARE FREE TO CHOOSE

Every knee should bow, and every tongue should confess that Jesus Christ is Lord. Knowing they should, some may still choose to reject Jesus. The word should in V.10-11 doesn't have a lexicon number as it was added in at translation. Some versions may say will instead. Even though some people recognize Jesus for who he is, they still will reject him. Just like Satan and the demons rejected him.

Philippians 2:9-11 Strongs

9 G1352 Wherefore G2316 God G2532 also G5251 hath highly exalted [G5656] G846 him G2532 , and G5483 given [G5662] G846 him G3686 a name G3588 which G5228 is above G3956 every G3686 name:

10 G2443 That G1722 at G3686 the name G2424 of Jesus G3956 every G1119 knee G2578 should bow [G5661] G2032 , of things in heaven G2532 , and G1919 things in earth G2532 , and G2709 things under the earth;

11 G2532 And G3956 that every G1100 tongue G1843 should confess [G5672] G3754 that G2424 Jesus G5547 Christ G2962 is Lord G1519 , to G1391 the glory G2316 of God G3962 the Father.

WE FOLLOW THE SHEPHERD

It's because of verses like this I feel so strongly about giving people freedom of thought. We may understand things differently from each other, but we all need to follow the path that God has laid out for us, working out our own salvation with fear and trembling.

Philippians 2:12-13 Strongs

12 G5620 Wherefore G3450 , my G27 beloved G2531 , as G5219 ye have G3842 always G5219 obeyed [G5656] G3361 , not G5613 as G1722 in G3450 my G3952 presence G3440 only G235 , but G3568 now G4183 much G3123 more G1722 in G3450 my G666 absence G2716 , work out [G5737] G1438 your own G4991 salvation G3326 with G5401 fear G2532 and G5156 trembling

13 G1063 For G2076 it is [G5748] G2316 God G3588 which G1754 worketh [G5723] G1722 in G5213 you G2532 both G2309 to will [G5721] G2532 and G1754 to do [G5721] G5228 of G2107 his good pleasure.

NO SALVATION BEFORE THE SAVIOR

Paul here looks forward to the resurrection of the dead. He knew he, like everyone else, follows Jesus in the resurrection from the dead. Saying that, how could anyone have preceded Jesus into heaven? Does this match your beliefs? If it doesn't, how does this verse fit into your understanding of where the OT faithful are and when they got there? What scriptures support your beliefs, and how do they blend with the other scriptures we have covered in this study?

Philippians 3:10-13 Strongs

10 G1097 That I may know [G5629] G846 him G2532 , and G1411 the power G846 of his G386 resurrection G2532 , and G2842 the fellowship G846 of his G3804 sufferings G4833 , being made conformable [G5746] G846 unto his G2288 death;

11 G1513 If by any means G2658 I might attain [G5661] G1519 unto G1815 the resurrection G3498 of the dead.

12 G3756 Not G3754 as though G2235 I had already G2983 attained [G5627] G2228 , either G2235 were already G5048 perfect [G5769] G1161 : but G1377 I follow after [G5719] G1499 , if G2638 that I may apprehend [G5632] G1909 that for G3739 which G2532 also G2638 I am apprehended [G5681] G5259 of G5547 Christ G2424 Jesus.

13 G80 Brethren G1473 , I G3049 count [G5736] G3756 not G1683 myself G2638 to have apprehended [G5760] G1161 : but G1520 this one thing G1950 I do, forgetting [G5740] G3303 those things G3694 which are behind G1161 , and G1901 reaching forth unto [G5740] G1715 those things which are before,

NEW CLOTHS FOR AN OLD BODY

Our new bodies are to be like Jesus' glorious body. When we are resurrected we are to be like him. We will be spiritual as he is. We will take on his form as children of God.

Philippians 3:21 Strongs

21 G3739 Who G3345 shall change [G5692] G2257 our G5014 vile G4983 body G1519 , that G846 it G1096 may be [G5635] G4832 fashioned like unto G846 his G1391 glorious G4983 body G2596 , according to G1753 the working G846 whereby he G1410 is able [G5738] G2532 even G5293 to subdue [G5658] G3956 all things G1438 unto himself.

GOD KNOWS OUR NAME

This book of life is the one that has the names of those who love the Lord written in it. The book that is used to identify the believers at God's judgement day.

Philippians 4:3 Strongs

3 G2532 And G2065 I intreat [G5719] G4571 thee G2532 also G1103 , true
G4805 yokefellow G4815 , help [G5732] G846 those women G3748 which
G4866 laboured [G5656] G3427 with me G1722 in G2098 the gospel
G3326 , with G2815 Clement G2532 also G2532 , and G3062 with other
G3450 my G4904 fellowlabourers G3739 , whose G3686 names G1722 are
in G976 the book G2222 of life.

Chapter 27: BOOK OF COLOSSIANS

OUR INHERITANCE IS IN THE FUTURE

Partakers of the inheritance, the word translated into inheritance means to be chosen by lot, by God. We are specifically chosen by God to be in his kingdom. What an honour he has bestowed upon us. We are to be translated, and placed into the kingdom.

Colossians 1:12-13 Strongs

12 G2168 Giving thanks [G5723] G3962 unto the Father G3588 , which G2427 hath made G2248 us G2427 meet [G5660] G1519 to G3310 be partakers G2819 of the inheritance G40 of the saints G1722 in G5457 light:

13 G3739 Who G4506 hath delivered [G5673] G2248 us G1537 from G1849 the power G4655 of darkness G2532 , and G3179 hath translated [G5656] G1519 us into G932 the kingdom G846 of his G26 dear G5207 Son:

G2819 κλῆρος - Strong's Greek Lexicon Number

κλῆρος

a lot;

κλῆρος a die (for drawing chances); by implication, a portion (as if so secured); by extension, an acquisition (especially a patrimony, figuratively)

Derivation: probably from G2806 (through the idea of using bits of wood, etc., for the purpose;

KJV Usage: heritage, inheritance, lot, part.

G2806

1) an object used in casting or drawing lots, which was either a pebble, or a potsherd, or a bit of wood

1a) the lots of several persons concerned, inscribed with their names, were thrown together into a vase, which was then shaken, and he whose lot fell out first upon the ground was the one chosen

2) what is obtained by lot, allotted portion

2a) a portion of the ministry common to the apostles

2b) used of the part which one will have in eternal salvation

2b1) of salvation itself

2b2) the eternal salvation which God has assigned to the saints

2c) of persons

2c1) those whose care and oversight has been assigned to one [allotted charge], used of Christian churches, the administration of which falls to the lot of presbyters

- Charge (Nouns, Adjective and Verbs), Chargeable
- Inherit, Inheritance
- Lot, Lots
- Portion

κλῆρος

klēros

klay'-ros

Probably from G2806 (through the idea of using bits of wood, etc., for the purpose); a die (for drawing chances); by implication a portion (as if so secured); by extension an acquisition (especially a patrimony, figuratively)

KJV Usage: heritage, inheritance, lot, part.

G3179 μεθίστημι - Strong's Greek Lexicon Number

μεθίστημι

to place in another way, to change

μεθίστημι , or (1 Cor. 13:2) UP9875: LEXEME NOT FOUND FOR STRONGS 3179 lemma no 1 to transfer, i.e. carry away, depose or (figuratively) exchange, seduce

Derivation: from G3326 and G2476;

KJV Usage: put out, remove, translate, turn away.

G3326 G2476

1) to transpose, transfer, remove from one place to another

1a) of change of situation or place

1b) to remove from the office of a steward

1c) to depart from life, to die

- Put

- Remove, Removing
- Turn

μεθίστημι, μεθιστάνω

methistēmi methistanō

meth-is'-tay-mee, -is-tan'-o

From G3326 and G2476; (second form used at 1 Corinthians 13:2) to transfer, that is, carry away, depose or (figuratively) exchange, seduce

JESUS IS OUR ALL IN ALL

Jesus is not only the son of the invisible God. He is the image of him. He was the one who created all things as the word of the Old Testament.

Colossians 1:15-17 Strongs

15 G3739 Who G2076 is [G5748] G1504 the image G517 of the invisible G2316 God G4416 , the firstborn G3956 of every G2937 creature:

16 G3754 For G1722 by G846 him G2936 were G3956 all things G2936 created [G5681] G1722 , that are in G3772 heaven G2532 , and G1909 that are in G1093 earth G3707 , visible G2532 and G517 invisible G1535 , whether G2362 they be thrones G1535 , or G2963 dominions G1535 , or G746 principalities G1535 , or G1849 powers G3956 : all things G2936 were created [G5769] G1223 by G846 him G2532 , and G1519 for G846 him:

17 G2532 And G846 he G2076 is [G5748] G4253 before G3956 all things G2532 , and G1722 by G846 him G3956 all things G4921 consist [G5758].

YOU CAN NOT COME BEFORE THE FIRST ONE

Jesus is the first born from the dead. When did Jesus die? He died on the cross, was buried, and on the third day rose again. If this was when Jesus died, and was the first born of the dead, the first to be resurrected to spiritual life. That would make it impossible for anyone to be born from the dead before he was. So everyone who had died before Jesus was resurrected, still has to be dead in their graves, waiting for their resurrection to take place. Which would exclude them from being in heaven, or hell.

Colossians 1:18-19 Strongs

18 G2532 And G846 he G2076 is [G5748] G2776 the head G4983 of the body G1577 , the church G3739 : who G2076 is [G5748] G746 the beginning G4416 , the firstborn G1537 from G3498 the dead G2443 ; that G1722 in G3956 all G846 things he G1096 might have [G5638] G4409 the preeminence [G5723].

19 G2106 For it pleased [G5656] G3754 the Father that G1722 in G846 him G2730 should G3956 all G4138 fulness G2730 dwell [G5658];

BY HIS SACRIFICE WE ARE FORGIVEN

It is only by his blood that we can be reconciled, and found acceptable in his sight.

Colossians 1:20-22 Strongs

20 G2532 And G1517 , having made peace [G5660] G1223 through G129 the blood G846 of his G4716 cross G1223 , by G846 him G604 to reconcile [G5658] G3956 all things G1519 unto G846 himself G1223 ; by G846 him G1535 , I say, whether G1909 they be things in G1093 earth G1535 , or G1722 things in G3772 heaven.

21 G2532 And G5209 you G5607 , that were [G5752] G4218 sometime G526 alienated [G5772] G2532 and G2190 enemies G1271 in your mind

G1722 by G4190 wicked G2041 works G1161 , yet G3570 now G604 hath he reconciled [G5656]

22 G1722 In G4983 the body G846 of his G4561 flesh G1223 through G2288 death G3936 , to present [G5658] G5209 you G40 holy G2532 and G299 unblameable G2532 and G410 unreproveable G846 in his G2714 sight:

WE WILL APPEAR WHEN GLORY COMES

We will appear when Christ appears. It's not clear in this scripture if we return with him, or are we changed at his return. To find out we would need to look at what other scriptures say about when we are changed.

Colossians 3:4 Strongs

4 G3752 When G5547 Christ G2257 , who is our G2222 life G5319 , shall appear [G5686] G5119 , then G5319 shall G5210 ye G2532 also G5319 appear [G5701] G4862 with G846 him G1722 in G1391 glory.

Chapter 28: BOOKS OF 1&2 THESSALONIANS

THE FIRST DAY OF THE REST OF OUR ETERNITY

Paul lays out the resurrection for believers. He plainly tells them what will happen to those who are dead, and to those who are alive at Christ's coming. V.13 talks about those which are asleep in the present text, as in, right now they are asleep. V.16 pictures the day of the Lord with Christ descending from heaven. That's when the dead in Christ shall rise first. Then we which are alive will be caught up together with them in the clouds, to meet the Lord in the air. This is the rapture of the believers. It is a noisy spectacle that the whole world will witness. Ushering in the beginning of the kingdom of God.

1 Thessalonians 4:13-17 Strongs

13 G1161 But G2309 I would G3756 not G2309 have [G5719] G5209 you G50 to be ignorant [G5721] G80 , brethren G4012 , concerning G2837 them which are asleep [G5772] G3363 , that G3076 ye sorrow [G5747] G3363 not G2532 , even G2531 as G3062 others G3588 which G2192 have [G5723] G3361 no G1680 hope.

14 G1063 For G1487 if G4100 we believe [G5719] G3754 that G2424 Jesus G599 died [G5627] G2532 and G450 rose again [G5627] G3779 , even so G2532 them also G2837 which sleep [G5685] G1223 in G2424 Jesus G71 will G2316 God G71 bring [G5692] G4862 with G846 him.

15 G1063 For G5124 this G3004 we say [G5719] G5213 unto you G1722

by G3056 the word G2962 of the Lord G3754 , that G2249 we G3588 which G2198 are alive [G5723] G4035 and remain [G5742] G1519 unto G3952 the coming G2962 of the Lord G5348 shall G3364 not G5348 prevent [G5661] G3588 them which G2837 are asleep [G5685].

16 G3754 For G2962 the Lord G846 himself G2597 shall descend [G5695] G575 from G3772 heaven G1722 with G2752 a shout G1722 , with G5456 the voice G743 of the archangel G2532 , and G1722 with G4536 the trump G2316 of God G2532 : and G3498 the dead G1722 in G5547 Christ G450 shall rise [G5698] G4412 first:

17 G1899 Then G2249 we G3588 which G2198 are alive [G5723] G4035 and remain [G5742] G726 shall be caught up [G5691] G260 together G4862 with G846 them G1722 in G3507 the clouds G1519 , to G529 meet G2962 the Lord G1519 in G109 the air G2532 : and G3779 so G2071 shall we G3842 ever G2071 be [G5704] G4862 with G2962 the Lord.

RESPOND TO GODS CALL WHILE YOU CAN

For those who are called by God to know Jesus, now is your day of salvation. Work out your own salvation with fear and trembling. We don't know when the bride groom will return. We must always be ready. We can't let up, relaxing our standards, drifting away from God. The return of Christ, for us personally could be the next time we cross the street. It could be the next time we pass a truck on the road, or go swimming. When we die, our race is done. We will have had our opportunity to make our election sure. We must walk in the light of day.

1 Thessalonians 5:1-5 Strongs

1 G1161 But G4012 of G5550 the times G2532 and G2540 the seasons G80 , brethren G2192 , ye have [G5719] G3756 no G5532 need G1125 that I write [G5745] G5213 unto you.

2 G1063 For G846 yourselves G1492 know [G5758] G199 perfectly G3754 that G2250 the day G2962 of the Lord G3779 so G2064 cometh [G5736]

G5613 as G2812 a thief G1722 in G3571 the night.

3 G1063 For G3752 when G3004 they shall say [G5725] G1515 , Peace G2532 and G803 safety G5119 ; then G160 sudden G3639 destruction G2186 cometh upon [G5731] G846 them G5618 , as G5604 travail G1722 upon G1064 a woman with child G2192 [G5723] G2532 ; and G1628 they shall G3364 not G1628 escape [G5632].

4 G1161 But G5210 ye G80 , brethren G2075 , are [G5748] G3756 not G1722 in G4655 darkness G2443 , that G2250 that day G2638 should overtake [G5632] G5209 you G5613 as G2812 a thief.

5 G5210 Ye G2075 are [G5748] G3956 all G5207 the children G5457 of light G2532 , and G5207 the children G2250 of the day G2070 : we are [G5748] G3756 not G3571 of the night G3761 , nor G4655 of darkness.

YOU'RE RESPONSIBLE FOR YOURSELF

As I have said at the start of this bible study, I am not trying to convince people to see things the way I do. I believe in freedom of thought, and I try not to be dogmatic. Yes I do have an opinion and will defend that opinion. But at the end of the day, it is up to each of us to follow our own conscience as God leads us. He will judge rightly as he knows our hearts. Let's make sure we follow his instructions and not take the easy way out by blindly following along were others may lead. Take the time and effort to prove all things, and keep what is good.

1 Thessalonians 5:21 Strongs

21 G1381 Prove [G5720] G3956 all things G2722 ; hold fast [G5720] G3588 that which G2570 is good.

GOD GIVES US A CHOICE, CHOOSE LIFE

Those that reject God will have everlasting destruction. They will never be in the presence of the Lord again. They will be dead for ever.

2 Thessalonians 1:8-9 Strongs

8 G1722 In G5395 flaming G4442 fire G1325 taking [G5723] G1557 vengeance G1492 on them that know [G5761] G3361 not G2316 God G2532 , and G5219 that obey [G5723] G3361 not G2098 the gospel G2257 of our G2962 Lord G2424 Jesus G5547 Christ:

9 G3748 Who G1349 shall be punished G5099 [G5692] G166 with everlasting G3639 destruction G575 from G4383 the presence G2962 of the Lord G2532 , and G575 from G1391 the glory G846 of his G2479 power;

WHEN HE RETURNS, WE WILL GLORIFY HIM

Christ will be glorified by all of his saints at his return.

2 Thessalonians 1:10 Strongs

10 G3752 When G2064 he shall come [G5632] G1740 to be glorified [G5683] G1722 in G846 his G40 saints G2532 , and G2296 to be admired [G5683] G1722 in G3956 all G4100 them that believe [G5723] G3754 (because G2257 our G3142 testimony G1909 among G5209 you G4100 was believed [G5681] G1722) in G1565 that G2250 day.

GODS PLAN IS SURE

Before Jesus returns certain events have to take place. Don't worry God has a plan and he is following it.

2 Thessalonians 2:1-4 Strongs

1 G1161 Now G2065 we beseech [G5719] G5209 you G80 , brethren G5228 , by G3952 the coming G2257 of our G2962 Lord G2424 Jesus G5547 Christ G2532 , and G2257 by our G1997 gathering together G1909 unto G846 him,

2 G1519 That G5209 ye G4531 be G3361 not G5030 soon G4531 shaken

[G5683] G575 in G3563 mind G3383 , or G2360 be troubled [G5745] G3383 , neither G1223 by G4151 spirit G3383 , nor G1223 by G3056 word G3383 , nor G1223 by G1992 letter G5613 as G1223 from G2257 us G5613 , as G3754 that G2250 the day G5547 of Christ G1764 is at hand [G5758].

3 G1818 Let G3361 no G5100 man G1818 deceive [G5661] G5209 you G2596 by G3367 any G5158 means G3754 : for G3362 that day shall not come, except G2064 there come [G5632] G646 a falling away G4412 first G2532 , and G444 that man G266 of sin G601 be revealed [G5686] G5207 , the son G684 of perdition;

4 G3588 Who G480 opposeth [G5740] G2532 and G5229 exalteth [G5746] G1909 himself above G3956 all G3004 that is called [G5746] G2316 God G2228 , or G4574 that is worshipped G5620 ; so G846 that he G5613 as G2316 God G2523 sitteth [G5658] G1519 in G3485 the temple G2316 of God G584 , shewing [G5723] G1438 himself G3754 that G2076 he is [G5748] G2316 God.

MEASURE TWICE CUT ONCE

At times people will use verses like this to not look at other possibilities and change their beliefs. Notice we are to stick with the beliefs taught by the apostles by word or epistle (written text). This is good when you have been taught the whole truth. It is nice to check our beliefs against all of the biblical teachings. Not only to refresh the truth it in our minds, but to also make corrections when they are needed.

2 Thessalonians 2:15 Strongs

15 G686 Therefore G3767 G80 , brethren G4739 , stand fast [G5720] G2532 , and G2902 hold [G5720] G3862 the traditions G3739 which G1321 ye have been taught [G5681] G1535 , whether G1223 by G3056 word G1535 , or G1223 G2257 our G1992 epistle.

Chapter 29: BOOKS OF 1&2 TIMOTHY

ALL WILL HAVE A TIME

Jesus is our only hope for salvation. He will be taught to all mankind.

1 Timothy 2:5-6 Strongs

5 G1063 For G1520 there is one G2316 God G2532 , and G1520 one G3316 mediator G2316 between God G2532 and G444 men G444 , the man G5547 Christ G2424 Jesus;

6 G3588 Who G1325 gave [G5631] G1438 himself G487 a ransom G5228 for G3956 all G3142 , to be testified G2398 in due G2540 time.

WHO CAN SEE GOD, WHO IS IMMORTAL?

No man can see him. No man has seen him. No man can approach the light of his dwelling. He alone has immortality. How does that fit with the idea of going to heaven right after we die? How does that fit with the belief that people can go to heaven and then come back? The bible tells us what is right, it doesn't tell us all of the things that are, or could be wrong.

1 Timothy 6:14-16 Strongs

14 G4571 That thou G5083 keep [G5658] G1785 this commandment G784 without spot G423 , unrebukeable G3360 , until G2015 the appearing G2257 of our G2962 Lord G2424 Jesus G5547 Christ:

15 G3739 Which G2398 in his G2540 times G1166 he shall shew [G5692] G3588 , who G3107 is the blessed G2532 and G3441 only G1413 Potentate G935 , the King G936 of kings [G5723] G2532 , and G2962 Lord G2961 of lords [G5723];

16 G3588 Who G3441 only G2192 hath [G5723] G110 immortality G3611 , dwelling [G5723] G5457 in the light G3762 which no man G676 can approach unto G3739 ; whom G444 no man G1492 hath seen [G5627] G3761 , nor G1410 can [G5736] G1492 see [G5629] G3739 : to whom G5092 be honour G2532 and G2904 power G166 everlasting G281 . Amen.

A GREAT PROMISE

In Jesus Christ we have the promise of life. Only through and by him can we have it. We don't have eternal life innately within ourselves. We didn't have access to it until it was made available through Jesus. If the promise was going to heaven, then going to heaven would be the promise. But it's not. The promise is life.

2 Timothy 1:1 Strongs

1 G3972 Paul G652 , an apostle G2424 of Jesus G5547 Christ G1223 by G2307 the will G2316 of God G2596 , according to G1860 the promise G2222 of life G3588 which G1722 is in G5547 Christ G2424 Jesus,

BY HIS GRACE WE ARE SAVED

God has chosen and called us specifically to come to Jesus before the world was created. We were part of his plan from the beginning. He will not start a good work and leave it incomplete. Not because of our good works, but because of his good grace.

2 Timothy 1:9 Strongs

9 G3588 Who G4982 hath saved [G5660] G2248 us G2532 , and G2564

called [G5660] G40 us with an holy G2821 calling G3756 , not G2596 according to G2257 our G2041 works G235 , but G2596 according to G2398 his own G4286 purpose G2532 and G5485 grace G3588 , which G1325 was given [G5685] G2254 us G1722 in G5547 Christ G2424 Jesus G4253 before G5550 the world began G166,

APPROVED BY UNDERSTANDING

Know what truth is, by what you can prove through the word of God.

2 Timothy 2:15 Strongs

15 G4704 Study [G5657] G3936 to shew [G5658] G4572 thyself G1384 approved G2316 unto God G2040 , a workman G422 that needeth not to be ashamed G3718 , rightly dividing [G5723] G3056 the word G225 of truth.

RESURRECTION IS YET TO COME

It seems like the truth of the resurrection, and different opinions concerning the afterlife have been a topic of debate for a long time. Let's be careful that it doesn't overthrow our faith.

2 Timothy 2:18 Strongs

18 G3748 Who G4012 concerning G225 the truth G795 have erred [G5656] G3004 , saying [G5723] G386 that the resurrection G1096 is past [G5755] G2235 already G2532 ; and G396 overthrow [G5719] G4102 the faith G5100 of some.

PREPARE FOR GOOD WORK

We may be in Gods house but if we don't purge ourselves of unrighteousness we will end up being vessels of dishonour.

2 Timothy 2:19-21 Strongs

19 G3305 Nevertheless G2310 the foundation G2316 of God G2476 standeth [G5707] [G5758] G4731 sure G2192 , having [G5723] G5026 this G4973 seal G2962 , The Lord G1097 knoweth [G5627] G5607 them that are [G5752] G846 his G2532 . And G868 , Let G3956 every one G3687 that nameth [G5723] G3686 the name G5547 of Christ G868 depart [G5628] G575 from G93 iniquity.

20 G1161 But G1722 in G3173 a great G3614 house G2076 there are [G5748] G3756 not G3440 only G4632 vessels G5552 of gold G2532 and G693 of silver G235 , but G2532 also G3585 of wood G2532 and G3749 of earth G2532 ; and G3739 some G3303 G1519 to G5092 honour G1161 , and G3739 some G1519 to G819 dishonour.

21 G1437 If G5100 a man G3767 therefore G1571 purge [G5661] G1438 himself G575 from G5130 these G2071 , he shall be [G5704] G4632 a vessel G1519 unto G5092 honour G37 , sanctified [G5772] G2532 , and G2173 meet G1203 for the master's use G2090 , and prepared [G5772] G1519 unto G3956 every G18 good G2041 work.

SATANIC TRAPS

What was the first lie recorded in the bible, and who told it? Does it have you in a snare?

2 Timothy 2:26 Strongs

26 G2532 And G366 that they may recover themselves [G5661] G1537 out of G3803 the snare G1228 of the devil G2221 , who are taken captive [G5772] G5259 by G846 him G1519 at G1565 his G2307 will.

DICTATED BY GOD

The scriptures won't lie, or contradict themselves.

2 Timothy 3:16 Strongs

16 G3956 All G1124 scripture G2315 is given by inspiration of God G2532 , and [G5624] is profitable G4314 for G1319 doctrine G4314 , for G1650 reproof G4314 , for G1882 correction G4314 , for G3809 instruction G1722 in G1343 righteousness:

JUDGED IN THE KINGDOM

In his kingdom, Christ will judge when he returns.

2 Timothy 4:1 Strongs

1 G1473 I G1263 charge [G5736] G3767 thee therefore G1799 before G2316 God G2532 , and G2962 the Lord G2424 Jesus G5547 Christ G3588 , who G3195 shall [G5723] G2919 judge [G5721] G2198 the quick [G5723] G2532 and G3498 the dead G2596 at G846 his G2015 appearing G2532 and G846 his G932 kingdom;

CROWNED AT THE RETURN OF JESUS

All those that love Jesus will receive their crowns on the day of his return.

2 Timothy 4:8 Strongs

8 G3063 Henceforth G606 there is laid up [G5736] G3427 for me G4735 a crown G1343 of righteousness G3739 , which G2962 the Lord G1342 , the righteous G2923 judge G591 , shall give [G5692] G3427 me G1722 at G1565 that G2250 day G1161 : and G3756 not G1698 to me G3440 only G235 , but G3956 unto all them G2532 also G25 that love [G5761] G846 his G2015 appearing.

G2250 ἡμέρα - Strong's Greek Lexicon Number

ἡμέρα

day

ἡμέρα day, i.e. (literally) the time space between dawn and dark, or the whole 24 hours (but several days were usually reckoned by the Jews as inclusive of the parts of both extremes); figuratively, a period (always defined more or less clearly by the context)

Derivation: feminine (with G5610 implied) of a derivative of ἧμαι (to sit; akin to the base of G1476) meaning tame, i.e. gentle;

KJV Usage: age, + alway, (mid-)day (by day, (-ly)), + for ever, judgment, (day) time, while, years.

G5610 G1476

1) the day, used of the natural day, or the interval between sunrise and sunset, as distinguished from and contrasted with the night

1a) in the daytime

1b) metaph., "the day" is regarded as the time for abstaining from indulgence, vice, crime, because acts of the sort are perpetrated at night and in darkness

2) of the civil day, or the space of twenty four hours (thus including the night)

2a) Eastern usage of this term differs from our western usage. Any part of a day is counted as a whole day, hence the expression "three days and three nights" does not mean literally three whole days, but at least one whole day plus part of two other days.

3) of the last day of this present age, the day Christ will return from heaven, raise the dead, hold the final judgment, and perfect his kingdom

4) used of time in general, i.e. the days of his life.

Chapter 30: BOOKS OF TITUS AND HEBREWS

A HOPE FOR ETERNITY

Paul has the hope of eternal life. He doesn't have it already. He doesn't have the hope of being in paradise because he already has eternal life naturally inside himself. Eternal life isn't part of us at birth. It is the free gift of God given to those who believe in Jesus. That's why it is important God does not lie, for it is only by the promise God made before the world began that we have the hope of eternal life. If it was by our own power or goodness we would be utterly hopeless.

Titus 1:1-2 Strongs

1 G3972 Paul G1401 , a servant G2316 of God G1161 , and G652 an apostle G2424 of Jesus G5547 Christ G2596 , according to G4102 the faith G2316 of God's G1588 elect G2532 , and G1922 the acknowledging G225 of the truth G3588 which G2596 is after G2150 godliness;

2 G1909 In G1680 hope G166 of eternal G2222 life G3739 , which G2316 God G893 , that cannot lie G1861 , promised [G5662] G4253 before G166 the world G5550 began;

HEIRS HAVE FUTURE REWARDS

We are heirs, meaning we are not yet in possession. We have the hope, meaning we are expecting to have it. To have what? To possess what? To have and possess eternal life. We don't have it yet, but it will be ours someday.

Titus 3:7 Strongs

7 G2443 That G1344 being justified by [G5685] G1565 his G5485 grace G1096 , we should be made [G5638] G2818 heirs G2596 according to G1680 the hope G166 of eternal G2222 life.

NO SALVATION TILL THE PRICE WAS PAID

The story of salvation wasn't written until Jesus was made perfect. Then they who obey can partake in salvation.

Hebrews 5:9 Strongs

9 G2532 And G5048 being made perfect [G5685] G1096 , he became [G5633] G159 the author G166 of eternal G4991 salvation G3956 unto all G5219 them that obey [G5723] G846 him;

UNDERSTANDING RESURRECTION IS A FOUNDATION OF CHRISTIANITY

It is good to exercise our spiritual senses Pro.27:17. As iron sharpens iron, we should be able to prove what we believe and articulate why. We should welcome the opportunity to discern the good and evil. If we aren't skilful in discerning the difference, how do we knowledgeably instruct others about Jesus and the fundamental questions of life?

Hebrews 5:14 Strongs

14 G1161 But G4731 strong G5160 meat G2076 belongeth to them that are [G5748] G5046 of full age G1223 , even those who by reason G1838 of use G2192 have [G5723] G145 their senses G1128 exercised [G5772] G4314 to G1253 discern G5037 both G2570 good G2532 and G2556 evil.

Once we have the fundamentals of repentance and faith, understanding the doctrine of baptism, laying on of hands, resurrection of the dead and eternal judgement, with the help of God we can go on to perfect our lives in the important things, loving God with all that we have, and reflecting Jesus in all that we do.

Hebrews 6:1-3 Strongs

1 G1352 Therefore G863 leaving [G5631] G746 the principles G3056 of the doctrine G5547 of Christ G5342 , let us go on [G5747] G1909 unto G5047 perfection G3361 ; not G2598 laying [G5734] G3825 again G2310 the foundation G3341 of repentance G575 from G3498 dead G2041 works G2532 , and G4102 of faith G1909 toward G2316 God,

2 G1322 Of the doctrine G909 of baptisms G5037 , and G1936 of laying on G5495 of hands G5037 , and G386 of resurrection G3498 of the dead G2532 , and G166 of eternal G2917 judgment.

3 G2532 And G5124 this G4160 will we do [G5692] G1437 , if G4007 G2316 God G2010 permit [G5725].

NOT WILLFULLY BAD BUT BE WILLFULLY GOOD

It won't go well for those who turn back to the world after having tasted God's salvation.

Hebrews 6:4-8 Strongs

4 G1063 For G102 it is impossible G530 for those who were once G5461 enlightened [G5685] G5037 , and G1089 have tasted [G5666] G2032 of the heavenly G1431 gift G2532 , and G1096 were made [G5679] G3353 partakers G40 of the Holy G4151 Ghost,

5 G2532 And G1089 have tasted [G5666] G2570 the good G4487 word G2316 of God G5037 , and G1411 the powers G165 of the world G3195 to come [G5723],

6 G2532 If G3895 they shall fall away [G5631] G340 , to renew them [G5721] G3825 again G1519 unto G3341 repentance G388 ; seeing they crucify G1438 to themselves G5207 the Son G2316 of God G388 afresh [G5723] G2532 , and G3856 put him to an open shame [G5723].

7 G1063 For G1093 the earth G3588 which G4095 drinketh in [G5631] G5205 the rain G2064 that cometh [G5740] G4178 oft G1909 upon G846 it G2532 , and G5088 bringeth forth [G5723] G1008 herbs G2111 meet G1565 for them G2532 G1223 by G3739 whom G1090 it is dressed [G5743] G3335 , receiveth [G5719] G2129 blessing G575 from G2316 God:

8 G1161 But G1627 that which beareth [G5723] G173 thorns G2532 and G5146 briers G96 is rejected G2532 , and G1451 is nigh G2671 unto cursing G3739 ; whose G5056 end G1519 is to G2740 be burned.

It seems to me that those who are backsliders, as we all can be, but don't reject God won't be forgotten by him either.

Hebrews 6:9-11 Strongs

9 G1161 But G27 , beloved G3982 , we are persuaded [G5769] G2909 better things G4012 of G5216 you G2532 , and G2192 things that accompany [G5746] G4991 salvation G1499 , though G2980 we G3779 thus G2980 speak [G5719].

10 G1063 For G2316 God G3756 is not G94 unrighteous G1950 to forget [G5635] G5216 your G2041 work G2532 and G2873 labour G26 of love G3739 , which G1731 ye have shewed [G5668] [G5625] G1731 [G5669] G1519 toward G846 his G3686 name G1247 , in that ye have ministered [G5660] G40 to the saints G2532 , and G1247 do minister [G5723].

11 G1161 And G1937 we desire [G5719] G1538 that every one G5216 of you G1731 do shew [G5733] G846 the same G4710 diligence G4314 to G4136 the full assurance G1680 of hope G891 unto G5056 the end:

IMPOSSIBLE FOR GOD TO LIE

God has promised it, he will do it. Jesus is the example for our hope, that we are heirs in him and will be in the kingdom of God.

Hebrews 6:16-20 Strongs

16 G1063 For G444 men G3303 verily G3660 swear [G5719] G2596 by G3187 the greater G2532 : and G3727 an oath G1519 for G951 confirmation G846 is to them G4009 an end G3956 of all G485 strife.

17 G1722 Wherein G3739 G2316 God G1014 , willing [G5740] G4054 more abundantly G1925 to shew [G5658] G2818 unto the heirs G1860 of promise G276 the immutability G846 of his G1012 counsel G3315 , confirmed [G5656] G3727 it by an oath:

18 G2443 That G1223 by G1417 two G276 immutable G4229 things G1722 , in G3739 which G102 it was impossible G2316 for God G5574 to lie [G5664] G2192 , we might have [G5725] G2478 a strong G3874 consolation G3588 , who G2703 have fled for refuge [G5631] G2902 to lay hold [G5658] G1680 upon the hope G4295 set before us [G5740]:

19 G3739 Which G2192 hope we have [G5719] G5613 as G45 an anchor G5590 of the soul G5037 , both G804 sure G2532 and G949 stedfast G2532 , and G1525 which entereth [G5740] G1519 into G2082 that within G2665 the veil;

20 G3699 Whither G4274 the forerunner G1525 is G5228 for G2257 us G1525 entered [G5627] G2424 , even Jesus G1096 , made [G5637] G749 an high priest G1519 for G165 ever G2596 after G5010 the order G3198 of Melchisedec.

ALL WILL KNOW GOD

I think this verse is talking about after Jesus returns, and the resurrection of his believers. After those days, the day of the lord, there will be no need to teach about the Lord because all will know him. This has not yet taken place. It is a time in the future when all will learn freely about the Lord.

Hebrews 8:10-11 Strongs

10 G3754 For G3778 this G1242 is the covenant G3739 that G1303 I wil make [G5695] G3624 with the house G2474 of Israel G3326 after G1565 those G2250 days G3004 , saith [G5719] G2962 the Lord G1325 ; I will put [G5723] G3450 my G3551 laws G1519 into G846 their G1271 mind G2532 , and G1924 write [G5692] G846 them G1909 in G846 their G2588 hearts G2532 : and G2071 I will be [G5704] G1519 to G846 them G2316 a God G2532 , and G846 they G2071 shall be [G5704] G1519 to G3427 me G2992 a people:

11 G2532 And G1321 they shall G3364 not G1321 teach [G5661] G1538 every man G846 his G4139 neighbour G2532 , and G1538 every man G846 his G80 brother G3004 , saying [G5723] G1097 , Know [G5628] G2962 the Lord G3754 : for G3956 all G1492 shall know [G5692] G3165 me G575 , from G3398 the least G846 G2193 to G3173 the greatest G846.

NEW TESTAMENT CAME INTO EFFECT AFTER THE DEATH OF JESUS

I believe these next verses clearly show us the New Testament promises didn't come into effect until after Jesus was crucified. We are only reconciled to God through the sacrifice of Jesus. His sacrifice was sufficient to atone for all of humanities sins, once and for all. No redemption could be found until after he died. Therefore although many people died with the hope of salvation, with the faith God would save them, it was not possible for salvation to be delivered to them until after Jesus had actually been crucified and had died. Not until his blood was shed was there a path to God, not until after his sacrifice was made could we be reconciled to God.

Hebrews 9:11-17 Strongs

11 G1161 But G5547 Christ G3854 being come [G5637] G749 an high priest G18 of good things G3195 to come [G5723] G1223 , by G3187 a greater G2532 and G5046 more perfect G4633 tabernacle G3756 , not G5499 made with hands G5123 , that is to say [G5748] G3756 , not G5026 of this G2937 building;

12 G3761 Neither G1223 by G129 the blood G5131 of goats G2532 and G3448 calves G1161 , but G1223 by G2398 his own G129 blood G1525 he entered in [G5627] G2178 once G1519 into G39 the holy place G2147 , having obtained [G5642] G166 eternal G3085 redemption for us .

13 G1063 For G1487 if G129 the blood G5022 of bulls G2532 and G5131 of goats G2532 , and G4700 the ashes G1151 of an heifer G4472 sprinkling [G5723] G2840 the unclean [G5772] G37 , sanctifieth [G5719] G4314 to G2514 the purifying G4561 of the flesh:

14 G4214 How much G3123 more G2511 shall G129 the blood G5547 of Christ G3739 , who G1223 through G166 the eternal G4151 Spirit G4374 offered [G5656] G1438 himself G299 without spot G2316 to God G2511 , purge [G5692] G5216 your G4893 conscience G575 from G3498 dead G2041 works G1519 to G3000 serve [G5721] G2198 the living [G5723] G2316 God?

15 G2532 And G5124 for this G1223 cause G2076 he is [G5748] G3316 the mediator G2537 of the new G1242 testament G3704 , that G1096 by means [G5637] G2288 of death G1519 , for G629 the redemption G3847 of the transgressions G1909 that were under G4413 the first G1242 testament G2564 , they which are called [G5772] G2983 might receive [G5632] G1860 the promise G166 of eternal G2817 inheritance.

16 G1063 For G3699 where G1242 a testament G318 is, there must also of necessity G5342 be [G5745] G2288 the death G1303 of the testator [G5642].

17 G1063 For G1242 a testament G949 is of force G1909 after G3498 men are dead G1893 : otherwise G2480 it is of G3379 no G2480 strength

[G5719] G3379 at all G3753 while G1303 the testator [G5642] G2198 liveth [G5719].

ONCE WAS ENOUGH

Our hope is through Christ alone. He has atoned for us, as the high priest did for Israel in the temple.His atonement was only made once. Otherwise he would have to live and die continually. Where the high priest made atonement every year, Jesus just lived one pure atoning life to bear the sins of many.

V27 is often quoted to disprove the resurrection of mankind. When read in context, this verse is not talking about the resurrection at all. But rather saying how Jesus didn't have to keep reliving a perfect life, from the beginning of time till the end of humanity, to be our sacrifice. He just had to live the one life that he lived. Those who say people can only live once seem to forget about the dead coming back to life through a miracle.

As a side point, in Dictionary.com describes dead as being asleep, not conscious or having any mental capacity, brain dead is used as a way to describe being dead. Death is not described as becoming a disembodied spirit, alive in a spiritual realm as some people believe. Death is the opposite of life.

As well the judgement will not be very effective if those being judged weren't alive to experience it. Those having died in their sins, will stand before judgement and give an account for themselves. That would demand they be brought back to life, making the assertion that man can't live more than once ineffectual. In order to justify your actions you must be alive to do so.

V28 For those who look for Christ, he will appear to them at his second coming and they will receive their salvation, at his second coming.

Hebrews 9:24-28 Strongs

24 G1063 For G5547 Christ G1525 is G3756 not G1525 entered [G5627] G1519 into G39 the holy places G5499 made with hands G499 , which are the figures G228 of the true G235 ; but G1519 into G3772 heaven G846 itself G3568 , now G1718 to appear [G5683] G4383 in the presence G2316 of God G5228 for G2257 us:

25 G3761 Nor G2443 yet that G4374 he should offer [G5725] G1438 himself G4178 often G5618 , as G749 the high priest G1525 entereth [G5736] G1519 into G39 the holy place G2596 every G1763 year G1722 with G129 blood G245 of others;

26 G1893 For then G1163 must [G5713] G846 he G4178 often G3958 have suffered [G5629] G575 since G2602 the foundation G2889 of the world G1161 : but G3568 now G530 once G1909 in G4930 the end G165 of the world G5319 hath he appeared [G5769] G1519 to G115 put away G266 sin G1223 by G2378 the sacrifice G846 of himself.

27 G2532 And G2596 as G3745 G606 it is appointed [G5736] G444 unto men G530 once G599 to die [G5629] G1161 , but G3326 after G5124 this G2920 the judgment:

28 G3779 So G5547 Christ G530 was once G4374 offered [G5685] G1519 to G399 bear [G5629] G266 the sins G4183 of many G553 ; and unto them that look [G5740] G846 for him G3700 shall he appear [G5701] G1537 G1208 the second time G5565 without G266 sin G1519 unto G4991 salvation.

dead

[ded] Show IPA adjective, dead·er, dead·est, noun, adverb

adjective

1.no longer living; deprived of life: dead people; dead flowers; dead animals.

2.brain-dead.

3.not endowed with life; inanimate: dead stones.

4.resembling death; deathlike: a dead sleep; a dead faint.

5.bereft of sensation; numb: He was half dead with fright. My leg feels dead.

a·live

[uh-lahyv] Show IPA

adjective

1.having life; living; existing; not dead or lifeless.

2.living (used for emphasis): the proudest man alive.

3.in a state of action; n force or operation; active: to keep hope alive.

4.full of energy and spirit; lively: Grandmother's more alive than most of her contemporaries.

5.having the quality of life; vivid; vibrant: The room was alive with color.

G4991 σωτηρία - Strong's Greek Lexicon Number

σωτηρία

a saving, deliverance, preservation, safety

σωτηρία rescue or safety (physically or morally)

Derivation: feminine of a derivative of G4990 as (properly, abstract) noun;

KJV Usage: deliver, health, salvation, save, saving.

G4990

1) deliverance, preservation, safety, salvation

1a) deliverance from the molestation of enemies

1b) in an ethical sense, that which concludes to the souls safety or salvation

1b1) of Messianic salvation

2) salvation as the present possession of all true Christians

3) future salvation, the sum of benefits and blessings which the Christians, redeemed from all earthly ills, will enjoy after the visible return of Christ from heaven in the consummated and eternal kingdom of God.

ONLY SAVED THROUGH JESUS

The law and sacrifices never saved anyone. The Law only showed people their sins, it didn't forgive them of their sins. Our sins are only forgiven by the sacrifice of Jesus. This is made clear by the following scriptures. Since sin can only be forgiven through Jesus, and his sacrifice is good for all of humanity from any time in history or future. Those who died before his sacrifice couldn't have their sins forgiven until after his sacrifice was complete. They could have the faith in Gods promise of salvation. They could have the hope of eternal life because they knew God would fulfil his promise. This hope and faith could not give them what they desired, only Jesus could. We have seen in previous verses how their faith and hope is realized at the return of Jesus. This leaves those that trust in God waiting for the day of the lord to arrive so they may be glorified in him.

Hebrews 10:1-12 Strongs

1 G1063 For G3551 the law G2192 having [G5723] G4639 a shadow G18 of good things G3195 to come [G5723] G3756 , and not G846 the very G1504 image G4229 of the things G1410 , can [G5736] G3763 never G846 with those G2378 sacrifices G3739 which G4374 they offered [G5719] G2596 year by year G1763 G1519 continually G1336 G5048 make G4334 the comers thereunto [G5740] G5048 perfect [G5658].

2 G1893 For then G302 would they G3756 not G3973 have ceased

[G5668] G4374 to be offered [G5746] G1223 ? because G3000 that the worshippers [G5723] G530 once G2508 purged [G5772] G2192 should have had [G5721] G3367 no G2089 more G4893 conscience G266 of sins.

3 G235 But G1722 in G846 those G364 sacrifices there is a remembrance again G266 made of sins G2596 every G1763 year.

4 G1063 For G102 it is not possible G129 that the blood G5022 of bulls G2532 and G5131 of goats G851 should take away [G5721] G266 sins.

5 G1352 Wherefore G1525 when he cometh [G5740] G1519 into G2889 the world G3004 , he saith [G5719] G2378 , Sacrifice G2532 and G4376 offering G2309 thou wouldest [G5656] G3756 not G1161 , but G4983 a body G2675 hast thou prepared [G5668] G3427 me:

6 G3646 In burnt offerings G2532 and G4012 sacrifices for G266 sin G2106 thou hast had G3756 no G2106 pleasure [G5656].

7 G5119 Then G2036 said I [G5627] G2400 , Lo [G5628] G2240 , I come [G5719] G1722 (in G2777 the volume G975 of the book G1125 it is written [G5769] G4012 of G1700 me G4160 ,) to do [G5658] G4675 thy G2307 will G2316 , O God.

8 G511 Above G3004 when he said [G5723] G3754 , G2378 Sacrifice G2532 and G4376 offering G2532 and G3646 burnt offerings G2532 and G4012 offering for G266 sin G2309 thou wouldest [G5656] G3756 not G3761 , neither G2106 hadst pleasure [G5656] G3748 therein; which G4374 are offered [G5743] G2596 by G3551 the law;

9 G5119 Then G2046 said he [G5758] G2400 , Lo [G5628] G2240 , I come [G5719] G4160 to do [G5658] G4675 thy G2307 will G2316 , O God G337 . He taketh away [G5719] G4413 the first G2443 , that G2476 he may establish [G5661] G1208 the second.

10 G1722 By G3739 the which G2307 will G2070 we are [G5748] G37 sanctified [G5772] G1223 through G4376 the offering G4983 of the body G2424 of Jesus G5547 Christ G2178 once for all .

11 G2532 And G3303 G3956 every G2409 priest G2476 standeth [G5707] [G5758] G2596 daily G2250 G3008 ministering [G5723] G2532 and G4374 offering [G5723] G4178 oftentimes G846 the same G2378 sacrifices G3748 , which G1410 can [G5736] G3763 never G4014 take away [G5629] G266 sins:

12 G1161 But G846 this man G4374 , after he had offered [G5660] G3391 one G2378 sacrifice G5228 for G266 sins G1519 for G1336 ever G2523 , sat down [G5656] G1722 on G1188 the right hand G2316 of God;

ONCE SAVED ALLWAYS SAVED?

Wilfully sinning is a bad life choice. Especially if you have the knowledge of God.

Hebrews 10:26-32 Strongs

26 G1063 For G2257 if we G264 sin [G5723] G1596 wilfully G3326 after G2983 that we have received [G5629] G1922 the knowledge G225 of the truth G620 , there remaineth [G5743] G3765 no more G2378 sacrifice G4012 for G266 sins,

27 G1161 But G5100 a certain G5398 fearful G1561 looking for G2920 of judgment G2532 and G4442 fiery G2205 indignation G3195 , which shall [G5723] G2068 devour [G5721] G5227 the adversaries.

28 G5100 He G114 that despised [G5660] G3475 Moses G3551 ' law G599 died [G5719] G5565 without G3628 mercy G1909 under G1417 two G2228 or G5140 three G3144 witnesses:

29 G4214 Of how much G5501 sorer G5098 punishment G1380 , suppose ye [G5719] G515 , shall he be thought worthy [G5701] G3588 , who G2662 hath trodden under foot [G5660] G5207 the Son G2316 of God G2532 , and G2233 hath counted [G5666] G129 the blood G1242 of the covenant G3739 , wherewith G1722 G37 he was sanctified [G5681] G2839 , an unholy thing G2532 , and G1796 hath done despite [G5660] G4151 unto

the Spirit G5485 of grace?

30 G1063 For G1492 we know [G5758] G2036 him that hath said [G5631] G1557 , Vengeance G1698 belongeth unto me G1473 , I G467 will recompense [G5692] G3004 , saith [G5719] G2962 the Lord G2532 . And G3825 again G2962 , The Lord G2919 shall judge [G5692] [G5719] G846 his G2992 people.

31 G5398 It is a fearful thing G1706 to fall [G5629] G1519 into G5495 the hands G2198 of the living [G5723] G2316 God.

32 G1161 But G363 call to remembrance [G5732] G4386 the former G2250 days G1722 , in G3739 which G5461 , after ye were illuminated [G5685] G5278 , ye endured [G5656] G4183 a great G119 fight G3804 of afflictions;

PAY DAY

The implication in needing patience is because we will receive our recompense, our reward, when he that shall come will come. That's when we receive our rewards as well as our eternal life. The day of the Lord is certainly a day to look forward to.

Hebrews 10:35-37 Strongs

35 G577 Cast G3361 not G577 away [G5632] G3767 therefore G5216 your G3954 confidence G3748 , which G2192 hath [G5719] G3173 great G3405 recompence of reward.

36 G1063 For G2192 ye have [G5719] G5532 need G5281 of patience G2443 , that G4160 , after ye have done [G5660] G2307 the will G2316 of God G2865 , ye might receive [G5672] G1860 the promise.

37 G1063 For G2089 yet G3397 a little G3745 while G3745 G2064 , and he that shall come [G5740] G2240 will come [G5692] G2532 , and G5549 will G3756 not G5549 tarry [G5692].

FAITH THAT GOD'S WORD IS SURE

By faith the elders obtained a good report. By faith we believe that God created all things.

Hebrews 11:1-3 Strongs

1 G1161 Now G4102 faith G2076 is [G5748] G5287 the substance G1679 of things hoped for [G5746] G1650 , the evidence G4229 of things G3756 not G991 seen [G5746].

2 G1063 For G1722 by G5026 it G4245 the elders G3140 obtained a good report [G5681].

3 G4102 Through faith G3539 we understand [G5719] G165 that the worlds G2675 were framed [G5771] G4487 by the word G2316 of God G1519 , so G3588 that things which G991 are seen [G5746] G1096 were G3361 not G1096 made [G5755] G1537 of G5316 things which do appear [G5730].

WITHOUT US THEY ARE NOT MADE PERFECT

I have often been told these next verses conclusively show that the faith filled people of old were saved by their faith and now that they are dead they are in paradise with God. Just look at Cain being righteous, Enoc was translated that he should not see death because he pleased God. And the list goes on, in fact it is the same train of thought to the end of the chapter. The subject doesn't change it is all contextually the same thought. That is why I lumped it all together rather than break it up into smaller sections. We are saved by faith undoubtedly, no ifs ands or buts. The problem I see, is with the contention that the faithful are now all in paradise or heaven. When you read to the last two verses, they put the rest of the chapter into perspective.

I may not have complete understanding on how God translated Enoch, or where he was translated too. But the last two verses make it clear to me where he isn't. As Abraham's belief and faith in God was accounted to him for righteousness in Gal.3:6-8, it didn't give him immortality or a pass to heaven instantly after death. Just like everyone else, he needs to wait for the return of Christ to be made perfect.

Hebrews 11:4-38 Strongs

4 G4102 By faith G6 Abel G4374 offered [G5656] G2316 unto God G4119 a more excellent G2378 sacrifice G3844 than G2535 Cain G1223 , by G3739 which G3140 he obtained witness [G5681] G1511 that he was [G5750] G1342 righteous G2316 , God G3140 testifying [G5723] G1909 of G846 his G1435 gifts G2532 : and G1223 by G846 it G599 he being dead [G5631] G2089 yet G2980 speaketh [G5731] [G5625] G2980 [G5719].

5 G4102 By faith G1802 Enoch G3346 was translated [G5681] G1492 that he should G3361 not G1492 see [G5629] G2288 death G2532 ; and G2147 was G3756 not G2147 found [G5712] G1360 , because G2316 God G3346 had translated [G5656] G846 him G1063 : for G4253 before G846 his G3331 translation G3140 he had this testimony [G5769] G2100 , that he pleased [G5760] G2316 God.

6 G1161 But G5565 without G4102 faith G102 it is impossible G2100 to please [G5658] G1063 him : for G4334 he that cometh [G5740] G2316 to God G1163 must [G5748] G4100 believe [G5658] G3754 that G2076 he is [G5748] G2532 , and G1096 that he is [G5736] G3406 a rewarder G1567 of them that diligently seek [G5723] G846 him.

7 G4102 By faith G3575 Noah G5537 , being warned of God [G5685] G4012 of G3369 things not G991 seen [G5746] G3369 as yet G2125 , moved with fear [G5685] G2680 , prepared [G5656] G2787 an ark G1519 to G4991 the saving G846 of his G3624 house G1223 ; by G3739 the which G2632 he condemned [G5656] G2889 the world G2532 , and G1096 became [G5633] G2818 heir G1343 of the righteousness G2596 which is by G4102 faith.

8 G4102 By faith G11 Abraham G2564 , when he was called [G5746] G1831 to go out [G5629] G1519 into G5117 a place G3739 which G3195 he should after [G5707] G2983 receive [G5721] G1519 for G2817 an inheritance G5219 , obeyed [G5656] G2532 ; and G1831 he went out [G5627] G3361 , not G1987 knowing [G5740] G4226 whither G2064 he went [G5736].

9 G4102 By faith G3939 he sojourned [G5656] G1519 in G1093 the land G1860 of promise G5613 , as G245 in a strange country G2730 , dwelling [G5660] G1722 in G4633 tabernacles G3326 with G2464 Isaac G2532 and G2384 Jacob G4789 , the heirs with him G846 of the same G1860 promise:

10 G1063 For G1551 he looked for [G5711] G4172 a city G2192 which hath [G5723] G2310 foundations G3739 , whose G5079 builder G2532 and G1217 maker G2316 is God.

11 G4102 Through faith G2532 also G4564 Sara G846 herself G2983 received [G5627] G1411 strength G1519 to G2602 conceive G4690 seed G2532 , and G5088 was delivered of a child [G5627] G3844 when she was past G2540 age G2244 G1893 , because G2233 she judged [G5662] G4103 him faithful G1861 who had promised [G5666].

12 G1352 Therefore G1080 sprang there [G5681] G2532 even G575 of G1520 one G2532 , and G5023 him G3499 as good as dead [G5772] G2531 , so many as G798 the stars G3772 of the sky G4128 in multitude G2532 , and G5616 as G285 the sand G3588 which G3844 is by G2281 the sea G5491 shore G382 innumerable.

13 G3778 These G3956 all G599 died [G5627] G2596 in G4102 faith G3361 , not G2983 having received [G5631] G1860 the promises G235 , but G1492 having seen [G5631] G846 them G4207 afar off G2532 , and G3982 were persuaded of [G5685] G2532 them, and G782 embraced [G5666] G2532 them, and G3670 confessed [G5660] G3754 that G1526 they were [G5748] G3581 strangers G2532 and G3927 pilgrims G1909 on G1093 the earth.

14 G1063 For G3004 they that say [G5723] G5108 such things G1718 declare plainly [G5719] G3754 that G1934 they seek [G5719] G3968 a country.

15 G2532 And G3303 truly G1487 , if G3421 they had been mindful [G5707] G1565 of that G575 country from G3739 whence G1831 they came out [G5627] G302 , they might G2192 have had [G5707] G2540 opportunity G344 to have returned [G5658].

16 G1161 But G3570 now G3713 they desire [G5734] G2909 a better G5123 country, that is [G5748] G2032 , an heavenly G1352 : wherefore G2316 God G1870 is G3756 not G1870 ashamed [G5736] G846 G1941 to be called [G5745] G846 their G2316 God G1063 : for G2090 he hath prepared [G5656] G846 for them G4172 a city.

17 G4102 By faith G11 Abraham G3985 , when he was tried [G5746] G4374 , offered up [G5754] G2464 Isaac G2532 : and G324 he that had received [G5666] G1860 the promises G4374 offered up [G5707] G3439 his only begotten son,

18 G4314 Of G3739 whom G2980 it was said [G5681] G3754 , That G1722 in G2464 Isaac G2564 shall G4671 thy G4690 seed G2564 be called [G5701]:

19 G3049 Accounting [G5666] G3754 that G2316 God G1415 was able G1453 to raise him up [G5721] G2532 , even G1537 from G3498 the dead G3606 ; from whence G2532 also G2865 he received [G5668] G846 him G1722 in G3850 a figure.

20 G4102 By faith G2464 Isaac G2127 blessed [G5656] G2384 Jacob G2532 and G2269 Esau G4012 concerning G3195 things to come [G5723].

21 G4102 By faith G2384 Jacob G599 , when he was a dying [G5723] G2127 , blessed [G5656] G1538 both G5207 the sons G2501 of Joseph G2532 ; and G4352 worshipped [G5656] G1909 , leaning upon G206 the top G846 of his G4464 staff.

22 G4102 By faith G2501 Joseph G5053 , when he died [G5723] G3421 , made mention [G5656] G4012 of G1841 the departing G5207 of the children G2474 of Israel G2532 ; and G1781 gave commandment [G5662] G4012 concerning G846 his G3747 bones.

23 G4102 By faith G3475 Moses G1080 , when he was born [G5685] G2928 , was hid [G5648] G5150 three months G5259 of G846 his G3962 parents G1360 , because G1492 they saw [G5627] G791 he was a proper G3813 child G2532 ; and G5399 they were G3756 not G5399 afraid [G5675] G935 of the king's G1297 commandment.

24 G4102 By faith G3475 Moses G1096 , when he was come [G5637] G3173 to years G720 , refused [G5662] G3004 to be called [G5745] G5207 the son G5328 of Pharaoh's G2364 daughter;

25 G138 Choosing [G5642] G3123 rather G4778 to suffer affliction [G5738] G2992 with the people G2316 of God G2228 , than G2192 to enjoy the pleasures [G5721] G619 G266 of sin G4340 for a season;

26 G2233 Esteeming G3680 the reproach G5547 of Christ G3187 greater G4149 riches G2233 than [G5666] G2344 the treasures G1722 in G125 Egypt G1063 : for G578 he had respect [G5707] G1519 unto G3405 the recompence of the reward.

27 G4102 By faith G2641 he forsook [G5627] G125 Egypt G3361 , not G5399 fearing [G5679] G2372 the wrath G935 of the king G1063 : for G2594 he endured [G5656] G5613 , as G3708 seeing [G5723] G517 him who is invisible.

28 G4102 Through faith G4160 he kept [G5758] G3957 the passover G2532 , and G4378 the sprinkling G129 of blood G3363 , lest G3645 he that destroyed [G5723] G4416 the firstborn G2345 should touch [G5632] G846 them.

29 G4102 By faith G1224 they passed through [G5627] G2063 the Red G2281 sea G5613 as G1223 by G3584 dry G3739 land : which G124 the Egyptians G3984 assaying G2983 to do [G5631] G2666 were drowned

[G5681].

30 G4102 By faith G5038 the walls G2410 of Jericho G4098 fell down
[G5627] G2944 , after they were compassed [G5685] G1909 about G2033
seven G2250 days.

31 G4102 By faith G4204 the harlot G4460 Rahab G4881 perished [G5639]
G3756 not G544 with them that believed not [G5660] G1209 , when she
had received [G5666] G2685 the spies G3326 with G1515 peace.

32 G2532 And G5101 what G3004 shall I G2089 more G3004 say [G5725]
G1063 ? for G5550 the time G1952 would fail [G5692] G3165 me G1334
to tell [G5740] G4012 of G1066 Gedeon G5037 , and G913 of Barak G2532
, and G4546 of Samson G2532 , and G2422 of Jephthae G1138 ; of David
G2532 also G5037 , and G4545 Samuel G2532 , and G4396 of the
prophets:

33 G3739 Who G1223 through G4102 faith G2610 subdued [G5662] G932
kingdoms G2038 , wrought [G5662] G1343 righteousness G2013 ,
obtained [G5627] G1860 promises G5420 , stopped [G5656] G4750 the
mouths G3023 of lions,

34 G4570 Quenched [G5656] G1411 the violence G4442 of fire G5343 ,
escaped [G5627] G4750 the edge G3162 of the sword G575 , out of G769
weakness G1743 were made strong [G5681] G1096 , waxed [G5675]
G2478 valiant G1722 in G4171 fight G2827 , turned to flight [G5656]
G3925 the armies G245 of the aliens.

35 G1135 Women G2983 received [G5627] G846 their G3498 dead G1537
raised to life again G386 G1161 : and G243 others G5178 were tortured
[G5681] G3756 , not G4327 accepting [G5666] G629 deliverance G2443 :
that G5177 they might obtain [G5632] G2909 a better G386 resurrection:

36 G1161 And G2087 others G2983 had [G5627] G3984 trial G1701 of
cruel mockings G2532 and G3148 scourgings G1161 , yea G2089 ,
moreover G1199 of bonds G2532 and G5438 imprisonment:

37 G3034 They were stoned [G5681] G4249 , they were sawn asunder [G5681] G3985 , were tempted [G5681] G599 , were slain [G5627] G1722 with G5408 the sword G3162 G4022 : they wandered about [G5627] G1722 in G3374 sheepskins G1722 and G122 goatskins G1192 G5302 ; being destitute [G5746] G2346 , afflicted [G5746] G2558 , tormented [G5746];

38 G3739 (Of whom G2889 the world G2258 was [G5713] G3756 not G514 worthy G4105 :) they wandered [G5746] G1722 in G2047 deserts G2532 , and G3735 in mountains G2532 , and G4693 in dens G2532 and G3692 caves G1093 of the earth.

These last two verses put all of the eleventh chapter into perspective. All of the people mentioned earlier in the chapter are said to have been saved by their faith. Now they received a good report through faith, but they did not receive the promise. Did not receive what promise? The promise of being made perfect. The promise of eternal life. God had something better in mind for us. They will not receive the promise of being made perfect until they receive it with us. To be made perfect and receive all of the promise they must wait for us. We receive it together at the same time. Paul didn't receive it when he died, he must wait for us, just as we will have to wait for those that come after us, and so on until the return of Christ. Then we will all receive it together on the day of the Lord.

Hebrews 11:39-40 Strongs

39 G2532 And G3778 these G3956 all G3140 , having obtained a good report [G5685] G1223 through G4102 faith G2865 , received [G5668] G3756 not G1860 the promise:

40 G2316 God G4265 having provided [G5671] G5100 some G2909 better G5100 thing G4012 for G2257 us G3363 , that G5048 they G5565 without G2257 us G5048 should G3363 not G5048 be made perfect [G5686].

FINISH YOUR RACE

I heard a sermon in which the minister exhorted us to run our race and not give up or run the wrong way. He said there were all these dead Christians in heaven cheering us on to the finish line. There is, metaphorically speaking, a great cloud of witness's. But it's only the memory of them and their faith in God that encourages us on. The stories of their lives and what they went through make us stronger. The deceased are waiting till the end of the relay race so that we will all partake together in celebration.

Hebrews 12:1-2 Strongs

1 G5105 Wherefore G2532 seeing we also G2192 are [G5723] G4029 compassed about [G5740] G2254 G5118 with so great G3509 a cloud G3144 of witnesses G659 , let G2249 us G659 lay aside [G5642] G3956 every G3591 weight G2532 , and G266 the sin G2139 which doth so easily beset G5143 us, and let us run [G5725] G1223 with G5281 patience G73 the race G4295 that is set before [G5740] G2254 us,

2 G872 Looking [G5723] G1519 unto G2424 Jesus G747 the author G2532 and G5051 finisher G4102 of our faith G3739 ; who G473 for G5479 the joy G4295 that was set before [G5740] G846 him G5278 endured [G5656] G4716 the cross G2706 , despising [G5660] G152 the shame G5037 , and G2523 is set down [G5656] G1722 at G1188 the right hand G2362 of the throne G2316 of God.

WHAT IS ALIVE

If we won't give reverence to God we won't live. If we aren't alive we are dead. Not live forever in the torments of hell. We measure light by how bright it is. Darkness isn't measured, as it's the absence of light. We can measure the signs of life, the responses of life, and the functions of life. Death is the absence of life. You aren't mostly dead, you're barely alive. You can't be dead and have thoughts, or feel pain as those are only attributes of life. As darkness is the complete absence of light, death is the complete absence of life.

Hebrews 12:9 Strongs

9 G1534 Furthermore G3303 G2192 we have had [G5707] G3962 fathers G2257 of our G4561 flesh G3810 which corrected G2532 us, and G1788 we gave them reverence [G5710] G5293 : shall we G3756 not G4183 much G3123 rather G5293 be in subjection [G5691] G3962 unto the Father G4151 of spirits G2532 , and G2198 live [G5692] ?

OUR SHEPHERD LEADS US TO PERFECTION

God works in us through Jesus to make us better during this life.

Hebrews 13:20-21 Strongs

20 G1161 Now G2316 the God G1515 of peace G321 , that brought again [G5631] G1537 from G3498 the dead G2257 our G2962 Lord G2424 Jesus G3173 , that great G4166 shepherd G4263 of the sheep G1722 , through G129 the blood G166 of the everlasting G1242 covenant,

21 G2675 Make G5209 you G2675 perfect [G5659] G1722 in G3956 every G18 good G2041 work G1519 to G4160 do [G5658] G846 his G2307 will G4160 , working [G5723] G1722 in G5213 you G2101 that which is wellpleasing G846 in his G1799 sight G1223 , through G2424 Jesus G5547 Christ G3739 ; to whom G1391 be glory G1519 for G165 ever G165 and ever G281 . Amen.

Chapter 31: BOOK OF JAMES

TRIED AND TRUE

The crown of life is reserved for those who love him and endure temptation.

James 1:12 Strongs

12 G3107 Blessed G435 is the man G3739 that G5278 endureth [G5719] G3986 temptation G3754 : for G1384 when he is tried G1096 [G5637] G2983 , he shall receive [G5695] G4735 the crown G2222 of life G3739 , which G2962 the Lord G1861 hath promised [G5662] G25 to them that love [G5723] G846 him.

EPIC FAIL

Sin produces death.

James 1:15 Strongs

15 G1534 Then G1939 when lust G4815 hath conceived [G5631] G5088 , it bringeth forth [G5719] G266 sin G1161 : and G266 sin G658 , when it is finished [G5685] G616 , bringeth forth [G5719] G2288 death.

LEADERS OF THE FACK

We are called by the will of God to Jesus. We are the first portion of all creatures to become the sons of God.

James 1:18 Strongs

18 G1014 Of his own will [G5679] G616 begat he [G5656] G2248 us G3056 with the word G225 of truth G1519 , that G2248 we G1511 should be [G5750] G5100 a kind G536 of firstfruits G846 of his G2938 creatures.

OUR WEAKNESS DISPLAYS HIS STRENGTH

God has chosen those the world has counted as inferior to show his greatness.

James 2:5 Strongs

5 G191 Hearken [G5657] G3450 , my G27 beloved G80 brethren G1586 , Hath G3756 not G2316 God G1586 chosen [G5668] G4434 the poor G5127 of this G2889 world G4145 rich G1722 in G4102 faith G2532 , and G2818 heirs G932 of the kingdom G3739 which G1861 he hath promised [G5662] G25 to them that love [G5723] G846 him?

FAITH BOOT CAMP

We are saved by faith, but here the bar is raised. God wants to see our faith in action so that it will grow and be alive in us. He wants us to put our faith into practise, to work it like a muscle and make it stronger.

James 2:17-26 Strongs

17 G2532 Even G3779 so G4102 faith G3362 , if G2192 it hath [G5725] G3362 not G2041 works G2076 , is [G5748] G3498 dead G2596 , being alone G1438.

18 G235 Yea G5100 , a man G2046 may say [G5692] G4771 , Thou G2192 hast [G5719] G4102 faith G2504 , and I G2192 have [G5719] G2041 works G1166 : shew [G5657] G3427 me G4675 thy G4102 faith G1537 without G4675 thy G2041 works G2504 , and I G1166 will shew [G5692] G4671

thee G3450 my G4102 faith G1537 by G3450 my G2041 works.

19 G4771 Thou G4100 believest [G5719] G3754 that G2076 there is [G5748] G1520 one G2316 God G4160 ; thou doest [G5719] G2573 well G1140 : the devils G2532 also G4100 believe [G5719] G2532 , and G5425 tremble [G5719].

20 G1161 But G2309 wilt [G5719] G1097 thou know [G5629] G5599 , O G2756 vain G444 man G3754 , that G4102 faith G5565 without G2041 works G2076 is [G5748] G3498 dead?

21 G1344 Was G3756 not G11 Abraham G2257 our G3962 father G1344 justified [G5681] G1537 by G2041 works G399 , when he had offered [G5660] G2464 Isaac G846 his G5207 son G1909 upon G2379 the altar?

22 G991 Seest thou [G5719] G3754 how G4102 faith G4903 wrought [G5707] G846 with his G2041 works G2532 , and G1537 by G2041 works G5048 was G4102 faith G5048 made perfect [G5681]?

23 G2532 And G1124 the scripture G4137 was fulfilled [G5681] G3004 which saith [G5723] G1161 , G11 Abraham G4100 believed [G5656] G2316 God G2532 , and G3049 it was imputed [G5681] G846 unto him G1519 for G1343 righteousness G2532 : and G2564 he was called [G5681] G5384 the Friend G2316 of God.

24 G3708 Ye see [G5719] G5106 then G3754 how that G1537 by G2041 works G444 a man G1344 is justified [G5743] G2532 , and G3756 not G1537 by G4102 faith G3440 only.

25 G3668 Likewise G1161 G2532 also G1344 was G3756 not G4460 Rahab G4204 the harlot G1344 justified [G5681] G1537 by G2041 works G5264 , when she had received [G5666] G32 the messengers G2532 , and G1544 had sent them out [G5631] G2087 another G3598 way?

26 G1063 For G5618 as G4983 the body G5565 without G4151 the spirit G2076 is [G5748] G3498 dead G3779 , so G4102 faith G5565 without G2041 works G2076 is [G5748] G3498 dead G2532 also.

PATIENCE BRINGS REWARDS

Be patient waiting for the coming of the Lord. It is important to look forward to the coming of the Lord because it is then we receive our promised eternal life.

James 5:7-8 Strongs

7 G3114 Be patient [G5657] G3767 therefore G80 , brethren G2193 , unto G3952 the coming G2962 of the Lord G2400 . Behold [G5628] G1092 , the husbandman G1551 waiteth [G5736] G5093 for the precious G2590 fruit G1093 of the earth G3114 , and hath long patience [G5723] G1909 for G846 it G2193 , until G302 G2983 he receive [G5632] G4406 the early G2532 and G3797 latter G5205 rain.

8 G3114 Be G5210 ye G2532 also G3114 patient [G5657] G4741 ; stablish [G5657] G5216 your G2588 hearts G3754 : for G3952 the coming G2962 of the Lord G1448 draweth nigh [G5758].

WHY WE STUDY

Here the believers are admonished to help each other leave their sin and follow in the righteousness of Jesus. Saving the sinner from death.

James 5:19-20 Strongs

19 G80 Brethren G1437 , if G5100 any G1722 of G5213 you G4105 do err [G5686] G575 from G225 the truth G2532 , and G5100 one G1994 convert [G5661] G846 him;

20 G1097 Let G846 him G1097 know [G5720] G3754 , that G1994 he which converteth [G5660] G268 the sinner G1537 from G4106 the error G846 of his G3598 way G4982 shall save [G5692] G5590 a soul G1537 from G2288 death G2532 , and G2572 shall hide [G5692] G4128 a multitude G2

66 of sins.

Chapter 32: BOOKS OF 1&2 PETER

OUR INCORRUPTIBLE INHERITANCE IS RESERVED UNTILL JESUS RETURNS

We are begotten of God, we have an inheritance of incorruptible immortality reserved for us in heaven. Through faith our salvation will be revealed on the Day of the Lord. We can rejoice in this even if now we are in great temptation. Our pure faith is more precious than worldly riches. We will receive praise, honour, and glory for it when Jesus Christ returns. That is why we anxiously look forward to that day.

1 Peter 1:3-7 Strongs

3 G2128 Blessed G2316 be the God G2532 and G3962 Father G2257 of our G2962 Lord G2424 Jesus G5547 Christ G3588 , which G2596 according to G846 his G4183 abundant G1656 mercy G313 hath begotten G2248 us G313 again [G5660] G1519 unto G2198 a lively [G5723] G1680 hope G1223 by G386 the resurrection G2424 of Jesus G5547 Christ G1537 from G3498 the dead,

4 G1519 To G2817 an inheritance G862 incorruptible G2532 , and G283 undefiled G2532 , and G263 that fadeth not away G5083 , reserved [G5772] G1722 in G3772 heaven G1519 for G5209 you,

5 G3588 Who G5432 are kept [G5746] G1722 by G1411 the power G2316 of God G1223 through G4102 faith G1519 unto G4991 salvation G2092 ready G601 to be revealed [G5683] G1722 in G2078 the last G2540 time.

6 G1722 Wherein G3739 G21 ye greatly rejoice [G5736] G737 , though

now G3641 for a season G1487 , if G1163 need [G5752] G2076 be [G5748] G3076 , ye are in heaviness [G5685] G1722 through G4164 manifold G3986 temptations:

7 G2443 That G1383 the trial G5216 of your G4102 faith G4183 , being much G5093 more precious G5553 than of gold G622 that perisheth [G5734] G1223 , though G1161 G1381 it be tried [G5746] G4442 with fire G2147 , might be found [G5686] G1519 unto G1868 praise G2532 and G5092 honour G2532 and G1391 glory G1722 at G602 the appearing G2424 of Jesus G5547 Christ:

WHEN IS GRACE BROUGHT TO US

Again, when are we to receive {V.9} the salvation of our souls? The grace that is to be brought to us is at the revealing of Jesus Christ. At his return on the Day of the Lord.

1 Peter 1:13 KJV Strongs

13 G1352 Wherefore G328 gird up [G5671] G3751 the loins G5216 of your G1271 mind G3525 , be sober [G5723] G1679 , and hope [G5657] G5049 to the end G1909 for G5485 the grace G5342 that is to be brought [G5746] G5213 unto you G1722 at G602 the revelation G2424 of Jesus G5547 Christ;

OUR JOB DESCRIPTION IN THE KINGDOM

Our job in the kingdom is to be priests under Jesus our chief priest. Called by God from the darkness of this world.

1 Peter 2:5 Strongs

5 G846 Ye G2532 also G5613 , as G2198 lively [G5723] G3037 stones G3618 , are built up [G5743] G4152 a spiritual G3624 house G40 , an holy G2406 priesthood G399 , to offer up [G5658] G4152 spiritual G2378 sacrifices G2144 , acceptable G2316 to God G1223 by G2424 Jesus G5547

Christ.

1 Peter 2:9-10 Strongs

9 G1161 But G5210 ye G1588 are a chosen G1085 generation G934 , a royal G2406 priesthood G40 , an holy G1484 nation G1519 , a peculiar G4047 G2992 people G3704 ; that G1804 ye should shew forth [G5661] G703 the praises G2564 of him who hath called [G5660] G5209 you G1537 out of G4655 darkness G1519 into G846 his G2298 marvellous G5457 light:

10 G3588 Which G4218 in time past G3756 were not G2992 a people G1161 , but G3568 are now G2992 the people G2316 of God G3588 : which G1653 had G3756 not G1653 obtained mercy [G5772] G1161 , but G3568 now G1653 have obtained mercy [G5685].

ONLY JESUS SAVES US

All were dead to their sins until Jesus by his stripes bore our sins, and healed us of them.

1 Peter 2:24 Strongs

24 G3739 Who G846 his own self G399 bare [G5656] G2257 our G266 sins G1722 in G846 his own G4983 body G1909 on G3586 the tree G2443 , that G2198 we G581 , being dead [G5637] G266 to sins G2198 , should live [G5661] G1343 unto righteousness G3739 : by G846 whose G3468 stripes G2390 ye were healed [G5681].

KNOW THE REASON FOR YOUR HOPE

You may have an opportunity to share your understanding of the bible and Gods plan of salvation with others. Possibly those you talk to won't totally agree with you. If you aren't sure yourself and can't show scriptural proof for your convictions, chances are you won't be taken as a credible source of information. Learning doesn't require agreeing with all you're taught. Sometimes you learn why you don't agree.

1 Peter 3:15 Strongs

15 G1161 But G37 sanctify [G5657] G2962 the Lord G2316 God G1722 in G5216 your G2588 hearts G1161 : and G2092 be ready G104 always G4314 to G627 give an answer G3956 to every man G154 that asketh [G5723] G5209 you G3056 a reason G4012 of G1680 the hope G1722 that is in G5213 you G3326 with G4240 meekness G2532 and G5401 fear:

HOW DOES THIS WORK

There are many very good commentaries on line for this section of scripture. Some give only the opinion of the author, some give a wide range of perspectives pointing out the short comings of each one. It seems like this has been a difficult section of scripture to understand for a long time. I don't have to try very hard to imagine someone from the first intended audience turning to his friend with a perplexed look on his face saying. "Whaaat"???

The first part of V18 seems to be straight forward. Jesus paid for our sins so that we could be reconciled to God. I think, the last part says that he died but was brought back to life by the spirit.

V19-20 seems to be the real puzzler. If he went to preach to spirits in prison while his body was in the tomb, then he wasn't fully dead as I understand death to be defined. To be dead is to recognize no sensory inputs, to cease from functioning mentally and physically. If he was preaching to spirits, then he would have had to be alive just not in a physical body. Which would make him not dead, but extremely physically challenged. We are repeatedly told in scripture Jesus had to die for our sins. Since I firmly believe that Jesus is my saviour, I must believe he was completely dead and was not just physically non-functioning.

As I pointed out there are many contradictory thoughts on this verse, I tend to go with the one that Augustine put forward as an explanation.

Jesus, who was the Word and created everything from the beginning, preached to the people in Noah's day by the Holy Spirit through Noah, who is called “a preacher of righteousness”. Those people were in the prison of their sins, but they would not heed the warnings and died in the flood, leaving only eight alive.

If I were to believe Jesus preached to imprisoned spirits while physically in the grave, to which spirits did he preach, human or demonic? And what did he preach? Did he preach to them repentance, or was he there to gloat and show that, he overcame them and that he won the victory over them? If it was to demonic spirits, they already knew that he had won. If he preached repentance to them, could they repent and receive forgiveness? Hadn't they made their choice? If he preached to human spirits, why such a limited group? If he did preach to human spirits, where did they get their immortality from? They were already dead and in their graves. Eternal life is a free gift from God for those who believe in Jesus. The only way to have immortality is to accept Jesus. How can there be human spirits alive that haven't accepted Jesus? How can there be human spirits alive before he returns to resurrect them?

It may seem like Augustine had a convoluted point of view, but to me choosing a different option can't be sustained by biblical scripture. When I look at the implications that occur from taking other points of view, I find there are too many scriptures going against those opinions. I must side with Augustine's thought on the subject. See also 2Peter 2:4-9.

1 Peter 3:18-20 Strongs

18 G3754 For G5547 Christ G2532 also G530 hath once G3958 suffered [G5627] G4012 for G266 sins G1342 , the just G5228 for G94 the unjust G2443 , that G4317 he might bring [G5632] G2248 us G2316 to God G2289 , being put to death [G5772] G3303 G4561 in the flesh G1161 , but G2227 quickened [G5685] G4151 by the Spirit:

19 G1722 By G3739 which G2532 also G4198 he went [G5679] G2784 and preached [G5656] G4151 unto the spirits G1722 in G5438 prison;

20 G4218 Which sometime G544 were disobedient [G5660] G3753 , when G530 once G3115 the longsuffering G2316 of God G1551 waited [G5711] G1722 in G2250 the days G3575 of Noah G2787 , while the ark G2680 was a preparing [G5746] G1519 , wherein G3739 G3641 few G5123 , that is [G5748] G3638 , eight G5590 souls G1295 were saved [G5681] G1223 by G5204 water.

LIVE FOR GOD ALWAYS

Jesus will judge every one that has lived. Believers need to live like it's their last day to be alive, striving for the perfection of Christ. In this world we will be judged by man, in the Kingdom of God we will be judged by Christ.

1 Peter 4:5-6 Strongs

5 G3739 Who G591 shall give [G5692] G3056 account G2192 to him that is [G5723] G2093 ready G2919 to judge [G5658] G2198 the quick [G5723] G2532 and G3498 the dead.

6 G1063 For G1519 for G5124 this cause G2097 was the gospel preached [G5681] G2532 also G3498 to them that are dead G2443 , that G2919 they might be judged [G5686] G3303 G2596 according to G444 men G4561 in the flesh G1161 , but G2198 live [G5725] G2596 according to G2316 God G4151 in the spirit.

KNOWING GOD PRODUCES MORE ACTIONS OF LOVE

We are called by God to learn the knowledge of God and Jesus so we may have grace and peace. By faith we will receive the promises. Then through the divine nature we will learn virtue, knowledge, temperance, patience, godliness, brotherly kindness, and charity. When we abound in these attributes we will abound in the knowledge of our Lord Jesus Christ.

When we reflect Jesus to the world we will make our calling a certainty.

Our actions are more important than our knowledge. Remind our brothers in Christ to keep these traits and to never forget that we have come from a sin filled life, into the glorious promise of God.

2 Peter 1:2-12 Strongs

2 G5485 Grace G2532 and G1515 peace G4129 be multiplied [G5684] G5213 unto you G1722 through G1922 the knowledge G2316 of God G2532 , and G2424 of Jesus G2257 our G2962 Lord,

3 G5613 According as G846 his G2304 divine G1411 power G1433 hath given [G5772] G2254 unto us G3956 all things G4314 that pertain unto G2222 life G2532 and G2150 godliness G1223 , through G1922 the knowledge G2564 of him that hath called [G5660] G2248 us G1223 to G1391 glory G2532 and G703 virtue:

4 G1223 Whereby G3739 G1433 are given [G5769] G2254 unto us G3176 exceeding great G2532 and G5093 precious G1862 promises G2443 : that G1223 by G5130 these G1096 ye might be [G5638] G2844 partakers G2304 of the divine G5449 nature G668 , having escaped [G5631] G5356 the corruption G1722 that is in G2889 the world G1722 through G1939 lust.

5 G2532 And G1161 G846 beside G5124 this G3923 , giving [G5660] G3956 all G4710 diligence G2023 , add [G5657] G1722 to G5216 your G4102 faith G703 virtue G1161 ; and G1722 to G703 virtue G1108 knowledge;

6 G1161 And G1722 to G1108 knowledge G1466 temperance G1161 ; and G1722 to G1466 temperance G5281 patience G1161 ; and G1722 to G5281 patience G2150 godliness;

7 G1161 And G1722 to G2150 godliness G5360 brotherly kindness G1161 ; and G1722 to G5360 brotherly kindness G26 charity.

8 G1063 For G5023 if these things G5225 be [G5723] G5213 in you G2532 , and G4121 abound [G5723] G2525 , they make [G5719] G3756 you that

ye shall neither G692 be barren G3761 nor G175 unfruitful G1519 in G1922 the knowledge G2257 of our G2962 Lord G2424 Jesus G5547 Christ.

9 G1063 But G3739 he that G3361 lacketh G3918 [G5748] G5023 these things G2076 is [G5748] G5185 blind G3467 , and cannot see afar off [G5723] G3024 , and hath forgotten G2983 [G5631] G2512 that he was purged from G846 his G3819 old G266 sins.

10 G1352 Wherefore G3123 the rather G80 , brethren G4704 , give diligence [G5657] G4160 to make [G5733] G5216 your G2821 calling G2532 and G1589 election G949 sure G1063 : for G4160 if ye do [G5723] G5023 these things G4218 , ye shall G4417 G3364 never G4218 fall G4417 [G5661]:

11 G1063 For G3779 so G1529 an entrance G2023 shall be ministered [G5701] G5213 unto you G4146 abundantly G1519 into G166 the everlasting G932 kingdom G2257 of our G2962 Lord G2532 and G4990 Saviour G2424 Jesus G5547 Christ.

12 G1352 Wherefore G272 I will G3756 not G272 be negligent [G5692] G5279 to put G5209 you G104 always G5279 in remembrance [G5721] G4012 of G5130 these things G2539 , though G1492 ye know [G5761] G2532 them, and G4741 be established [G5772] G1722 in G3918 the present [G5752] G225 truth.

TRANSFIGURATION PART FOUR

At the transfiguration Peter saw Jesus with Moses and Elijah. This is recorded in Mathew, Mark, and Luke. Earlier in the study we covered these passages. I find it interesting what stood out to Peter was the majesty of Jesus being audibly confirmed by God. Even years later what stuck in his memory so vividly was hearing the voice from heaven. Seeing Moses and Elijah didn't even rate a footnote.

2 Peter 1:16-18 Strongs

16 G1063 For G1811 we have G3756 not G1811 followed [G5660] G4679 cunningly devised [G5772] G3454 fables G1107 , when we made known [G5656] G5213 unto you G1411 the power G2532 and G3952 coming G2257 of our G2962 Lord G2424 Jesus G5547 Christ G235 , but G1096 were [G5679] G2030 eyewitnesses G1565 of his G3168 majesty.

17 G1063 For G2983 he received [G5631] G3844 from G2316 God G3962 the Father G5092 honour G2532 and G1391 glory G5342 , when there came [G5685] G5107 such G5456 a voice G846 to him G5259 from G3169 the excellent G1391 glory G3778 , This G2076 is [G5748] G3450 my G27 beloved G5207 Son G1519 , in G3739 whom G1473 I G2106 am well pleased [G5656].

18 G2532 And G5026 this G5456 voice G5342 which came [G5685] G1537 from G3772 heaven G2249 we G191 heard [G5656] G5607 , when we were [G5752] G4862 with G846 him G1722 in G40 the holy G3735 mount.

THE DAY OF JUDGEMENT IS COMMING

It is odd that while Jesus was in the tomb he would have gone to preach to the imprisoned spirits from the time of Noah. When here God says they are to be reserved until the day of judgement to be punished along with other sinners, and fallen angels.

2 Peter 2:4-9 Strongs

4 G1063 For G1487 if G2316 God G5339 spared [G5662] G3756 not G32 the angels G264 that sinned [G5660] G235 , but G5020 cast them down to hell [G5660] G3860 , and delivered [G5656] G4577 them into chains G2217 of darkness G5083 , to be reserved [G5772] G1519 unto G2920 judgment;

5 G2532 And G5339 spared [G5662] G3756 not G744 the old G2889 world G235 , but G5442 saved [G5656] G3575 Noah G3590 the eighth G2783 person, a preacher G1343 of righteousness G1863 , bringing in [G5660] G2627 the flood G2889 upon the world G765 of the ungodly;

6 G2532 And G5077 turning G4172 the cities G4670 of Sodom G2532 and G1116 Gomorrha G5077 into ashes [G5660] G2632 condemned [G5656] G2692 them with an overthrow G5087 , making [G5761] G5262 them an ensample G3195 unto those that after should [G5723] G764 live ungodly [G5721];

7 G2532 And G4506 delivered [G5673] G1342 just G3091 Lot G2669 , vexed [G5746] G5259 with G766 the filthy G391 conversation G1722 of G113 the wicked:

8 G1063 (For G1342 that righteous man G1460 dwelling [G5723] G1722 among G846 them G990 , in seeing G2532 and G189 hearing G928 , vexed [G5707] G1342 his righteous G5590 soul G2250 from day G1537 to G2250 day G459 with their unlawful G2041 deeds;)

9 G2962 The Lord G1492 knoweth [G5758] G4506 how to deliver [G5738] G2152 the godly G1537 out of G3986 temptations G1161 , and G5083 to reserve [G5721] G94 the unjust G1519 unto G2250 the day G2920 of judgment G2849 to be punished [G5746]:

THE LATTER END IS WORSE

For those called by God now, we need to count the cost when we accept Jesus and his redemption. God is faithful to finish the good work he starts in us. He won't give up on us, but we can choose to turn our backs on him. The fate of those who do, won't be good. We will all get one chance at salvation. Don't waist yours.

2 Peter 2:20-22 Strongs

20 G1063 For G1487 if G668 after they have escaped [G5631] G3393 the pollutions G2889 of the world G1722 through G1922 the knowledge G2962 of the Lord G2532 and G4990 Saviour G2424 Jesus G5547 Christ G1707 , they are G3825 again G1707 entangled [G5651] G5125 therein G1161 , and G1096 overcome [G5754] G2274 [G5736] G2078 , the latter end G5501 is worse G846 with them G4413 than the beginning.

21 G1063 For G2258 it had been [G5713] G2909 better G846 for them G3361 not G1921 to have known [G5760] G3598 the way G1343 of righteousness G2228 , than G1921 , after they have known [G5631] G1994 it, to turn [G5658] G1537 from G40 the holy G1785 commandment G3860 delivered [G5685] G846 unto them.

22 G1161 But G4819 it is happened [G5758] G846 unto them G3588 according to G227 the true G3942 proverb G2965 , The dog G1994 is turned G1909 to G2398 his own G1829 vomit G1994 again [G5660] G2532 ; and G5300 the sow G3068 that was washed [G5671] G1519 to G2946 her wallowing G1004 in the mire.

A NEW WORLD IS COMING

God want's everyone to repent and be saved, however he won't force us to accept him, he will let us choose our own fate, life or death.

The day of the Lord will be longer than one earth day. V.8 God doesn't only count a day using the revolution of the earth. He will keep his promise.

This world and heavens will be burnt up and will melt away. If, as some people think, mankind stays in the physical realm, where do we survive physically at this time of melting?

We look for a new heaven and earth according to his promise. He has promised us new spiritual bodies, and we will be dwelling righteously in them. We will no longer need this physical earth to sustain life. We will be able to dwell with Jesus for we will be like him.

2 Peter 3:7-13 Strongs

7 G1161 But G3772 the heavens G2532 and G1093 the earth G3568 , which are now G846 , by the same G3056 word G1526 are [G5748] G2343 kept in store [G5772] G5083 , reserved [G5746] G4442 unto fire G1519 against G2250 the day G2920 of judgment G2532 and G684 perdition

G765 of ungodly G444 men.

8 G1161 But G27 , beloved G2990 , be G3361 not G5209 G2990 ignorant [G5720] G1520 of this one G5124 thing G3754 , that G3391 one G2250 day G3844 is with G2962 the Lord G5613 as G5507 a thousand G2094 years G2532 , and G5507 a thousand G2094 years G5613 as G3391 one G2250 day.

9 G2962 The Lord G1019 is G3756 not G1019 slack [G5719] G1860 concerning his promise G5613 , as G5100 some men G2233 count [G5736] G1022 slackness G235 ; but G3114 is longsuffering [G5719] G1519 to G2248 us-ward G3361 , not G1014 willing [G5740] G5100 that any G622 should perish [G5641] G235 , but G3956 that all G5562 should come [G5658] G1519 to G3341 repentance.

10 G1161 But G2250 the day G2962 of the Lord G2240 will come [G5692] G5613 as G2812 a thief G1722 in G3571 the night G1722 ; in G3739 the which G3772 the heavens G3928 shall pass away [G5695] G4500 with a great noise G1161 , and G4747 the elements G3089 shall melt [G5701] G2741 with fervent heat [G5746] G1093 , the earth G2532 also G2532 and G2041 the works G1722 that are therein G846 G2618 shall be burned up [G5691].

11 G3767 Seeing then G3956 that all G5130 these things G3089 shall be dissolved [G5746] G4217 , what manner G1163 of persons ought [G5748] G5209 ye G5225 to be [G5721] G1722 in G40 all holy G391 conversation G2532 and G2150 godliness,

12 G4328 Looking for [G5723] G2532 and G4692 hasting [G5723] G3952 unto the coming G2250 of the day G2316 of God G1223 , wherein G3739 G3772 the heavens G4448 being on fire [G5746] G3089 shall be dissolved [G5701] G2532 , and G4747 the elements G5080 shall melt [G5743] G2741 with fervent heat [G5746]?

13 G1161 Nevertheless G4328 we G2596 , according to G846 his G1862 promise G4328 , look for [G5719] G2537 new G3772 heavens G2532 and

G2537 a new G1093 earth G1722 , wherein G3739 G2730 dwelleth [G5719] G1343 righteousness.

Chapter 33: BOOKS OF 1 JOHN AND JUDE

A PROMISE IS IN THE FUTURE

The promise of God is eternal life.

1 John 2:25 Strongs

25 G2532 And G3778 this G2076 is [G5748] G1860 the promise G3739 that G846 he G1861 hath promised [G5662] G2254 us G166 , even eternal G2222 life.

FOR WE WILL BE LIKE HIM

Not only eternal life, but we are to be the sons of God. We don't know how we will appear, but we do know that we will be like him for we shall see him as he is.

1 John 3:1-3 Strongs

1 G1492 Behold [G5628] G4217 , what manner G26 of love G3962 the Father G1325 hath bestowed [G5758] G2254 upon us G2443 , that G2564 we should be called [G5686] G5043 the sons G2316 of God G1223 : therefore G5124 G2889 the world G1097 knoweth [G5719] G2248 us G3756 not G3754 , because G1097 it knew [G5627] G846 him G3756 not.

2 G27 Beloved G3568 , now G2070 are we [G5748] G5043 the sons G2316 of God G2532 , and G5319 it doth G3768 not yet G5319 appear [G5681] G5101 what G2071 we shall be [G5704] G1161 : but G1492 we know [G5758] G3754 that G1437 , when G5319 he shall appear [G5686] G2071 ,

we shall be [G5704] G3664 like G846 him G3754 ; for G3700 we shall see [G5695] G846 him G2531 as G2076 he is [G5748].

3 G2532 And G3956 every man G2192 that hath [G5723] G5026 this G1680 hope G1909 in G846 him G48 purifieth [G5719] G1438 himself G2531 , even as G1565 he G2076 is [G5748] G53 pure.

PROOF OF LOVE

Jesus is the appeasement for our sins.

1 John 4:10 Strongs

10 G1722 Herein G5129 G2076 is [G5748] G26 love G3754 , not G3756 that G2249 we G25 loved [G5656] G2316 God G235 , but G3754 that G846 he G25 loved [G5656] G2248 us G2532 , and G649 sent [G5656] G846 his G5207 Son G2434 to be the propitiation G4012 for G2257 our G266 sins.

WHO CAN SAY THEY HAVE SEEN GOD

No one, has seen (looked on, beheld, gazed at, viewed), God at any time (ever).

1 John 4:12 Strongs

12 G3762 No man G2300 hath seen [G5766] G2316 God G4455 at any time G1437 . If G25 we love [G5725] G240 one another G2316 , God G3306 dwelleth [G5719] G1722 in G2254 us G2532 , and G846 his G26 love G2076 is [G5748] G5048 perfected [G5772] G1722 in G2254 us.

GOD IS LOVE. FILL YOURSELF UP.

Jesus is the saviour of the world. Those that believe in Jesus will live in God and God in them.

1 John 4:14-16 Strongs

14 G2532 And G2249 we G2300 have seen [G5766] G2532 and G3140 do testify [G5719] G3754 that G3962 the Father G649 sent [G5758] G5207 the Son G4990 to be the Saviour G2889 of the world.

15 G3739 Whosoever G302 G3670 shall confess [G5661] G3754 that G2424 Jesus G2076 is [G5748] G5207 the Son G2316 of God G2316 , God G3306 dwelleth [G5719] G1722 in G846 him G2532 , and G846 he G1722 in G2316 God.

16 G2532 And G2249 we G1097 have known [G5758] G2532 and G4100 believed [G5758] G26 the love G3739 that G2316 God G2192 hath [G5719] G1722 to G2254 us G2316 . God G2076 is [G5748] G26 love G2532 ; and G3306 he that dwelleth [G5723] G1722 in G26 love G3306 dwelleth [G5719] G1722 in G2316 God G2532 , and G2316 God G1722 in G846 him.

ABSENCE OF LIFE EQUALS DEAD

If we have the son of God, we have eternal life. If we don't have the son of God, we don't have eternal life. If we have eternal life, we will live eternally with God in his Kingdom. If we don't have eternal life, we will die in the fires of Gehenna and be dead for the rest of eternity.

1 John 5:10-13 Strongs

10 G4100 He that believeth [G5723] G1519 on G5207 the Son G2316 of God G2192 hath [G5719] G3141 the witness G1722 in G1438 himself G4100 : he that believeth [G5723] G3361 not G2316 God G4160 hath made [G5758] G846 him G5583 a liar G3754 ; because G4100 he believeth [G5758] G3756 not G1519 G3141 the record G3739 that G2316 God G3140 gave [G5758] G4012 of G846 his G5207 Son.

11 G2532 And G3778 this G2076 is [G5748] G3141 the record G3754 , that G2316 God G1325 hath given [G5656] G2254 to us G166 eternal G2222

life G2532 , and G3778 this G2222 life G2076 is [G5748] G1722 in G846 his G5207 Son.

12 G2192 He that hath [G5723] G5207 the Son G2192 hath [G5719] G2222 life G2192 ; and he that hath [G5723] G3361 not G5207 the Son G2316 of God G2192 hath [G5719] G3756 not G2222 life.

13 G5023 These things G1125 have I written [G5656] G5213 unto you G4100 that believe [G5723] G1519 on G3686 the name G5207 of the Son G2316 of God G2443 ; that G1492 ye may know [G5762] G3754 that ye G2192 have [G5719] G166 eternal G2222 life G2532 , and G2443 that G4100 ye may believe [G5725] G1519 on G3686 the name G5207 of the Son G2316 of God.

WALK THE WALK NOT TALK THE TALK

People who say they are believers but don't know God, are said to be like trees without fruit. Fit only to be tore out by the roots. Twice dead suggests that after being judged by God the wicked will die again. As we have read before, the wicked will be thrown into the fires of Gehenna where they will die a second time.

Jude 1:12-13 Strongs

12 G3778 These G1526 are [G5748] G4694 spots G1722 in G5216 your G26 feasts of charity G4910 , when they feast [G5740] G5213 with you G4165 , feeding [G5723] G1438 themselves G870 without fear G3507 : clouds G504 they are without water G4064 , carried about [G5746] G5259 of G417 winds G1186 ; trees G5352 whose fruit withereth G175 , without fruit G1364 , twice G599 dead [G5631] G1610 , plucked up by the roots [G5685];

13 G66 Raging G2949 waves G2281 of the sea G1890 , foaming out [G5723] G1438 their own G152 shame G4107 ; wandering G792 stars G3739 , to whom G5083 is reserved [G5769] G2217 the blackness G4655 of darkness G1519 for G165 ever.

KEEP YOUR CUP OVERFLOWING

Eternal life is through Jesus.

Jude 1:21 Strongs

21 G5083 Keep [G5657] G1438 yourselves G1722 in G26 the love G2316 of God G4327 , looking for [G5740] G1656 the mercy G2257 of our G2962 Lord G2424 Jesus G5547 Christ G1519 unto G166 eternal G2222 life.

Chapter 34: BOOK OF REVELATION

THE RETURN
I feel it is important to keep in mind the book of Revelation is about the revealing of Jesus Christ. It is a message for us, the servants of Jesus from God. It was passed on to John by one of God's angels. It primarily is to tell us how Jesus will be revealed to the world.

Revelation 1:1 Strongs

1 G602 The Revelation G2424 of Jesus G5547 Christ G3739 , which G2316 God G1325 gave [G5656] G846 unto him G1166 , to shew [G5658] G846 unto his G1401 servants G3739 things which G1163 must [G5748] G1722 shortly G5034 G1096 come to pass [G5635] G2532 ; and G649 he sent [G5660] G4591 and signified [G5656] G1223 it by G846 his G32 angel G846 unto his G1401 servant G2491 John:

NO ONE COULD BE SAVED UNTILL WASHED BY JESUS
Jesus was the first begotten of the dead. He was the first one to be brought back from the dead. He was the first one to be resurrected to spirit filled life. No one preceded him. He was the first.

Revelation 1:5 Strongs

5 G2532 And G575 from G2424 Jesus G5547 Christ G4103 , who is the faithful G3144 witness G4416 , and the first begotten G1537 of

G3498 the dead G2532 , and G758 the prince G935 of the kings G1093 of the earth G25 . Unto him that loved [G5660] G2248 us G2532 , and G3068 washed [G5660] G2248 us G575 from G2257 our G266 sins G1722 in G846 his own G129 blood,

GODS KINGS AND PRIESTS SERVE OTHERS

We will be the kings and priests in the Kingdom. Kings over who? Priests to who?

Revelation 1:6 Strongs

6 G2532 And G4160 hath made [G5656] G2248 us G935 kings G2532 and G2409 priests G2316 unto God G2532 and G846 his G3962 Father G846 ; to him G1391 be glory G2532 and G2904 dominion G1519 for G165 ever G165 and ever G281 . Amen.

A REALLY BIG SHOW

The return of Jesus won't be done in secret. Every eye shall see him.

Revelation 1:7 Strongs

7 G2400 Behold [G5628] G2064 , he cometh [G5736] G3326 with G3507 clouds G2532 ; and G3956 every G3788 eye G3700 shall see [G5695] G846 him G2532 , and G3748 they also which G1574 pierced [G5656] G846 him G2532 : and G3956 all G5443 kindreds G1093 of the earth G2875 shall wail [G5695] G1909 because G846 of him G3483 . Even so G281 , Amen.

OPPOSITES IN FACT

Jesus was alive, and was dead. Opposites of each other. As much as he was alive, he was dead. The definition of dead is not just bodily but cognitively as well. We don't measure death. We measure life. Is there brain function, is there breath or a pulse? Death is the absence of these things. When you stop functioning on all levels of life, then you are dead. Jesus was dead, but now because God resurrected him out of the tomb, he is alive for evermore. He holds the keys to hell and death, he alone can save us.

Revelation 1:18 Strongs

18 G2532 G2198 I am he that liveth [G5723] G2532 , and G1096 was [G5633] G3498 dead G2532 ; and G2400 , behold [G5628] G1510 , I am [G5748] G2198 alive [G5723] G1519 for G165 evermore G165 G281 , Amen G2532 ; and G2192 have [G5719] G2807 the keys G86 of hell G2532 and G2288 of death.

WE NEED EARS THAT HEAR

This is the first time we are told about the tree of life since the Garden of Eden. We are told its location. Jesus tells us we can eat from the Tree of Life if we overcome.

Revelation 2:7 Strongs

7 G2192 He that hath [G5723] G3775 an ear G191 , let him hear [G5657] G5101 what G4151 the Spirit G3004 saith [G5719] G1577 unto the churches G846 ; To him G3528 that overcometh [G5723] G1325 will I give [G5692] G5315 to eat [G5629] G1537 of G3586 the tree G2222 of life G3739 , which G2076 is [G5748] G1722 in G3319 the midst G3857 of the paradise G2316 of God.

SECOND DEATH DEMANDS A SECOND LIFE

Reminiscent of twice dead, those that overcome won't be hurt by the second death.

Revelation 2:11 Strongs

11 G2192 He that hath [G5723] G3775 an ear G191 , let him hear

[G5657] G5101 what G4151 the Spirit G3004 saith [G5719] G1577 unto the churches G1528 ; He that overcometh [G5723] G91 shall G3364 not G91 be hurt [G5686] G1537 of G1208 the second G2288 death.

GOOD WORKS BANK OF GOD

We will receive according to our works. This receiving is not eternal life which is a free gift of God. But a separate receiving according to our works. We need to store up our treasures in heaven.

Revelation 2:23 Strongs

23 G2532 And G615 I will kill [G5692] G846 her G5043 children G1722 with G2288 death G2532 ; and G3956 all G1577 the churches G1097 shall know [G5695] G3754 that G1473 I G1510 am [G5748] G3588 he which G2045 searcheth [G5723] G3510 the reins G2532 and G2588 hearts G2532 : and G1325 I will give [G5692] G1538 unto every one G5213 of you G2596 according to G5216 your G2041 works.

Matthew 6:19-20 Strongs

19 G2343 Lay G3361 not G2343 up [G5720] G5213 for yourselves G2344 treasures G1909 upon G1093 earth G3699 , where G4597 moth G2532 and G1035 rust G853 doth corrupt [G5719] G2532 , and G3699 where G2812 thieves G1358 break through [G5719] G2532 and G2813 steal [G5719]:

20 G1161 But G2343 lay up [G5720] G5213 for yourselves G2344 treasures G1722 in G3772 heaven G3699 , where G3777 neither G4597 moth G3777 nor G1035 rust G853 doth corrupt [G5719] G2532 , and G3699 where G2812 thieves G1358 do G3756 not G1358 break through [G5719] G3761 nor G2813 steal [G5719]:

KINGS AND PRIESTS OF GOD

The followers of Jesus are again told they will rule over people in the Kingdom. What people would this be? Where are they from? What happens to them? How long will they be there? When do they get to accept Jesus, or have they already?

Revelation 2:26-27 Strongs

26 G2532 And G3528 he that overcometh [G5723] G2532 , and G5083 keepeth [G5723] G3450 my G2041 works G891 unto G5056 the end G846 , to him G1325 will I give [G5692] G1849 power G1909 over G1484 the nations:

27 G2532 And G4165 he shall rule [G5692] G846 them G1722 with G4464 a rod G4603 of iron G5613 ; as G4632 the vessels G2764 of a potter G4937 shall they be broken to shivers [G5743] G2504 : even G5613 as G2504 I G2983 received [G5758] G3844 of G3450 my G3962 Father.

STICK TO YOUR PATH

The Sardis church had problems. But there were still a few Jesus would claim for his own. This verse shows us that if we fall away from our Lord, there is a point of no coming back. Some had their names in the book of life, but because of their actions, their names will be blotted out. They were as good as there. But in the end, their names will not be confessed to the Father. Church, listen and heed this warning from God.

Revelation 3:4-6 Strongs

4 G2192 Thou hast [G5719] G3641 a few G3686 names G2532 even G1722 in G4554 Sardis G3739 which G3435 have G3756 not G3435 defiled [G5656] G846 their G2440 garments G2532 ; and G4043 they shall walk [G5692] G3326 with G1700 me G1722 in G3022

white G3754 : for G1526 they are [G5748] G514 worthy.

5 G3528 He that overcometh [G5723] G3778 , the same G4016 shall be clothed [G5698] G1722 in G3022 white G2440 raiment G2532 ; and G1813 I will G3364 not G1813 blot out [G5692] G846 his G3686 name G1537 out of G976 the book G2222 of life G2532 , but G1843 I will confess [G5698] G846 his G3686 name G1799 before G3450 my G3962 Father G2532 , and G1799 before G846 his G32 angels.

6 G2192 He that hath [G5723] G3775 an ear G191 , let him hear [G5657] G5101 what G4151 the Spirit G3004 saith [G5719] G1577 unto the churches.

HE ALONE IS WORTHY OF ALL PRAISE

As with most things in life, and in the bible, this next set of scriptures has many differing interpretations. My goal with this bible study is not to tell you what to think about a particular scripture or topic. Rather, to give sound biblical reasoning, supported by scripture, that would cause you to give some credence to the possibility of another points of view. In doing so you will examine your own beliefs and put them to the test of scripture to see if they stand up to it. Such examining should strengthen your faith, not weaken it, for you will be sure of where it comes from. Even if you don't agree, you may see how others might agree and be ready to gently point out the misunderstanding. I want to have liberty and discussion in the peripheral, and unity on the essential. We may not agree, but we should defend each other’s liberty of thought.

Who the four beasts and four and twenty elders are, where they are from, is not what I wanted to highlight here. Rather, I want to use these scriptures to show the stature of Jesus and his pivotal role in salvation. For he is worthy of our praise and worship. He alone is our redeemer.

Revelation 5:8-14 Strongs

8 G2532 And G3753 when G2983 he had taken [G5627] G975 the book G5064 , the four G2226 beasts G2532 and G5064 four G1501 and twenty G4245 elders G4098 fell down [G5627] G1799 before G721 the Lamb G2192 , having [G5723] G1538 every one of them G2788 harps G2532 , and G5552 golden G5357 vials G1073 full [G5723] G2368 of odours G3739 , which G1526 are [G5748] G4335 the prayers G40 of saints.

9 G2532 And G103 they sung [G5719] G2537 a new G5603 song G3004 , saying [G5723] G1488 , Thou art [G5748] G514 worthy G2983 to take [G5629] G975 the book G2532 , and G455 to open [G5658] G4973 the seals G846 thereof G3754 : for G4969 thou wast slain [G5648] G2532 , and G59 hast redeemed [G5656] G2248 us G2316 to God G1722 by G4675 thy G129 blood G1537 out of G3956 every G5443 kindred G2532 , and G1100 tongue G2532 , and G2992 people G2532 , and G1484 nation;

10 G2532 And G4160 hast made [G5656] G2248 us G2257 unto our G2316 God G935 kings G2532 and G2409 priests G2532 : and G936 we shall reign [G5692] G1909 on G1093 the earth.

11 G2532 And G1492 I beheld [G5627] G2532 , and G191 I heard [G5656] G5456 the voice G4183 of many G32 angels G2943 round about G2362 the throne G2532 and G2226 the beasts G2532 and G4245 the elders G2532 : and G706 the number G846 of them G2258 was [G5713] G3461 ten thousand G3461 times ten thousand G2532 , and G5505 thousands G5505 of thousands;

12 G3004 Saying [G5723] G3173 with a loud G5456 voice G514 , Worthy G2076 is [G5748] G721 the Lamb G4969 that was slain [G5772] G2983 to receive [G5629] G1411 power G2532 , and G4149 riches G2532 , and G4678 wisdom G2532 , and G2479 strength G2532 , and G5092 honour G2532 , and G1391 glory G2532 , and G2129 blessing.

13 G2532 And G3956 every G2938 creature G3739 which G2076 is [G5748] G1722 in G3772 heaven G2532 , and G1722 on G1093 the earth G2532 , and G5270 under G1093 the earth G2532 , and G3739 such as G2076 are [G5748] G1909 in G2281 the sea G2532 , and G3956 all G1722 that are in G846 them G191 , heard I [G5656] G3004 saying [G5723] G2129 , Blessing G2532 , and G5092 honour G2532 , and G1391 glory G2532 , and G2904 power G2521 , be unto him that sitteth [G5740] G1909 upon G2362 the throne G2532 , and G721 unto the Lamb G1519 for G165 ever G165 and ever.

14 G2532 And G5064 the four G2226 beasts G3004 said [G5707] G281 , Amen G2532 . And G5064 the four G1501 and twenty G4245 elders G4098 fell down [G5627] G2532 and G4352 worshipped [G5656] G2198 him that liveth [G5723] G1519 for G165 ever G165 and ever.

REST UNTILL ALL ARE READY

Those given the white robes were to rest for a little season until other servants of Jesus are killed. What kind of rest are they to have? Where are they going to rest? These questions aren't addressed in this passage. To get a clue as to what the answers may be, we should consult the bible, to see what God tells us where other people will be waiting. David and the other kings of Israel said that they would be sleeping in their graves, waiting for their salvation.

Revelation 6:11 Strongs

11 G2532 And G3022 white G4749 robes G1325 were given [G5681] G1538 unto every one of them G2532 ; and G4483 it was said [G5681] G846 unto them G2443 , that G373 they should rest [G5672] G2089 yet G3398 for a little G5550 season G2193 , until G846 their G4889 fellowservants G2532 also G2532 and G846 their G80 brethren G3195 , that should [G5723] G615 be killed [G5745] G5613 as G2532 G846 they G3739 were, should G4137 be fulfilled [G5695].

DAY OF RECKONING BEGINS

Some people may think the seals of Revelation's have been opened already. Few think the sixth seal has already happened. I think it would be hard to miss.

Revelation 6:12-14 Strongs

12 G2532 And G1492 I beheld [G5627] G3753 when G455 he had opened [G5656] G1623 the sixth G4973 seal G2532 , and G2400 , lo [G5628] G1096 , there was [G5633] G3173 a great G4578 earthquake G2532 ; and G2246 the sun G1096 became [G5633] G3189 black G5613 as G4526 sackcloth G5155 of hair G2532 , and G4582 the moon G1096 became [G5633] G5613 as G129 blood;

13 G2532 And G792 the stars G3772 of heaven G4098 fell [G5627] G1519 unto G1093 the earth G5613 , even as G4808 a fig tree G906 casteth [G5719] G846 her G3653 untimely figs G4579 , when she is shaken [G5746] G5259 of G3173 a mighty G417 wind.

14 G2532 And G3772 the heaven G673 departed [G5681] G5613 as G975 a scroll G1507 when it is rolled together [G5746] G2532 ; and G3956 every G3735 mountain G2532 and G3520 island G2795 were moved [G5681] G1537 out of G846 their G5117 places.

This is the start of the day of the Lord. It lasts for more than one earth day. Jesus doesn't return to fight against the Beast and Antichrist for quite a while.

Revelation 6:17 Strongs

17 G3754 For G3173 the great G2250 day G846 of his G3709 wrath G2064 is come [G5627] G2532 ; and G5101 who G1410 shall be able [G5736] G2476 to stand [G5683]?

AS LONG AS PEOPLE ARE ALIVE GOD MAY CALL
John is seeing a vision of what is to come. The people in white robes are the ones that come out of great tribulation.

Revelation 7:14 Strongs

14 G2532 And G2046 I said [G5758] G846 unto him G2962 , Sir G4771 , thou G1492 knowest [G5758] G2532 . And G2036 he said [G5627] G3427 to me G3778 , These G1526 are they [G5748] G2064 which came [G5740] G1537 out of G3173 great G2347 tribulation G2532 , and G4150 have washed [G5656] G846 their G4749 robes G2532 , and G3021 made G4749 them G846 G3021 white [G5656] G1722 in G129 the blood G721 of the Lamb.

IT'S THE END OF THE WORLD AS WE KNOW IT
Christ still hasn't returned yet in these verses. The second coming is still being looked forward to by the faithful at this time. It is important to note the seventh seal is made up of seven angels, each with a specific job to do.

Revelation 8:1-2 Strongs

1 G2532 And G3753 when G455 he had opened [G5656] G1442 the seventh G4973 seal G1096 , there was [G5633] G4602 silence G1722 in G3772 heaven G5613 about the space of G2256 half an hour.

2 G2532 And G1492 I saw [G5627] G2033 the seven G32 angels G3739 which G2476 stood [G5758] G1799 before G2316 God G2532 ; and G846 to them G1325 were given [G5681] G2033 seven G4536 trumpets.

The angel opening the sixth seal reveals four angels who are loosed to deliver the punishments of the sixth seal on mankind.

Revelation 9:14-15 Strongs

14 G3004 Saying [G5723] G1623 to the sixth G32 angel G3739 which G2192 had [G5707] G4536 the trumpet G3089 , Loose [G5657] G5064 the four G32 angels G3588 which G1210 are bound [G5772] G1909 in G3173 the great G4215 river G2166 Euphrates.

15 G2532 And G5064 the four G32 angels G3089 were loosed [G5681] G3588 , which G2090 were prepared [G5772] G1519 for G5610 an hour G2532 , and G2250 a day G2532 , and G3376 a month G2532 , and G1763 a year G2443 , for to G615 slay [G5725] G5154 the third part G444 of men.

HIS VISION WAS LIKE REALITY

This vision that John has is very realistic. So real he could taste it.

Revelation 10:9-10 Strongs

9 G2532 And G565 I went [G5627] G4314 unto G32 the angel G3004 , and said [G5723] G846 unto him G1325 , Give [G5628] G3427 me G974 the little book G2532 . And G3004 he said [G5719] G3427 unto me G2983 , Take [G5628] G2532 it, and G2719 eat G846 it G2719 up [G5628] G2532 ; and it G4087 shall make G4675 thy G2836 belly G4087 bitter [G5692] G235 , but G2071 it shall be [G5704] G1722 in G4675 thy G4750 mouth G1099 sweet G5613 as G3192 honey.

10 G2532 And G2983 I took [G5627] G974 the little book G1537 out of G32 the angel's G5495 hand G2532 , and G2719 ate G846 it G2719 up [G5627] G2532 ; and G2258 it was [G5713] G1722 in G3450 my G4750 mouth G1099 sweet G5613 as G3192 honey G2532 : and G3753 as soon as G5315 I had eaten [G5627] G846 it G3450 , my G2836 belly G4087 was bitter [G5681].

END TIME OVERVUE
This section of scripture takes us to the time of the two witnesses during the tribulation. Then the seventh angel sounded and proclaims that Gods kingdom is here, and he shall reign for ever and ever. V18 It's not till after this takes place that the dead are judged and the righteous receive their rewards.

Revelation 11:11-19 Strongs

11 G2532 And G3326 after G5140 three G2250 days G2532 and G2255 an half G4151 the Spirit G2222 of life G1537 from G2316 God G1525 entered [G5627] G1909 into G846 them G2532 , and G2476 they stood [G5627] G1909 upon G846 their G4228 feet G2532 ; and G3173 great G5401 fear G4098 fell [G5627] G1909 upon G2334 them which saw [G5723] G846 them.

12 G2532 And G191 they heard [G5656] G3173 a great G5456 voice G1537 from G3772 heaven G3004 saying [G5723] G846 unto them G305 , Come up [G5628] G5602 hither G2532 . And G305 they ascended up [G5627] G1519 to G3772 heaven G1722 in G3507 a cloud G2532 ; and G846 their G2190 enemies G2334 beheld [G5656] G846 them.

13 G2532 And G1722 the same G1565 G5610 hour G1096 was there [G5633] G3173 a great G4578 earthquake G2532 , and G1182 the tenth part G4172 of the city G4098 fell [G5627] G2532 , and G1722 in G4578 the earthquake G615 were slain [G5681] G3686 G444 of men G2033 seven G5505 thousand G2532 : and G3062 the remnant G1096 were [G5633] G1719 affrighted G2532 , and G1325 gave [G5656] G1391 glory G2316 to the God G3772 of heaven.

14 G1208 The second G3759 woe G565 is past [G5627] G2532 ; and G2400 , behold [G5628] G5154 , the third G3759 woe G2064 cometh [G5736] G5035 quickly.

15 G2532 And G1442 the seventh G32 angel G4537 sounded
[G5656] G2532 ; and G1096 there were [G5633] G3173 great
G5456 voices G1722 in G3772 heaven G3004 , saying [G5723]
G932 , The kingdoms G2889 of this world G1096 are become
[G5633] G2257 the kingdoms of our G2962 Lord G2532 , and G846
of his G5547 Christ G2532 ; and G936 he shall reign [G5692]
G1519 for G165 ever G165 and ever.

16 G2532 And G5064 the four G2532 and G1501 twenty G4245
elders G3588 , which G2521 sat [G5740] G1799 before G2316 God
G1909 on G846 their G2362 seats G4098 , fell [G5627] G1909 upon
G846 their G4383 faces G2532 , and G4352 worshipped [G5656]
G2316 God,

17 G3004 Saying [G5723] G2168 , We give G4671 thee G2168
thanks [G5719] G2962 , O Lord G2316 God G3841 Almighty
G3588 , which G5607 art [G5752] [G5625] G3801 G2532 , and
G2258 wast [G5713] [G5625] G3801 G2532 , and G2064 art to
come [G5740] [G5625] G3801 G3754 ; because G2983 thou hast
taken to thee [G5758] G4675 thy G3173 great G1411 power G2532 ,
and G936 hast reigned [G5656].

18 G2532 And G1484 the nations G3710 were angry [G5681]
G2532 , and G4675 thy G3709 wrath G2064 is come [G5627]
G2532 , and G2540 the time G3498 of the dead G2919 , that they
should be judged [G5683] G2532 , and G1325 that thou shouldest
give [G5629] G3408 reward G4675 unto thy G1401 servants G4396
the prophets G2532 , and G40 to the saints G2532 , and G5399 them
that fear [G5740] G4675 thy G3686 name G3398 , small G2532 and
G3173 great G2532 ; and G1311 shouldest destroy [G5658] G1311
them which destroy [G5723] G1093 the earth.

19 G2532 And G3485 the temple G2316 of God G455 was opened
[G5648] G1722 in G3772 heaven G2532 , and G3700 there was seen
[G5681] G1722 in G846 his G3485 temple G2787 the ark G846 of
his G1242 testament G2532 : and G1096 there were [G5633] G796

lightnings G2532 , and G5456 voices G2532 , and G1027 thunderings G2532 , and G4578 an earthquake G2532 , and G3173 great G5464 hail.

DESCRIPTION OF THE WORLD RULING BEAST

Chapter 12 brakes out from the time line, and we flash back to the birth of Jesus.

Revelation 12:2-3 Strongs

2 G2532 And G2192 she being [G5723] G1722 with G1064 child G2896 cried [G5719] G5605 , travailing in birth [G5723] G2532 , and G928 pained [G5746] G5088 to be delivered [G5629].

3 G2532 And G3700 there appeared [G5681] G243 another G4592 wonder G1722 in G3772 heaven G2532 ; and G2400 behold [G5628] G3173 a great G4450 red G1404 dragon G2192 , having [G5723] G2033 seven G2776 heads G2532 and G1176 ten G2768 horns G2532 , and G2033 seven G1238 crowns G1909 upon G846 his G2776 heads.

PROTECTED BY GOD

During the tribulation the church is taken to a place of safety prepared by God in the wilderness.

Revelation 12:6 Strongs

6 G2532 And G1135 the woman G5343 fled [G5627] G1519 into G2048 the wilderness G3699 , where G2192 she hath [G5719] G5117 a place G2090 prepared [G5772] G575 of G2316 God G2443 , that G5142 they should feed [G5725] G846 her G1563 there G5507 a thousand G1250 two hundred G1835 and threescore G2250 days.

Satan chases the church into the place God has prepared for it. It is safe there during the tribulation and the opening of the remaining seals.

Revelation 12:13-17 Strongs

13 G2532 And G3753 when G1404 the dragon G1492 saw [G5627] G3754 that G906 he was cast [G5681] G1519 unto G1093 the earth G1377 , he persecuted [G5656] G1135 the woman G3748 which G5088 brought forth [G5627] G730 the man child .

14 G2532 And G1135 to the woman G1325 were given [G5681] G1417 two G4420 wings G3173 of a great G105 eagle G2443 , that G4072 she might fly [G5741] G1519 into G2048 the wilderness G1519 , into G846 her G5117 place G3699 , where G5142 she is nourished [G5743] G1563 for a time G2540 G2532 , and G2540 times G2532 , and G2255 half G2540 a time G575 , from G4383 the face G3789 of the serpent.

15 G2532 And G3789 the serpent G906 cast [G5627] G1537 out of G846 his G4750 mouth G5204 water G5613 as G4215 a flood G3694 after G1135 the woman G2443 , that G4160 he might cause [G5661] G5026 her G4216 to be carried away of the flood.

16 G2532 And G1093 the earth G997 helped [G5656] G1135 the woman G2532 , and G1093 the earth G455 opened [G5656] G846 her G4750 mouth G2532 , and G2666 swallowed up [G5627] G4215 the flood G3739 which G1404 the dragon G906 cast [G5627] G1537 out of G846 his G4750 mouth.

17 G2532 And G1404 the dragon G3710 was wroth [G5681] G1909 with G1135 the woman G2532 , and G565 went [G5627] G4160 to make [G5658] G4171 war G3326 with G3062 the remnant G846 of her G4690 seed G3588 , which G5083 keep [G5723] G1785 the commandments G2316 of God G2532 , and G2192 have [G5723] G3141 the testimony G2424 of Jesus G5547 Christ.

THE EVIL EMPIRE

Chapter 13 tells us about the government ruling the political and military establishments of the world. All of mankind will worship him except those that love the Lord.

Revelation 13:6-8 Strongs

6 G2532 And G455 he opened [G5656] G846 his G4750 mouth G1519 in G988 blasphemy G4314 against G2316 God G987 , to blaspheme [G5658] G846 his G3686 name G2532 , and G846 his G4633 tabernacle G2532 , and G4637 them that dwell [G5723] G1722 in G3772 heaven.

7 G2532 And G1325 it was given [G5681] G846 unto him G4160 to make [G5658] G4171 war G3326 with G40 the saints G2532 , and G3528 to overcome [G5658] G846 them G2532 : and G1849 power G1325 was given [G5681] G846 him G1909 over G3956 all G5443 kindreds G2532 , and G1100 tongues G2532 , and G1484 nations.

8 G2532 And G3956 all G2730 that dwell [G5723] G1909 upon G1093 the earth G4352 shall worship [G5692] G846 him G3739 , whose G3686 names G1125 are G3756 not G1125 written [G5769] G1722 in G976 the book G2222 of life G721 of the Lamb G4969 slain [G5772] G575 from G2602 the foundation G2889 of the world.

This world ruling government gives power to the beast of the tribulation.

Revelation 13:15-17 Strongs

15 G2532 And G846 he G1325 had power [G5681] G1325 to give [G5629] G4151 life G1504 unto the image G2342 of the beast G2443 , that G1504 the image G2342 of the beast G2980 should G2532 both G2980 speak [G5661] G2532 , and G4160 cause

[G5661] G3745 that as many as G302 would G4352 G3361 not G4352 worship [G5661] G1504 the image G2342 of the beast G2443 should be killed G615 [G5686].

16 G2532 And G4160 he causeth [G5719] G3956 all G3398 , both small G2532 and G3173 great G2532 , G4145 rich G2532 and G4434 poor G2532 , G1658 free G2532 and G1401 bond G2443 , to G846 G1325 receive [G5661] G5480 a mark G1909 in G846 their G1188 right hand G5495 G2228 , or G1909 in G846 their G3359 foreheads:

17 G2532 And G3363 that no G5100 man G1410 might [G5741] G59 buy [G5658] G2228 or G4453 sell [G5658] G1508 , save he G2192 that had [G5723] G5480 the mark G2228 , or G3686 the name G2342 of the beast G2228 , or G706 the number G846 of his G3686 name.

MESSENGERS OF GOD

The context of this passage is end time. V.6 tells us about an angel preaching to all people dwelling on the earth.

Revelation 14:6-7 Strongs

6 G2532 And G1492 I saw [G5627] G243 another G32 angel G4072 fly [G5740] G1722 in G3321 the midst of heaven G2192 , having [G5723] G166 the everlasting G2098 gospel G2097 to preach [G5658] G2730 unto them that dwell [G5723] G1909 on G1093 the earth G2532 , and G3956 to every G1484 nation G2532 , and G5443 kindred G2532 , and G1100 tongue G2532 , and G2992 people,

7 G3004 Saying [G5723] G1722 with G3173 a loud G5456 voice G5399 , Fear [G5676] G2316 God G2532 , and G1325 give [G5628] G1391 glory G846 to him G3754 ; for G5610 the hour G846 of his G2920 judgment G2064 is come [G5627] G2532 : and G4352 worship [G5657] G4160 him that made [G5660] G3772 heaven

G2532 , and G1093 earth G2532 , and G2281 the sea G2532 , and G4077 the fountains G5204 of waters.

Then another angel followed with a different message to the same people. People that dwell on the earth.

Revelation 14:8 Strongs

8 G2532 And G190 there followed [G5656] G243 another G32 angel G3004 , saying [G5723] G897 , Babylon G4098 is fallen [G5627] G4098 , is fallen [G5627] G3173 , that great G4172 city G3754 , because G4222 she made G3956 all G1484 nations G4222 drink [G5758] G1537 of G3631 the wine G2372 of the wrath G846 of her G4202 fornication.

This third angel who is preaching to people that dwell on the earth before the return of Jesus. Tells them that if they worship the beast or receive his mark they will be punished by God in front of the angels and Jesus, and the smoke of their torment will rise up for ever and ever.

They are tormented day and night if they worship the beast, his image, or receive his mark. Some people think this proves that people who are tormented in the fires of Gehenna will have no rest there day nor night for all eternity. If we believe that, then we would have to not believe eternal life is reserved for those who love and believe in Jesus. We would find ourselves at odds with many beloved scriptures like John.3:15-16. They tell us the only way to be saved and receive the gift of eternal life is to believe in Jesus. Jesus is our Savior, our only hope. To say that those who are in the fires of Gehenna will consciously be there eternally, is saying there is no need to accept Jesus to have eternal life. We only need him for eternal pleasure. We would have to rewrite Gods statement that the wages of sin is death, to say the wages of sin is eternal punishment. Change, the free gift of God is eternal life, to, the free gift of God is eternal bliss.

I think while they are alive during the tribulation they will be tormented day and night. If we understand the scripture this way, we have no problem with scriptures that say, only through Jesus do we have salvation and immortality. I believe the only way we can receive eternal life is through accepting Christ, do you?

Revelation 14:9-11 Strongs

9 G2532 And G5154 the third G32 angel G190 followed [G5656] G846 them G3004 , saying [G5723] G1722 with G3173 a loud G5456 voice G1536 , If any man G4352 worship [G5719] G2342 the beast G2532 and G846 his G1504 image G2532 , and G2983 receive [G5719] G5480 his mark G1909 in G846 his G3359 forehead G2228 , or G1909 in G846 his G5495 hand,

10 G846 The same G2532 G4095 shall drink [G5695] G1537 of G3631 the wine G2372 of the wrath G2316 of God G3588 , which G2767 is poured out [G5772] G194 without mixture G1722 into G4221 the cup G846 of his G3709 indignation G2532 ; and G928 he shall be tormented [G5701] G1722 with G4442 fire G2532 and G2303 brimstone G1799 in the presence G40 of the holy G32 angels G2532 , and G1799 in the presence G721 of the Lamb:

11 G2532 And G2586 the smoke G846 of their G929 torment G305 ascendeth up [G5719] G1519 for G165 ever G165 and ever G2532 : and G2192 they have [G5719] G3756 no G372 rest G2250 day G2532 nor G3571 night G3588 , who G4352 worship [G5723] G2342 the beast G2532 and G846 his G1504 image G2532 , and G1536 whosoever G2983 receiveth [G5719] G5480 the mark G846 of his G3686 name.

THAT'S A BAD TAT
People living in the tribulation and have the mark of the beast are tormented severely for following the beast.

Revelation 16:2 Strongs

2 G2532 And G4413 the first G565 went [G5627] G2532 , and G1632 poured out [G5656] G846 his G5357 vial G1909 upon G1093 the earth G2532 ; and G1096 there fell [G5633] G2556 a noisome G2532 and G4190 grievous G1668 sore G1519 upon G444 the men G3588 which G2192 had [G5723] G5480 the mark G2342 of the beast G2532 , and G4352 upon them which worshipped [G5723] G846 his G1504 image.

Revelation 16:9-11 Strongs

9 G2532 And G444 men G2739 were scorched [G5681] G3173 with great G2738 heat G2532 , and G987 blasphemed [G5656] G3686 the name G2316 of God G3588 , which G2192 hath [G5723] G1849 power G1909 over G5025 these G4127 plagues G2532 : and G3340 they repented [G5656] G3756 not G1325 to give [G5629] G846 him G1391 glory.

10 G2532 And G3991 the fifth G32 angel G1632 poured out [G5656] G846 his G5357 vial G1909 upon G2362 the seat G2342 of the beast G2532 ; and G846 his G932 kingdom G1096 was [G5633] G4656 full of darkness [G5772] G2532 ; and G3145 they gnawed [G5711] G846 their G1100 tongues G1537 for G4192 pain,

11 G2532 And G987 blasphemed [G5656] G2316 the God G3772 of heaven G1537 because of G846 their G4192 pains G2532 and G1537 G846 their G1668 sores G2532 , and G3340 repented [G5656] G3756 not G1537 of G846 their G2041 deeds.

JESUS WINS

This is a great verse because it again tells us that Jesus wins.

Revelation 17:14 Strongs

14 G3778 These G4170 shall make war [G5692] G3326 with G721 the Lamb G2532 , and G721 the Lamb G3528 shall overcome [G5692] G846 them G3754 : for G2076 he is [G5748] G2962 Lord G2962 of lords G2532 , and G935 King G935 of kings G2532 : and G3326 they that are with G846 him G2822 are called G2532 , and G1588 chosen G2532 , and G4103 faithful.

THE DAY OF THE LORD

This is describing of the return of Jesus. The beast and the false prophet are cast into a lake of fire. Most of their followers are eaten by the birds.

Revelation 19:19-21 Strongs

19 G2532 And G1492 I saw [G5627] G2342 the beast G2532 , and G935 the kings G1093 of the earth G2532 , and G846 their G4753 armies G4863 , gathered together [G5772] G4160 to make [G5658] G4171 war G3326 against G2521 him that sat [G5740] G1909 on G2462 the horse G2532 , and G3326 against G846 his G4753 army.

20 G2532 And G2342 the beast G4084 was taken [G5681] G2532 , and G3326 with G5127 him G5578 the false prophet G4160 that wrought [G5660] G4592 miracles G1799 before G846 him G1722 , with G3739 which G4105 he deceived [G5656] G2983 them that had received [G5631] G5480 the mark G2342 of the beast G2532 , and G4352 them that worshipped [G5723] G846 his G1504 image G1417 . These both G906 were cast [G5681] G2198 alive [G5723] G1519 into G3041 a lake G4442 of fire G2545 burning [G5746] G1722 with G2303 brimstone.

21 G2532 And G3062 the remnant G615 were slain [G5681] G1722

with G4501 the sword G2521 of him that sat [G5740] G1909 upon G2462 the horse G3588 , which G1607 sword proceeded [G5740] G1537 out of G846 his G4750 mouth G2532 : and G3956 all G3732 the fowls G5526 were filled [G5681] G1537 with G846 their G4561 flesh.

SATAN IS BANISHED AND BOUND

Here Satan is bound in the bottomless pit for a thousand years. He is sealed so that he can't deceive the nations till after the thousand years is over. Then he is set free to deceive people again for a little season.

Revelation 20:1-3 Strongs

1 G2532 And G1492 I saw [G5627] G32 an angel G2597 come down [G5723] G1537 from G3772 heaven G2192 , having [G5723] G2807 the key G12 of the bottomless pit G2532 and G3173 a great G254 chain G1909 in G846 his G5495 hand.

2 G2532 And G2902 he laid hold on [G5656] G1404 the dragon G744 , that old G3789 serpent G3739 , which G2076 is [G5748] G1228 the Devil G2532 , and G4567 Satan G2532 , and G1210 bound [G5656] G846 him G5507 a thousand G2094 years,

3 G2532 And G906 cast [G5627] G846 him G1519 into G12 the bottomless pit G2532 , and G2808 shut G846 him G2808 up [G5656] G2532 , and G4972 set a seal [G5656] G1883 upon G846 him G3363 , that G4105 he should deceive [G5661] G1484 the nations G3363 no G2089 more G891 , till G5507 the thousand G2094 years G5055 should be fulfilled [G5686] G2532 : and G3326 after G5023 that G846 he G1163 must [G5748] G3089 be loosed [G5683] G3398 a little G5550 season.

SAINTS RULE

During this thousand years, those who resisted the beast and stayed true to God become rulers and judges with Christ.

Revelation 20:4 Strongs

4 G2532 And G1492 I saw [G5627] G2362 thrones G2532 , and G2523 they sat [G5656] G1909 upon G846 them G2532 , and G2917 judgment G1325 was given [G5681] G846 unto them G2532 : and G5590 I saw the souls G3990 of them that were beheaded [G5772] G1223 for G3141 the witness G2424 of Jesus G2532 , and G1223 for G3056 the word G2316 of God G2532 , and G3748 which G4352 had G3756 not G4352 worshipped [G5656] G2342 the beast G3777 , neither G846 his G1504 image G2532 , G3756 neither G2983 had received [G5627] G5480 his mark G1909 upon G846 their G3359 foreheads G2532 , or G1909 in G846 their G5495 hands G2532 ; and G2198 they lived [G5656] G2532 and G936 reigned [G5656] G3326 with G5547 Christ G5507 a thousand G2094 years.

NOW THEY GET THEIR CHANCE TO CHOOSE

Here we see clearer there is more than one resurrection and that different people have different resurrections, at different times.

Revelation 20:5 Strongs

5 G1161 But G3062 the rest G3498 of the dead G326 lived G3756 not G326 again [G5656] G2193 until G5507 the thousand G2094 years G5055 were finished [G5686] G3778 . This G4413 is the first G386 resurrection.

BELIEVERS ARE RESURRECTED TO IMMORTALLITY AND RULERSHIP

Those that are in the first resurrection are blessed and will reign with Jesus during the thousand years when Satan is bound. They will be immortal because the second death has no power over them.

Revelation 20:6 Strongs

6 G3107 Blessed G2532 and G40 holy G2192 is he that hath [G5723] G3313 part G1722 in G4413 the first G386 resurrection G1909 : on G5130 such G1208 the second G2288 death G2192 hath [G5719] G3756 no G1849 power G235 , but G2071 they shall be [G5704] G2409 priests G2316 of God G2532 and G5547 of Christ G2532 , and G936 shall reign [G5692] G3326 with G846 him G5507 a thousand G2094 years.

THE WAR TO END ALL WARS

Satan will be released from the pit and he deceives those mortal people who live after the thousand years. There are a lot of people that will be deceived and go to fight against the saints. God destroys them with fire and they die.

Revelation 20:7-9 Strongs

7 G2532 And G3752 when G5507 the thousand G2094 years G5055 are expired [G5686] G4567 , Satan G3089 shall be loosed [G5701] G1537 out of G846 his G5438 prison,

8 G2532 And G1831 shall go out [G5695] G4105 to deceive [G5658] G1484 the nations G3588 which G1722 are in G5064 the four G1137 quarters G1093 of the earth G1136 , Gog G2532 and G3098 Magog G4863 , to gather G846 them G4863 together [G5629] G1519 to G4171 battle G706 : the number G3739 of whom G5613 is as G285 the sand G2281 of the sea.

9 G2532 And G305 they went up [G5627] G1909 on G4114 the breadth G1093 of the earth G2532 , and G2944 compassed G3925 the camp G40 of the saints G2944 about [G5656] G2532 , and G25 the beloved [G5772] G4172 city G2532 : and G4442 fire G2597 came down [G5627] G575 from G2316 God G1537 out of G3772 heaven G2532 , and G2719 devoured [G5627] G846 them.

EVIL REMOVED

Satan finally is imprisoned and put away from God and his people. He is cast into the lake of fire where the beast and false prophet are. Satan will be tormented there for ever. As the deceiver of mankind, all of the sins committed by mankind can be traced back to Satan. We have had our part in them as well, but he is the instigator of all sin. He will be held to account for what he has done. His penalty will be an eternity of torment in the lake of fire. The beast and false prophet were physical people. When they were thrown into the lake that burned with fire and brimstone they would have died and burned up, though their ashes remain. Satan is a spirit being, he is immortal. When he is confined in the lake of fire, he will be tormented there forever and ever.

Revelation 20:10 Strongs

10 G2532 And G1228 the devil G4105 that deceived [G5723] G846 them G906 was cast [G5681] G1519 into G3041 the lake G4442 of fire G2532 and G2303 brimstone G3699 , where G2342 the beast G2532 and G5578 the false prophet G2532 are, and G928 shall be tormented [G5701] G2250 day G2532 and G3571 night G1519 for G165 ever G165 and ever.

THE KING IS HERE

God and his throne are revealed.

Revelation 20:11 Strongs

11 G2532 And G1492 I saw [G5627] G3173 a great G3022 white G2362 throne G2532 , and G2521 him that sat [G5740] G1909 on G846 it G575 , from G3739 whose G4383 face G1093 the earth G2532 and G3772 the heaven G5343 fled away [G5627] G2532 ; and G2147 there was found [G5681] G3756 no G5117 place G846

for them.

SALVATION ONLY THROUGH JESUS

Mankind is judged by their works. The dead come from their graves where they have been waiting for this day to arrive. They are all judged and they will all be found lacking, for all have sinned and are worthy of death. Those who aren't in the book of life are cast into the lake of fire and die. This takes place after Gods final battle with Satan and those who allowed themselves to be influenced by him.

Revelation 20:12-15 Strongs

12 G2532 And G1492 I saw [G5627] G3498 the dead G3398 , small G2532 and G3173 great G2476 , stand [G5761] G1799 before G2316 God G2532 ; and G975 the books G455 were opened [G5681] G2532 : and G243 another G975 book G455 was opened [G5681] G3739 , which G2076 is [G5748] G2222 the book of life G2532 : and G3498 the dead G2919 were judged [G5681] G1537 out of G1125 those things which were written [G5772] G1722 in G975 the books G2596 , according to G846 their G2041 works.

13 G2532 And G2281 the sea G1325 gave up [G5656] G3498 the dead G3588 which G1722 were in G846 it G2532 ; and G2288 death G2532 and G86 hell G1325 delivered up [G5656] G3498 the dead G3588 which G1722 were in G846 them G2532 : and G2919 they were judged [G5681] G1538 every man G2596 according to G846 their G2041 works.

14 G2532 And G2288 death G2532 and G86 hell G906 were cast [G5681] G1519 into G3041 the lake G4442 of fire G3778 . This G2076 is [G5748] G1208 the second G2288 death.

15 G2532 And G1536 whosoever G2147 was G3756 not G2147 found [G5681] G1125 written [G5772] G1722 in G976 the book G2222 of life G906 was cast [G5681] G1519 into G3041 the lake

G4442 of fire.

LIVING WITH OUR FATHER
God comes to the earth to live with his children.

Revelation 21:1-3 Strongs

1 G2532 And G1492 I saw [G5627] G2537 a new G3772 heaven G2532 and G2537 a new G1093 earth G1063 : for G4413 the first G3772 heaven G2532 and G4413 the first G1093 earth G3928 were passed away [G5627] G2532 ; and G2076 there was [G5748] G3756 no G2089 more G2281 sea.

2 G2532 And G1473 I G2491 John G1492 saw [G5627] G40 the holy G4172 city G2537 , new G2419 Jerusalem G2597 , coming down [G5723] G575 from G2316 God G1537 out of G3772 heaven G2090 , prepared [G5772] G5613 as G3565 a bride G2885 adorned [G5772] G846 for her G435 husband.

3 G2532 And G191 I heard [G5656] G3173 a great G5456 voice G1537 out of G3772 heaven G3004 saying [G5723] G2400 , Behold [G5628] G4633 , the tabernacle G2316 of God G3326 is with G444 men G2532 , and G4637 he will dwell [G5692] G3326 with G846 them G2532 , and G846 they G2071 shall be [G5704] G846 his G2992 people G2532 , and G2316 God G846 himself G2071 shall be [G5704] G3326 with G846 them G846 , and be their G2316 God.

GOD WILL HAVE HIS QUIVER FULL
We will become the children of God. The unpleasant things of our lives will be gone, we will be living in the kingdom of God with God. We will inherit all things.

Revelation 21:4-7 Strongs

4 G2532 And G2316 God G1813 shall wipe away [G5692] G3956 all G1144 tears G575 from G846 their G3788 eyes G2532 ; and G2071 there shall be [G5704] G3756 no G2089 more G2288 death G3777 , neither G3997 sorrow G3777 , nor G2906 crying G3777 , neither G3756 G2071 shall there be [G5704] G2089 any more G4192 pain G3754 : for G4413 the former things G565 are passed away [G5627].

5 G2532 And G2521 he that sat [G5740] G1909 upon G2362 the throne G2036 said [G5627] G2400 , Behold [G5628] G4160 , I make [G5719] G3956 all things G2537 new G2532 . And G3004 he said [G5719] G3427 unto me G1125 , Write [G5657] G3754 : for G3778 these G3056 words G1526 are [G5748] G228 true G2532 and G4103 faithful.

6 G2532 And G2036 he said [G5627] G3427 unto me G1096 , It is done [G5754] G1473 . I G1510 am [G5748] G1 Alpha G2532 and G5598 Omega G746 , the beginning G2532 and G5056 the end G1473 . I G1325 will give [G5692] G1372 unto him that is athirst [G5723] G1537 of G4077 the fountain G5204 of the water G2222 of life G1432 freely.

7 G3528 He that overcometh [G5723] G2816 shall inherit [G5692] G3956 all things G2532 ; and G2071 I will be [G5704] G846 his G2316 God G2532 , and G846 he G2071 shall be [G5704] G3427 my G5207 son.

LIVE OR DIE BY YOUR CHOICES

Those that are wicked. Those who choose evil will die in the lake of fire. This is their second death. Their second life was when they were resurrected. Some were resurrected to learn of God for the first time but chose to refuse him. Others had rejected him during this present life and were resurrected to face the choices they had made and account for them. We all will get one opportunity to believe and obey.

Revelation 21:8 Strongs

8 G1161 But G1169 the fearful G2532 , and G571 unbelieving G2532 , and G948 the abominable [G5772] G2532 , and G5406 murderers G2532 , and G4205 whoremongers G2532 , and G5332 sorcerers G2532 , and G1496 idolaters G2532 , and G3956 all G5571 liars G846 , shall have their G3313 part G1722 in G3041 the lake G3588 which G2545 burneth [G5746] G4442 with fire G2532 and G2303 brimstone G3603 : which is [G5748] G1208 the second G2288 death.

HIS KINGDOM HAS COME

Those that eat from the tree of life will reign with God and Jesus for ever and ever. They will have immortality. The curse of death will be gone. The believers will become spirit, living with God, seeing him as he is, having no need of the temporal things like the sun.

Revelation 22:2-5 Strongs

2 G1722 In G3319 the midst G4113 of the street G846 of it G2532 , and G2532 on either G1782 side G1782 G4215 of the river G3586 , was there the tree G2222 of life G4160 , which bare [G5723] G1427 twelve G2590 manner of fruits G591 , and yielded [G5723] G846 her G2590 fruit G2596 every G1538 G1520 G3376 month G2532 : and G5444 the leaves G3586 of the tree G1519 were for G2322 the healing G1484 of the nations.

3 G2532 And G2071 there shall be [G5704] G3756 no G2089 more G3956 G2652 curse G2532 : but G2362 the throne G2316 of God G2532 and G721 of the Lamb G2071 shall be [G5704] G1722 in G846 it G2532 ; and G846 his G1401 servants G3000 shall serve [G5692] G846 him:

4 G2532 And G3700 they shall see [G5695] G846 his G4383 face G2532 ; and G846 his G3686 name G1909 shall be in G846 their

G3359 foreheads.

5 G2532 And G2071 there shall be [G5704] G3756 no G3571 night G1563 there G2532 ; and G5532 they need G3756 no G3088 candle G2192 [G5719] G2532 , neither G5457 light G2246 of the sun G3754 ; for G2962 the Lord G2316 God G5461 giveth G846 them G5461 light [G5719] G2532 : and G936 they shall reign [G5692] G1519 for G165 ever G165 and ever.

DO GOOD WORKS WHILE WE CAN

We will be rewarded according to our works.

Revelation 22:12 Strongs

12 G2532 And G2400 , behold [G5628] G2064 , I come [G5736] G5035 quickly G2532 ; and G3450 my G3408 reward G3326 is with G1700 me G591 , to give [G5629] G1538 every man G5613 according as G846 his G2041 work G2071 shall be [G5704].

TREE OF LIFE GIVES ETERNAL LIFE

Those that follow the commandments of Jesus will have access to the tree of life. Those who don't follow his commands won't have access to the tree of life. They will die.

Revelation 22:14-15 Strongs

14 G3107 Blessed G4160 are they that do [G5723] G846 his G1785 commandments G2443 , that G846 they G2071 may have [G5704] G1849 right G1909 to G3586 the tree G2222 of life G2532 , and G1525 may enter [G5632] G4440 in through the gates G1519 into G4172 the city.

15 G1161 For G1854 without G2965 are dogs G2532 , and G5333 sorcerers G2532 , and G4205 whoremongers G2532 , and G5406

murderers G2532 , and G1496 idolaters G2532 , and G3956 whosoever G5368 loveth [G5723] G2532 and G4160 maketh [G5723] G5579 a lie.

Chapter 35: FITTING ALL OF THE PUZZLE PIECES TOGETHER

Well that about sums it up. We have gone through the bible and read the scriptures pertaining to eternal life, heaven, hell, kingdom of God, resurrection, immortality and ideas coming close to those topics. I included the Hebrew, and Greek-English translations so it would be easier to see the words the original writers used. When we look into what exactly the word used means, our understanding of the scriptures may take on new meaning. Let's look at how these scriptures paint a picture of what God has in store for humanity. Making sure we use all verses to build a non-contradictory seamless portrait. We may have to realign our beliefs to match the scriptures or at least give some merit to a different point of view, but isn't that why we do bible studies? So we can get closer to the mind of God in all of our ways.

As I have pointed out earlier in this study, God through his word teaches truth. He doesn't refute all possible errors. There are statements about things being wrong, but it's not an exhaustive list covering every possible sin or specific error spanning all of mankind's history and future. God teaches us what is true and correct and we stray from those teachings at our own peril. If our beliefs and doctrines don't match what God has described as true we should consider our beliefs and doctrines as untrue. They may make us feel good and comfort us at times, but God won't leave us uncomforted in his truth. It is ultimately more comforting to know the truth of God, his plan and what he says he will do, than it is to be comforted by error and doctrines his bible doesn't support.

For example as I write this in the year 2013, some people I have had discussions with on the topic will say to me, “if people just die and don't go to heaven at death, what about all the people that say they have gone to heaven and came back? They have seen loved ones there and can at times describe seeing God and Jesus, what about these eyewitness accounts?”

There have been a lot of books and stories with this theme of people returning from heaven or to their bodies after death. I personally know honest God fearing people that have had similar experiences. I'm not disputing their experience, only their perception of it, John 1:18, John 3:13. When John eats the scroll in, Revelation 10:9-10 it is so real to him he can taste it. The book of Revelations is about what he saw and experienced. He doesn't tell us he died and had an out of body experience, his perspective was that it was a vision, he was in the spirit, Rev 1:10. As a child in the sixties I don't recall as many stories of people coming back from the dead as I hear about nowadays. I think that it is due to the medical system getting better. Now a days there are more people surviving close encounters with death, and their perceptions come back with them.

Can we ignore what is taught in the bible, 1 Timothy 6:14-16 and use these perceptions and stories to form our beliefs and doctrines? I don't think we should, 1 John 4:12. Rather we should look to understand their perceptions within the truth God provides. Cholera and other sicknesses were once thought to be plagues from God, but we have found them to be plagues of our own making from not following God. We've learned how to cure and avoid illnesses once thought of as divine punishment. In doing so we haven't bypassed God. We've only learned more about how his creation works, and how to work within it. As we learn more about ourselves, we may discover why some of us have these vivid God themed near death experiences. Only time will tell, but it is always best to stick with the truth God gives us through the bible. He has designed its knowledge to be timeless truths for all ages.

Rather than trying to disprove or prove every possible argument about what may happen to humanity, or the state of humans after they die, I have shown what I find the bible to be saying about these topics. Using the Strongs concordance to give clarity to the words used, as well as trying to fully understand the meanings the KJV translators intended for a word when translating the original text, we can get closer to understanding Gods plans.

Chapter 36: MANKIND WAS CREATED MORTAL

At the start of this bible study we were looking to see if mankind has eternal life in and of himself. For that is the question we need answered, if we are to fully understand, where we go when we die. We looked at all of the verses in order and took the ones that applied to our topic. Are we born with eternal life of some sort? Is there a part of us that has conscious eternal life separate from our body? Does the bible support the idea of an immortal soul, or does it teach us we are mortal and will die? The only chance at immortality we have is through the sacrifice of Jesus, our acceptance of it, and him as ruler over our lives. The verses we find addressing mankind being created with immortality are as follows.

Gen.2:7, According to the KJV scholars, they used the word soul to mean mortality, the exact opposite of what most people think it means. If we are to fully understand God's plan for mankind we need to be convinced of this first point. Ideas abound about how our body, soul and spirit are separate and they live autonomously from each other. Those ideas are not supported by this verse. The KJV scholars are clear that the definition of soul was to include mortal. That means it will die, it is not eternal. It dies when the body dies. In fact the soul is our body.

Gen.3:22-24, God bars mankind from the garden keeping them away from the tree of life so they could not eat of it's fruit and live forever. Clearly immortality wasn't within mankind's possession or part of them at this time. If an eternal spirit or soul is within our possession now, it must have been obtained after being expelled from the Garden of Eden. We weren't created with immortality in the beginning and didn't have it in the garden.

Genesis 5:26-27, Here we see that Mathusala died. The word died is in reference to a mortal life terminating. We aren't referred to as living consciously in another place or state.

Genesis 6:3, States that man is flesh and will die after living a limited time.

Genesis 49:33, Gave up the ghost, or died.

Joshua 23:14, Talks of returning back to the earth. Mortal flesh turning back to dirt.

2 Samuel 7:12, 1 Kings 2:10, 1 Kings 11:43. These verses liken death to sleeping. They aren't awake or conscious somewhere else, but dead in their graves as if asleep.

Job 4:17 In this conversation with Job, man is said to be mortal.

Psalms 115:17 The dead don't praise God for they are silent.

Ecclesiastes 9:5-6 The dead know nothing.

None of these verses tell us man is immortal or that there is a part of us that lives on without our body. We have to read into the scripture what we want to find, for those conclusions to be met. When we look at what the verses say, the original words used and only use the list of meanings the translators intended for those words, questions of mankind having an immortal soul, or a spirit that lives on, does not come up, Psalms 6:5. It's only when we are expecting the bible to support what we've always believed, that we wish it would say more, or be clearer on a particular subject. The people of faith from the Old Testament didn't think they were going to live on somewhere else, Acts 23:6, Acts 24:14-15. They were expecting to go back to the earth they were made from, Joshua 23:14, Job 10:20-22

They did have a faith God would not leave them there, Psalms 49:15. They knew God would be faithful to his promises of salvation, Job 19:25-26. They knew those promises would be fulfilled when he came to punish the wicked and reward the righteous for their deeds. They knew this reckoning would take place at the end of the world, at the time they knew of as, the day of the Lord, Acts 2:20-21, 2 Corinthians 4:14. A time like no other, when God would set things right and settle accounts, Job 21:22-33, Psalms 98:8-9.

Until that day came they expected to sleep with their fathers in the place of the dead, Psalms 55:15, Acts 2:34-35, 1 Corinthians 15:6. Knowing nothing of the world of the living, having no thoughts or cares, Acts 13:36. Being in the deep sleep of death until awakened by God's call to arise, Job 14:14,Ezekiel 37:1-14.

When Jesus came and said he had the keys to eternal life, John 3:36, saying if people were to believe on him they would have eternal life, John 1:12-13 John 3:14-15, John 6:47, it was a message, Job19:25-26, 1 Corinthians 15:12-26, that was new to them. The message of Jesus was radically different than anything they had heard before. They knew they didn't possess eternal life, John 6:49. They knew they would rot in their graves, Ecclesiastes 12:7. They knew all thought and brain activity would stop when their bodies died. They knew they didn't have an immortal soul, Ecclesiastes 3:19-22, or spirit that would live on consciously
outside of their body somewhere, Psalms 115:17. They knew it was by Gods spirit they had life, Job 27:3, Ecclesiastes 12:7. That is why even the scholars, the lawyers of the Old Testament and law, came to ask Jesus how they could receive eternal life, Matthew 19:16, Mark 10:17, Luke 10:25, Luke 18:18. They came seeking what they did not already possess, eternal life, John 6:49. This fact supports what we have found in the study of OT scriptures. The bible does not teach that mankind was created with an immortal soul, or spirit or anything that lives on past the dieing of the physical body. All that

those from the OT could hope on was the promise of God to bring them back in his good time, Proverbs 12:28, Isaiah 26:19-21, Romans 11:16-36

Chapter 37: WE ARE ONLY SAVED BY THE BLOOD OF JESUS

The promises of resurrection God gave to the faithful were true and binding on God. He would not, nor could he, not follow through with them. He had said they would come true, and he cannot lie or not follow through with his promises, Numbers 23:19, Titus 1:1-2, Hebrews 6:16-20. God speaks in the bible as if the dead are alive because it's a forgone conclusion they will be, Matthew 22:32, Mark 12:26-27, Luke 20:38, Romans 4:17, Romans 4:20-25. God will bring them back to life, 1 John 2:25, they will have new bodies, 1 Corinthians 15:35-44, Titus 3:7. Jesus is the proof of this hoped for transformation being possible. His is the example for us to follow. Just as assuredly as he was resurrected from the dead and lives, Acts 2:31, 1Corinthians 15:12-26, so will we. He is the first and we will follow as God's plan unfolds.

People will say that Heb.11, teaches the faithful of the OT are in heaven because their faith saved them, Galatians 3:6-8, Hebrews 11:1-38. We can only be saved through Jesus and his shed blood, Revelation 1:5 John 6:57-58, John 14:6. When we read to the end of Heb.11 we will see that, Hebrews 11:39-40, teaches us they are asleep in their graves waiting for us, waiting for the end time and Christ's return, when we will all receive the fulfilment of God's promise together. So that not only the faithful from the OT but the faithful believers from the AD age as well, all believers who die before the return of Jesus, 1 Corinthians 15:32-33, Galatians 3:29, will be waiting, so that we will all receive immortality together at the same time when Jesus returns. Till then we will sleep with our fathers, Daniel 12:2-3.

Here in John Jesus teaches plainly that he will come and get his followers, he won't lose any, John 10:28-29. And when does he say this will take place, John 6:39, John 6:40, John 6:44, John 6:54? He repeats himself four times so we are sure to get it. I will raise him up “on the last day”. Some may say “the last day” could be our last day of life. To do that would be to ignore the clear reference to the day of the Lord, Acts 2:20-21, Zechariah 14:1. Jesus is saying when we die we must wait until his return, then all of the faithful followers of God will be raised to glory together, Revelation 6:11. It is then we receive immortality as promised.

The second immutable truth. We can only be saved through the sacrifice Jesus provided for us, John 6:57-58, Acts 13:38-39, demands that his atonement be made before any are saved. He didn't let himself be crucified and murdered to fulfil an IOU, Revelation 1:5. He came and died to fulfil the promise to those having died in faith trusting God would somehow save them, Job 19:25-26, Mark 16:16. He came and died to cover the sins for all of humanity, past, present and future, Romans 5:1-21, 1 Corinthians 15:12-26. Whoever believes in Jesus can have eternal life, Luke 23:39-43, John 3:16, Acts 4:12. Jesus' temptation and pull towards sin was real and something he had to struggle with being human. The consequences for humanity were dire if he had at any time given into those temptations as there would not have been any perfect sacrifice to remove our sins.

He came into the world to save us, John 3:17. To bridge the gulf that separated humans from their heavenly father. That bridge was not built until Jesus had finished what he came to earth to do. He would have gladly saved us from sin, Matthew 1:21, by another method, if one existed, Matthew 26:39-42, Luke 22:41-45. No other way could be found. There is no other way to be with God, Galatians 2:16-21,

1Timothy 2:5-6. It was impossible for any human to be with God until after Jesus' sacrifice was completed, Acts 10:43, Hebrews 5:9. The salvation of all humanity rested on his shoulders, Hebrews 9:11-17. Some people could not have been already redeemed and with God in heaven before the redemptive power of Christ was available, John 14:6, Colossians 1:15-22, Hebrews 9:24-28. Saying someone could precede Jesus into heaven, puts into question the forgiveness brought to us exclusively through Jesus. It also diminishes the consequences for us if Jesus had failed.

Our only hope of forgiveness did not come cheap. It had a high price and was virtually unobtainable. It was extremely difficult for Jesus to live sinlessly. It was no walk in the park. If he had failed and given into temptation all of the promises made to mankind by God would have evaporated, 1 Corinthians 15:30-34, and satin would have won. There would have been no salvation for anyone, past, present, or future, Romans 3:9-12. The consequences were real, the trials were real, and the possibility for failure was real. Jesus was fighting for our lives, 1 John 5:10-13.

That is why it is only through Jesus we can find forgiveness and have eternal life, John 1:12-13, 2 Timothy 1:1. It is only through him that we can be saved from our sins, John 11:25-27, John 3:18, 1 John 4:14-16. Nothing we can do will save us. Our attempts are feeble, John 5:36-40, Acts 13:38-39. Only with the covering blood of Jesus can we be acceptable to God, Romans 6:22-23. We are cleansed through the washing of his blood, giving us access to our father, Hebrews 10:1-12. That cleansing, and access was only possible after Jesus had died, 1 Peter 2:24.

This plan had been worked out from the beginning, 2 Timothy 1:9. God had it all worked out ahead of time. God knows how it will end. He alone knows when it will end, Matthew 24:36. Knowing how it turns out doesn't mean you don't have to do the work to make it come about the way you want. If the effort wasn't put in, the results wouldn't have been there. Jesus had to do the work of his father to get the results that were planned for. He had to stay focused and keep on the time-line they had meticulously worked out.

Chapter 38: THE FIRSTFRUITS ARE TO BECOME THE KINGS AND PRIESTS OF GOD

When do we receive eternal life and become the adopted sons of God? The faithful and those who are called and accept Jesus need to always be ready to meet him for we don't know when our time of personal character development will come to an end. They will be raised into eternal life at the return of Jesus to the earth Revelation 1:18, Matthew 24:36-44, Luke 17:26-37, Romans 8:11, John 6:39, 40, 44, 54 Colossians 3:4, 1 Thessalonians 4:13-17, 2 Timothy 4:1, James 5:7-8, 1 Peter 1:3-7, Revelation 1:7. At this time we will be born into our new spirit bodies Matthew 25:41-46, Luke 18:18-30. These bodies will be similar to the spirit body Jesus had after he was resurrected John 3:1-12 Philippians 3:21 1 John 3:1-3, the exact description is not revealed to us through the bible 1Corinthians 15:35-47.

At the return of Jesus the beast and false prophet make war against him and his followers. The church also, called the bride of Christ, will have been in a place of safety for the previous three and a half years Revelation 12:6, the two witnesses preach about God to the rest of the world during this time but are killed just before Jesus returns Revelation 11:11-19, Revelation 13:6-8. Those that heed their message are relentlessly persecuted during this time of great tribulation 2 Thessalonians 2:1-4, Revelation 12:13-17, Revelation 13:15-17. The battle is a bloody one as the Beast does his best to get rid of Christ and his followers Revelation 19:19-21, Zechariah 14:1-

21. All of the followers of Jesus, as well as the faithful that died before Jesus was crucified are resurrected together at his return to the earth at this second coming Hosea 13:14, Luke 14:13-14, John 5:24-29, 1 Corinthians 15:12-26, 1 Peter 1:13 Revelation 20:6. They join with him in the air just as he is returning to the earth, changed in the blink of an eye into spiritual children of God John 11:21-24, Acts 24:14-15, 1 Corinthians 15:51-52, Ephesians 4:30.

When the dust settles though, it is Jesus and his followers that are victorious. Then Satan is bound and thrown into the bottomless pit for a thousand years Revelation 20:1-3. There are still people alive on the earth. This is not the culmination of Gods plan, it's still incomplete as only the first fruits of mankind have been harvested Romans 8:28-34. The harvest of the majority of mankind is still to take place Revelation 20:5. The ones who survived the tribulation will still have to decide if they want to follow God. They will be guided by the first fruits of salvation who will be their kings and priests in the kingdom. 1 Corinthians 6:2-3, 1 Peter 2:5-10, Revelation 1:6, Revelation 2:26-27, Revelation 20:4. This time of piece with Satan locked up will last for a thousand years. It will be a thousand years of no satanic influences on mankind. Generations will come and go and only know about God and his way of piece. Lives will be lived in Gods way of love without the influence of evil.

Those accepting God and his love through Jesus during these thousand years will inherit eternal life as children of God John 3:36, John 5:24-29, Revelation 2:7. Those rejecting that love and adoption will die Acts 13:46 and wait in their graves the same way as their forefathers before them did. All those that live during the thousand years will have their opportunity to be able to choose God, or reject him.

Chapter 39: WHAT HAPPENS AFTER THAT

After the thousand years are over it will be time for the second resurrection. Daniel 12:2-3, Acts 24:14-15, 1 Corinthians 15:12-26, Ephesians 5:14. The vast majority of humanity that never knew God and Ezekiel 37 those who were born in the wrong time or on the wrong continent, John 5:21 those who had their eyes blinded to Gods love John 6:45, Romans 11:1-12, Romans 11:16-36, the person that Opra was concerned for, the person who never had an opportunity to hear of Jesus John 12:39-40, 1 Peter 4:5-6, perhaps one of your loved ones that died not knowing the way to salvation through Jesus, Matthew 22:23-32, Mark 12:18-27 they will now have their chance to accept the free gift offered by Jesus Hebrews 8:10-11. Those that died while infants will be able to live a life with the knowledge of God explained to them Isaiah 65:17-25, John 5:24-29. This will be the time for these people to come to God and accept his adoption as sons and daughters Revelation 2:7. They will have a hundred years to learn of God and make their choice Isaiah 66:22-24. A full lifetime will be given them so they can spiritually mature and be sure of their decision to follow Jesus. God is not a fan of the "hard sell" he wants people to willingly accept him. People who will not alter their choice the next day, or the next decade. They will be choosing to become eternal beings and their decision will be final. God desires all to come to him and live 1 Corinthians 15:48-50. He doesn't want to lose any. He will not force us to come to him. We must choose him.

At the end of this hundred years Satan is again released. He sways mankind to once again make war against those that follow God and his ways of love Revelation 20:7-9. This will be the war to end all wars. This will be Satan's last opportunity to lead mankind astray Ezekiel 38, Ezekiel 39. When this battle is over he and his cohort demons are cast into the lake of fire and brimstone where they are in torment for the rest of eternity Revelation 20:10. The fate of Satan is to spend eternity in anguish, separated from God and his family. The very fate he would have us believe is waiting for us, if we don't accept Jesus. Those who make war against the saints living in peace die in this final battle and are fed to the wild beasts of the earth. Their death is now permanent James 1:15. They not only had their opportunity to accept God, but got to live his way of life without Satan influencing them to sin. As mortal humans who have died, they will be forgotten. They will never be brought back to life again.

It is now when the great white throne day of judgement arrives John 5:22-29, 2 Peter 2:4-9, Revelation 20:11. This is the final resurrection for those that had their eyes opened to the truth and love of God but wilfully chose to reject him John 11:45-53, Acts 13:46, Acts 24:14-15, James 1:15, Jude 1:12-13. All those who rejected Jesus while they were alive will now be judged 2 Timothy 4:1, and found worthy of death Mark 16:16 for there is no other salvation available to them Daniel 12:2-3. They will come face to face with their short comings and have to admit to their choice of sin over Jesus Revelation 2:11. All those brought back to mortal life in this resurrection will receive the punishment for their sins and choices Malachi 4:1-3, Matthew 5:29-30, Matthew 10:28, Matthew 13:40-42, Matthew 13:49-50, Matthew 18:7-9.They will die Matthew 25:41-46, Mark 16:16, Luke 3:17, Luke 12:5. This is the second death Revelation 20:12-15, Revelation 21:2-5, Revelation 21:8. These people had their opportunity to know and follow God in this life but willingly rejected him. God will honour their decision to not abide in love and let them choose death. The grave and death will now be abolished as there will be no more humans left to endure them Hosea 13:14. All of humanity will have had their passage through them 1 Corinthians 15:53-58.

There are no second chances if we have been given the opportunity to come to God John 15:21-25, Romans 1:6-7, Luke 9:62. God will make sure all will be given that opportunity. At some point in everyone's consciousness God will give us an opportunity to choose to be one of his children, and join his family. He won't force himself on us. It will be our free choice of life or death. Many will choose death rather than live in Gods life of love. But it will be their choice to make and it will last for eternity. No one will be able to say they never had the opportunity of immortality made available to them Philippians 2:9-11. God is not a respecter of persons and loves us all Acts 10:34-36. His will is that none should perish 2 Peter 3:7-13.

Finally everyone who has ever lived will have had the chance to know God. Some will have loved him and become one of his children Romans 8:14-23. Their names are found written in the book of life Philippians 4:3 and born as spirit beings the likes of which we cannot yet fully comprehend John 20:26-27, 1 Corinthians 15:35-47. Others will reject him and the free gift of life he offers and choose death. They will get what they want and never again have life 2 Thessalonians 1:8-9. It will be our choice and it will be eternal. Life or death Deuteronomy 30:19. What we will become if we choose life is not now apparent to us. But we can trust the one who is taking us there Romans 8:28-34.He only wants the best for us for he is our father of love, the king of glory. Which choice will you make?

We may have eternal life in the kingdom of God but we will also be rewarded for our efforts in becoming better people Hebrews 10:35-37, Revelation 22:12, 1 Corinthians 3:8-15. Having eternal life is good and is preferable to death, as in The Parable of the Talents, God will see to it that we are rewarded for how we used the talents he has given each of us Galatians 6:7-10, Revelation 22:14-15. Our jobs as Christians don't end with conversion, they only just begin James 1:12, James 2:17-26, 1 John 4:12, Mark 9:36-37. We each must run our race and never stop striving for the perfection of Jesus

Philippians 1:20-24, Philippians 3:10-13, Hebrews 13:20-21, 2 Peter 1:2-12. Stating that our goal is perfection, makes Christians look like hypocrites, as we are forever falling short of our desired objectives. We may never get it right but we must never stop trying Hebrews 12:1-2 Revelation 2:23.

At last God will descend to earth with the new Jerusalem so the whole family can live together John 14:2-3, 1 Corinthians 15:27-28, 2 Thessalonians 1:10, Revelation 21:1-3. This is what we were born for. To be the children of our most high God John 17:2-3, Revelation 21:4-7. What we will do as a family has not been shown, but we will be together as a family living in love John 14:2. The family of God Ephesians 2:6-7.

Chapter 40: GOD WILL SAVE ALL THAT CHOOSE TO BE SAVED

I believe the resurrections to be the only scripturally supported plan in which all of humanity has the opportunity to come to know Jesus as saviour. The plan as I have laid out, mirrors the holy days God gave the Israelites to follow in their worship of him. Getting to know the holy days and understanding the symbolism they represent gives you many insights about God that others may miss. From Jesus being our Passover sacrifice at the start of the Hebrew year, the Holy Spirit being poured out at Pentecost, to God coming to dwell with his children, represented by The Last Great Day of the Feast of Tabernacles, all of the holy days he instituted have significance within his planned schedule for humanity, and they all point to Jesus as our saviour. If we want to get to know God and what he has in store for us and humanity the relevance of knowing about the holy days should not be ignored.

Many people will say they believe God will give all humans an opportunity to know him but can't give many details on when or how. With them I agree. God will give all people at some point in their consciousness an opportunity to accept him. The main difference is that this plan can show, from scripture, when their opportunity will arise. Having this belief frees me of heartaches over loved ones who have died, not apparently knowing Jesus. It also gives hope to those who are not called by God in this life.

I spread the good news about Christ Acts 11:14 not in an effort to save a lost and sick world from the fires of hell, but so that through my efforts God will be able to draw those he wants at this time to Jesus John 16:25-29, Acts 8:26-39, Romans 1:6-7, Romans 10:13-17. If he chooses not to draw them now Acts 13:48, 1 Corinthians 1:9, Ephesians 1:4-5,I know he will be able to save them at a future time Romans 11:13-15, Romans 11:25-36, if they choose to be saved John 8:24. Not that they will have a second chance at salvation but if God doesn't draw them now, they simply cannot come to Jesus for salvation in this life John 6:65-66, John 12:39-40. Just as the scales miraculously fell from Saul's eyes to see the salvation of Jesus Christ, so must we have our eyes opened to Jesus by God John 15:16-19,John 17:2-3,Romans 8:28-34, Romans 11:16-24.

If he does draw us out of the world in this life Acts 16:14, Romans 1:6-7, 1 Corinthians 1:24-29, 2 Timothy 1:9, James 2:5, Ephesians 2:6-7, James 1:18 we must make our election sure for this will be our time for salvation 2 Corinthians 6:2, 1 Thessalonians 5:1-5, Hebrews 12:9, Mrk9:42-48, Revelation 17:14. Those who have their eyes opened to Jesus but spurn him will not be in his kingdom Mark 10:17-31, John 12:42-43, Revelation 3:4-6. They will have their part in the lake of fire Mathew 10: 32-33, John 15:21-25, John 11:45-53. If we turn back to the world, can we crucify Jesus twice Hebrews 10:26-32? If we have tasted of Gods deliverance, our life path must be set towards him and not reject him for other passions Job 16:22, Hebrews 6:4-8, James 5:19-20, 2 Peter 2:20-22, Jude 1:21, Mrk9:49-50. He knows our weaknesses and sinful nature, however we must guard our hearts to not turn from him 1 Corinthians, 5:5, Hebrews 6:9-11.

God wants all people to come to him Acts 13:48. He loves us and wants the best for us all 1 John 4:10. He longs that we should choose life with him. This is his heart, what he would prefer to have happen. As creator of all things I find it odd God would create a system that would kill off, if others are correct, the majority of humanity. Think about it. The only way to be saved is to accept Jesus as your saviour John20:31, Acts 4:12, Romans 10:9-10, John 20:31. Therefore if you didn't get the opportunity to hear about Jesus then you must be tormented for the rest of eternity, or so says the status quo. Why would God create such a system? He knows the end from the beginning, he would have seen the potential problems that would come up. Would have he sent his only begotten son to suffer and die for only those who could hear about him now during this life, knowing the majority of his potential children would never get to learn of the life altering powers in the name of Jesus? I argue no, he would not. As a loving father he would, as the scriptures show, try to get as many as will accept him, born into eternal life.

The traditional thoughts of mortality and the afterlife give God a small return on his investment. One line from the song, "Here I am to worship", by Chris Tomlin goes, "I'll never know how much it cost to see my sin upon that cross". It highlights the steep price paid not only by Jesus but also the Father to save us from our sins and make us acceptable. It was not easy. It did not come cheap Luke 22:41-45. We are children of God because a ransom of great price was paid on our behalf. God as a shrewd investor will get all he can from his efforts. He will get all those who will willingly accept his offer of life Colossians 1:12-13. The scriptures describe to us how and when humanity gets to choose that life. Each in their time Job 14:14, 1 Corinthians 15:12-26. God will not let even one slip from his hand John 10:28-29. We will all get our time to freely choose him.

Some of the people I shared these concepts with have said, "That would be nice if it were true." Inferring that what I am stating as fact, is a fantasy not supported by biblical scripture. I find it intriguing they would find the ideas positive ones. Why would they think, it would be a nice thing, for all people to have an opportunity to accept the life giving sacrifice of Jesus? Is it because they have a conflict with the thought many people will be in the tortures of Hell never having had the opportunity to know of Jesus? If the traditional teachings are right there is no other option given for them.

To have your sins forgiven you must rely on Jesus. Only Jesus can save us from our sins. To rely on Jesus you must know of him. Those who never had the opportunity to know, or rely on Jesus are, in the traditional understanding, doomed to torment. This would include any child that had died without accepting Jesus. To make an allowance for them to be forgiven, on the basis of age would be denying them the right to reject living with God. God could be potentially forcing them to be with him against their will. He will never do that, for he wants children who love him and want to be with him.

All of the bible scriptures telling us about the resurrections are accurate Hebrews 6:1-3. People in the OT who said they would see their redeemer in their own flesh are right. They will be resurrected to mortal life as described in Ezekiel. Those who have accepted Jesus are as Paul explains, resurrected to a new spiritual body like the one Jesus has. All of the resurrection accounts are accurate because they don't all take place at the same time. There is a plan for everyone, each has their own time. Each has their own decision to make, a decision that will lead to life or death.

Resurrection versus don't seem to have a place to fit, in the traditional understanding of the afterlife. To truly understand God, to get to know and appreciate him we need, to use all of the scriptures he has given us. We need to see how they fit together and not incorporate worldly concepts into the truth of God. Ideas not from God and not from his bible, are just that, ungodly and unbiblical. These ungodly ideas don't bring us closer to God and his love but lead us astray and away from God.

When God told ancient Israel to kill the inhabitants of the Promised Land, every man woman and child, he wasn't being mean by condemning them all to a tortured fate in hell. He was putting them in a safe place until they are resurrected to life and finally have an opportunity to learn of Jesus. Humanity is carnal, the only way to be cleansed is to be redeemed by Jesus. In order to conclusively prove that mankind cannot live a life of love acceptable to God, he let them try. Even when given ten rules to follow, that could make them acceptable, mankind was still unable to live in love. At the end, no one will be able to say they don't need Jesus to be cleansed of sin. For all will have fallen short of the glory of God. The legacy from generations of trial and error will be plain for all to see. Those who reject the life God offers, will get their wish and not receive life. They will be allowed to die and stay that way for the rest of eternity. Those who willingly accept, will receive eternal life.

I know some of the readers of this bible study won't agree with my assessment of the scriptures we have covered. That's alright, God gave us minds to think with and freedom of thought to ponder his personality and plans. If he had wanted us all to be yellow pencils he wouldn't have given us the capacity for individual personalities and ideas Mrk9:41. As long as we have the essentials for life with him, it is mostly a moot point if I should die and go directly to be with him, or if I sleep in my grave until he resurrects me. The end result will be the same. I'll be with him after I die.

My main ambition is to open people to the realization that the Bible will support viewpoints not held by the majority of Christians 2 Thessalonians 2:15. Giving others the room for religious freedom of thought is an important tool for expanding the good news about Jesus. If tolerance to different ideas was totally rejected it is doubtful Patrick would have been sent back to Ireland in the fifth century, or that Martin Luther and Menno Simons, would have gotten far with the reformation. Someone has to be open to different ideas and be willing to search the scriptures like the Berean Jews were in order to find the truths about Jesus and his father Acts 17:11, 2 Timothy 2:18.

The advancement of Christianity comes with diversity. What appeals and makes sense to some, will seem foolish to others. We don't have to all agree on the peripheral, only with the essential Acts 16:31, Mark 9:38-40. We can hold fast to our beliefs and know they are accurate only when we are not afraid they may be shown lacking through scriptural testing Acts 18:24-26,2 Timothy 3:16, Hebrews 5:14. Proving all things and holding our cherished doctrines to the truth of the Bible can only bring us closer to the heart of God Acts 19:1-7, 1 Thessalonians 5:2, 2 Timothy 2:15, 1 Peter 3:15. As God leads us by his Holy Spirit we will grow closer to him Philippians 2:12-13, 2 Timothy 2:26.

Perhaps this is not a topic God's spirit is making you interested in, you may be led somewhere else of Gods choosing. But let's not limit God in the peripheral by telling others there is only one way that is correct and the Bible only supports the status quo 2 Timothy 2:18.

Finding the scriptural answers, for when you are searching for immortality, gives us insights to God and his plan for salvation that others miss. This knowledge can lead us into the true meaning for our lives, as well as giving us a glimpse at the potential that is waiting for us, as children of God. We can rest assured that in the end God wins and will take care of us Revelation 21:1-3.

Scripture Index – Sorted Alphabetically

About the Author

Clayton Carlson is a published freelance author within the Christian genre. He writes articles and bible studies for the Biblists.com web site, and has audio books and articles appearing on various podcast websites.

As a Biblist in the Berean tradition, at *biblists.com* Clayton Carlson shares biblical truths and studies the Bible to fully understand scripture by reviewing original texts of ancient believers while exploring modern theology.

Acts 17:10-11
10 And the brethren immediately sent away Paul and Silas by night unto Berea: who coming thither went into the synagogue of the Jews.

11 These were more noble than those in Thessalonica, in that they received the word with all readiness of mind, and searched the scriptures daily, whether those things were so.

As a biblist, he holds the Bible to be the sole source for Christian faith.

2 Timothy 3:16
16 All scripture is given by inspiration of God, and is profitable for doctrine, for reproof, for correction, for instruction in righteousness:

While respecting the essential beliefs that make us Christian, he believes it is important for Christians to have a solid understanding of scripture and not outsource the beliefs that form their faith.

2 Timothy 3:15 [15] And that from a child thou hast known the holy scriptures, which are able to make thee wise unto salvation through faith which is in Christ Jesus.

1 Peter 3:15
[15] But sanctify the Lord God in your hearts: and be ready always to give an answer to every man that asketh you a reason of the hope that is in you with meekness and fear:

To acquire a comprehensive view of biblical scripture, he finds the definitions of words used in a particular bible passage, then considers the original meaning and how it aligns with other similar passages in the old and new testaments.

He looks at a specific biblical topic like a jigsaw puzzle. Each verse is part of the puzzle. As he looks at each scripture that is pertinent to the topic, he then puts the pieces together to find Gods picture. He believes the Bible does not contradict itself and that all verses form a cohesive whole.

Isaiah 28:10
[10] For precept must be upon precept, precept upon precept; line upon line, line upon line; here a little, and there a little:

By example; when understanding what the bible says about heaven, hell and eternal life, the chapters and sections in this book walk you sequentially through relevant biblical verses that mention or allude to heaven, hell, or immortality. The scriptural discoveries in this book may not align with traditional Christian doctrine or more specifically, contemporary beliefs, but he feels that understanding the Word of God is of utmost importance.

Romans 3:4

[4] God forbid: yea, let God be true, but every man a liar; as it is written, That thou mightest be justified in thy sayings, and mightest overcome when thou art judged.

Connect with Clayton Carlson

I really appreciate you reading my book! Please rate this book on the website you found it or leave a comment about any of my books on my website or Facebook:

Visit my website: http://www.biblists.com/

Friend me on Facebook: https://www.facebook.com/biblists

www.ingramcontent.com/pod-product-compliance
Lightning Source LLC
LaVergne TN
LVHW051726080426
835511LV00018B/2902
9781988226019